CHRISTIANITY:

Some Non-Christian Appraisals

Edited by DAVID W. McKAIN

With an introduction by ROBERT LAWSON SLATER

GREENWOOD PRESS, PUBLISHERS
WESTPORT, CONNECTICUT

Library of Congress Cataloging in Publication Data
McKain, David W
Christianity : some non-Christian appraisals.

Reprint of the ed. published by McGraw-Hill, New York.
Bibliography: p.
1. Christianity and other religions--Addresses, essays, lectures. I. Title.
[BR127.M22 1976 291 76-966
ISBN 0-8371-8144-5

Originally published in 1964 by McGraw-Hill Book Company, New York

Reprinted with the permission of David W. McKain

Reprinted in 1976 by Greenwood Press, a division of Williamhouse-Regency Inc.

Library of Congress Catalog Card Number 76-966

ISBN 0-8371-8144-5

Printed in the United States of America

ACKNOWLEDGMENTS

Ahmandia Anjuman-I-Ishaat-I-Islam, Lahore, India; Mauliv Muhammad Ali's *Muhammad and Christ* (1921).

George Allen & Unwin, Ltd., London; S. Radhakrishnan's *East and West in Religion* (1933), Masaharu Anesaki's "How Christianity Appeals to a Japanese Buddhist" from the *Hibbert Journal,* vol. IV, no. 1 (1905), M. Amir Ali's "Christianity from the Islâmic Standpoint" from the *Hibbert Journal,* vol. IV, no. 2 (1906).

George Allen & Unwin, Ltd., London, and Harper & Row, Publishers, Incorporated, New York; Daisetz Teitaro Suzuki's *Mysticism: Christian and Buddhist,* copyright 1957 by D. T. Suzuki.

Martin Buber, for his essay "Church, State, Nation, Jewry" (1933), translated by William Hallo.

Arthur A. Cohen, for his essay "The Temper of Jewish Anti-Christianity" (1964).

The John Day Company Inc., New York, and Dennis Dobson, Ltd., London; Ananda K. Coomaraswamy's *Am I My Brother's Keeper?*, copyright 1943, 1944, 1945, 1946, 1947 by the John Day Company.

Djambatan N. V., Amsterdam; M. Kamel Hussein's *City of Wrong,* translated by Kenneth Cragg, copyright 1959 by Djambatan N. V.

Nahum N. Glatzer, for a selection from Franz Rosenzweig's *Star of Redemption,* translated by William Hallo.

The Jewish Publication Society of America, Philadelphia; Leo Baeck's *Judaism and Christianity,* translated by Walter Kaufmann, copyright 1958 by the Jewish Publication Society of America.

Fumio Masutani, for selections from his *A Comparative Study of Buddhism and Christianity* (1957).

Navajivan Trust, Navajivan, India; M. Gandhi's *The Mahatma and the Mission* (1941), edited by Clifford Manshardt.

Philosophical Library, Inc., New York; Swami Akhilananda's *Hindu View of Christ,* copyright 1949 by Philosophical Library, Inc.

Daisetz Teitaro Suzuki, for his essay "Knowledge and Innocence," which appeared in *New Directions 17*.

Waverley Book Company, Ltd., London; Khuda Bukhsh's "A Mohammedan View of Christendom" from *An Outline of Christianity,* vol. 5.

EDITOR'S PREFACE

I was led to compile this volume of non-Christian appraisals of Christianity by the absence of any similar collection. It follows that I believe such a collection *should* be made available for the reader eager to increase his understanding of Christianity from the perspectives afforded by critical positions other than his own.

Paul Tillich's analysis of the problem of Christianity and its encounter with the world religions as a historical problem and not a theological one is not entirely convincing in the light of our present historical moment.[1] The serious historical problem of today must be seen as the potentially serious theological problem of tomorrow. Tillich's position, although more liberal than most, reflects the traditional Christian attitude of isolationism and what can only be regarded as fear. As much as most Christians may disapprove, an interreligious dialogue is already under way, and its impact is being felt inside and outside the walls of Christendom.

The selections from this dialogue have been limited to twentieth-century writings from the literature of four non-Christian religions: Hinduism, Buddhism, Judaism, and Islam. Selections within each religion have been made on the basis of the writer's achievement; this has been determined, first, by his overall contribution to the literature of his culture and religion and, second, by the influence of his thought and work on the Christian West.

Since I have made the non-Christian at least as important as his point of view, I have given more than the usual biographical information at the beginning of each selection. Each section and each essay within that section speaks for itself; consequently, I have avoided either understating or overstating and—perhaps even more offensive—merely paraphrasing.

From the editor's point of view, therefore, there is no unfolding of a theme, no theological position, no integrating argument. It cannot even be said that the points of view presented here—Hindu, Buddhist, Jewish, and Moslem—represent the "official" or "typical"

[1] Paul Tillich, *Christianity and the Encounter of the World Religions*, Columbia University Press, New York, p. 45.

persuasions of those religions. Of course, it is true that certain trends can be found and that others can be predicted, but the significances of the isolated characteristics should not be allowed to obscure what is really of importance—that all religions are made up of men and that the concern of all religious men is God.

I wish to thank many friends and strangers who have advised, helped, or encouraged me in editing this anthology.

CONTENTS

JUDAISM

ISLAM

THE COMING GREAT DIALOGUE

by Robert Lawson Slater

One of the notable new facts of this twentieth century is the growing dialogue between Christians, Jews, Hindus, Buddhists, and other believers. As the term "dialogue" implies, this amounts to something more than an *interest* in other religions. Such an interest is indeed manifest. In the last ten years it has meant in America a spate of new introductions to the subject of world religions, a good many of them in popular paperback editions, along with revised editions of older books, some of them written twenty, thirty, or more years ago.

Various reasons may be assigned for this growing interest. When Buddhist monks in Saigon set themselves on fire in public thoroughfares, they shock not only the immediate observers. They also shock a wider world into new understanding of the strength, persistence, and social impact of religious motives. But there is no need to travel as far as Saigon today to find zealous Buddhists. A Christian in New York or Chicago who wants to meet with a Buddhist congregation need not even leave his own city. The very fact that such meeting is increasingly possible in a world brought more closely together by better facilities for travel and communication is in itself one reason for the development of interest in the faiths of other men.

Among Christians, however, there is still a disposition to regard the subject of world religions as only of peripheral interest. In a good many theological colleges it has a very small place in the curriculum, and among church people generally it remains a subject associated with efforts to whip up an interest in missionary efforts abroad.

Yet there are increasing signs of a new outlook—a new and more realistic appraisal of the situation and a new approach to it. The fact that more and more writers should be referring to what they call "the coming great dialogue" is one evidence of this change of view. Dialogue means conversation. It is a term used, for example, with reference to what the characters in a novel say to each other as distinguished from what they do. It is also used to describe a particular literary form in which an author sets different opinions side by side by attributing them to fictitious spokesmen engaged in discussion. There was a vogue at one time for books on the art of conversation. To be a good conversationalist, it was insisted, one should not be too talkative, claiming all the say. A good conversationalist knows when to be silent, give his attention to others, and invite their opinion. He is, in brief, a good listener.

In a good sense, there may be dialogue without any spoken exchange. A book is read in the spirit of dialogue when one is mindful of the author who wrote it and is listening hard to what he may say implicitly as well as explicitly. Thus Emerson wrote of himself as engaging in conversation with Plato and other great minds of the past. In this broad sense "dialogue with other religions" may mean a reading of texts and scriptures with recognition of the fact that they bring us into the presence of the believers who wrote them and the living believers who read them today. It is therefore dialogue in which all may share. At the same time, it may be conceived that religious teachers and others have a special responsibility in developing an attitude to other believers which will allow them a hearing. Strictly speaking, however, there is no such thing as a dialogue between religions, for the engagement is not between abstractions but between believers. There are some who go further. They see the coming dialogue as something more than an engagement between man and man as they ask what the Spirit may be saying to the churches today through the invigorating challenge presented by other believers.

Dialogue, then, goes a step further than any mere academic desire to know about other religions and what they may stand for. Dialogue bespeaks a desire to *hear from* other believers, not just a desire to *know more about* them. It suggests an exchange of views and a give-and-take in which both parties to the discussion may learn.

In the past, one barrier in the way of such dialogue has been the brute fact of physical distance—the near impossibility of any coming together on the part, say, of Christians living in Tennessee and Buddhists living in Thailand. For the greater part of human history the major world religions have gone more or less their separate ways, dividing the earth between them. For example, Hinduism, as the name implies, has been very much a religion of India and scarcely anywhere else. Buddhism, born in India, has traveled mainly south and northeast. Moreover, Buddhists have tended to divide into two separate camps as they have traveled in these two different directions, with Theravada Buddhists mainly concentrated in Southeast Asia and Mahayana Buddhists mainly inhabiting Tibet, China, Korea, and Japan. Similarly we have "Orthodox Christians," significantly called Eastern Orthodox, and Catholics and Protestants dividing Western Europe more or less between them. Moslems, it is true, seem determined to go everywhere, and Christians at one time had a very alarmed awareness of their invasiveness, but in more recent times Moslems too have been largely confined to particular regions.

Not that opportunity and occasion for dialogue has been entirely lacking in the past; nor is dialogue altogether strange or unknown in the history of the world's great religions. For example, the Tarim basin in Central Asia has been described as a very crossroads of religions—Brahminism, Buddhism, Manichaeism, Zoroastrianism, Chinese religions, and Christianity—during the centuries when the Mahayana Buddhist missionaries from northern India were introducing their faith to China. Whether we have here one explanation of the striking parallelism between certain aspects of Christian and Buddhist thought is still an open question, but that there was some kind of exchange is certainly conceivable and even probable. And we are learning more and more today about the exchange which took place between Christians and Moslems when, in the seventh and succeeding centuries, Moslems advanced far beyond Arabia, establishing a sprawling empire which brought, among other things, acquaintance with Hellenistic Christian thought. Asked recently why Moslems, by and large, do not exhibit the same interest in the comparative study of religion which has been shown by other believers today, a Moslem scholar in Iran replied: "The challenge of other religions is no new thing for us Moslems. It belongs to our past. We have learned to live with it. We are not, therefore, nearly so excited about it as some of you Christians seem to be." Hindus might say much the same, for Hinduism not only bears traces of the persistent dialogue between itself and its own rebellious stepchild, Buddhism; it has lived side by side with the Christian church established in south India in the early centuries of the Christian faith; and it has felt the impact of Moslem empire in its midst. There was certainly dialogue enough at the court of Akbar the Great, who built his famous capital House of Worship in the sixteenth century. Besides his own Moslem divines, Akbar invited Hindu sages, Jain teachers, Zoroastrian priests, and Jesuit missionaries to his court to discuss religion and ended by proposing his own synthesis.

Among all the world's believers it is perhaps Christians who have been least exposed to the challenge which promotes dialogue. There was dialogue indeed in the earlier centuries of the Christian era, of which Justin Martyr's *Dialogue with Trypho, a Jew* is a notable example. In modern times, the challenging Christian missionary enterprise has aroused counterchallenge and has also stimulated and largely prepared the way for the new interest in other religions. But for the greater period of their history Christians have had the Western world very much to themselves. The dominance of the Christian faith in the West is indicated by the term "Christendom" and the long-cherished persuasion that Western civilization is essentially Christian civilization. Where there was any Christian approach to the study of other religions, it seldom amounted to dialogue. Even the impact of the Moslem world did little to change the Christian outlook. The contribution of Moslem culture to Christian European culture is, of course, unquestionable, but there was little that was specifically Islamic in this contribution. The hostile attitude to Islam *as a religion* is indicated by the fact that Dante, in his *Divine Comedy,* placed the philosopher Avicenna along with Mohammed the Prophet and his son-in-law Ali in Hell, although he was kind enough to allow Averroes, the interpreter of Aristotle, a place in

Limbo. It has been plausibly argued that what indeed resulted from the Christian-Moslem encounter was an attitude of hostility to non-Christian religions in general rather than any disposition to understand them better. As for the Jewish faith, it was generally held that Christians knew all they needed to know about it from the Old Testament. The great Hindu-Buddhist tradition, so far as Christians in the West were concerned, was altogether outside their world. The *Encyclopaedia Britannica* had no article on Buddhism until late in the nineteenth century (1875).

Even at the present time the majority of Christians in the West behave as if the only religious teaching which confronts their world is Christian teaching. Most of the books written to commend the Christian faith to those who do not accept it are addressed to unbelievers who may be regarded as nurtured in the Christian tradition which they reject rather than to believers holding to some rival faith. Dr. Hendrik Kraemer is shrewdly right in saying that while the present situation may be compared with that which prevailed in earlier centuries of the Christian era rather than with the situation which Christians have taken for granted for the greater part of their history, the dialogue which present conditions demand has scarcely begun. It is still the *coming* dialogue.

The first condition of dialogue has been met—there is now both opportunity and very apparent need for dialogue—but the second condition, which is a change of outlook and a disposition to engage in dialogue, is still largely absent. Comparatively few Christians seem to realize either the radical change of outlook which the times demand or the gravity of the situation from the Christian standpoint. It is not primarily a question of Christians realizing the tremendous change in the world situation which brings Ramakrishna teachers, Buddhist missionaries, and Hindu savants to nearly all the larger cities in the Western world today, together with thousands of students from overseas who are aliens to the Christian faith. It is much more important how Christians respond to the changed situation. Many of them foolishly ignore it. Others just as foolishly deplore it, seeing it only as threatening allegiance to their faith rather than as spelling new opportunity for the fuller understanding both of the faith of others and of their own faith. There is also a need for far more adequate appreciation of what the coming dialogue may require, both in preparation and in the engagement itself: how much there is to learn; how much there is to unlearn!

There are, however, some few encouraging signs that a change of outlook has begun. Who would have expected, even a decade ago, to hear a body like the Anglican Congress, assembled in Toronto, say calmly, firmly, and boldly that God may be speaking to men through other faiths than their own? Or who would have expected so conservative a Christian as Dr. Hendrik Kraemer to sound a clarion call to dialogue, saying (albeit with due qualification, as might be expected) that it is the ". . . high duty of the Christian participants to show openness of mind and eagerness to learn"? [1]

There have also been, in recent years, a number of books which have begun to make a significant contribution to the dialogue. One such is Professor Ninian Smart's *A Dialogue of Religions*,[2] which returns to the literary form of dialogue exemplified by Justin Martyr. Professor Smart presents a Christian, a Jew, a Hindu, a Buddhist from Ceylon, and a Buddhist from Japan engaged in a discussion of religious issues. The characters are imaginary, but the arguments presented are in a different category: they reflect the author's wide reading in the field of world religions and come, as it were, from the texts he has studied and from the lips of other believers he has met. "In my country," the Christian party to the dialogue says, "I find that arguments about religion tend too much to be confined to the dispute between faith and agnosticism; while on the other hand, the relations between the major religions of the world are often obscured by the cultural and political dress in which they are clothed. Wouldn't it be illuminating to see whether we can attain some degree of understanding on the principles, if any, underlying the doctrinal differences between us." [3]

This attempt to arrive at understanding is integral to the whole purpose of dialogue, and it is interesting to compare what Professor Smart has to say with what the late Werner Jaeger observed with reference to the purpose and spirit of Justin Martyr's dialogue. In

[1] Hendrik Kraemer, *World Cultures and World Religions: The Coming Dialogue*, Philadelphia, 1960, p. 369.
[2] Ninian Smart, *A Dialogue of Religions*, London, 1960.
[3] *Ibid.*, p. 16.

the second century Christians had to confront a large, hostile, critical pagan world.

> [They] had to find some common ground with the people they addressed if they wanted to reach an understanding. That compelled them to take a more rational approach to their own cause, in order to make it possible for others to join them in a real discussion. Most of them chose a didactic form of speech, answering possible objections or slander, but the situation itself led to a revival of the dialogue form as we find it in Justin Martyr's dialogue with Trypho, which is a classic example not of external imitation of a rigidified literary pattern but of a true effort by the partners in the dialogue to understand each other instead of asking questions only for the sake of refutation.[4]

In a number of respects the two dialogues are very different. But the broad aim in each is similar. What is attempted is a meeting of minds and better understanding of the different positions represented. This is perhaps more apparent in Professor Smart's dialogue than in Justin Martyr's. Justin does most of the talking and teaching, and he does not seem to be learning much in the dialogue itself. It is the Jew, Trypho, who says at the end: "We have found more than we expected. If only we could do this more often." But when we consider what has gone into the making of this literary dialogue, a different Justin comes into view—the Justin who must be learner before he can be author, the Justin who is seeking to understand why such a man as Trypho should oppose and reject Christianity, on what grounds he does so, how he conceives the Christian position, and how it may be presented to him in a way which may lead him to reconsider his attitude. This obviously involves an effort on Justin's part to understand the Jewish faith, not as a Christian might see it, but as a Jew sees it. For this very reason what Justin has to say in the dialogue should be illuminating to Christians as well as to Jews. This indeed may be part of his purpose. But he will only be illuminating insofar as he honestly and fairly states the Jewish

[4] Werner Jaeger, *Early Christianity and Greek Paideia,* The Belknap Press, 1961, p. 27.

view. Professor Smart puts this point explicitly: ". . . the demand for fairness is one reason for the dialogue form."[5]

It is a similar demand which meets us today when we ask how the coming great dialogue may be conducted. What is proposed is certainly not a library of books after the literary model of Justin's dialogue but rather a return to the outlook, spirit, and purpose which prompted it, a return in keeping with the fact that there has been a return to much the same conditions as those which existed in Justin's day. They are conditions which, now as then, present a serious challenge. Christians are called upon, now as then, to defend their faith and affirm it anew to critical, maybe hostile audiences in terms which may carry conviction. At the same time the conditions mean a new opportunity to gain insight in the encounter, including new insight regarding the Christian faith itself.

Anything done, said, or written which may contribute to the spirit that should inform this coming dialogue and promote a better understanding of the faiths by which other men live may be regarded as a contribution to the dialogue itself. This present volume may be welcomed in this light. For one of the things Christians most need to know if they are to be ready for the encounter is how the Christian faith is understood by those who do not share it. The editor is to be congratulated on providing such an informative anthology. It cannot have been an easy task. For Dr. Kraemer is again shrewdly right in saying that at the present time there is not nearly as much interest in the Christian faith on the part of Moslems, Buddhists, and others as there is interest in the religions of the Orient on the part of people in the West today.

A Moslem scholar recently came to see me expressly to make this very point. The majority of Moslems, he said, knew little or nothing about Christian thought; nor were they likely to give much heed to books written by Christians. He himself was one of the comparatively few Moslems concerned with better mutual understanding between Moslems and Christians. Was there not a need for books written on Christianity by Moslems similar to those

[5] Smart, *op. cit.*, p. 13.

dation in the West might not be prepared to finance a Moslem writer willing to make the inquiry required for such a book.

My reply was perhaps discouraging. I felt that any work commissioned in such a way would surely be suspect in Moslem eyes. But I agreed with my visitor in regard to the lack of Moslem interest. I myself cannot claim any special knowledge of the Moslem world. But such as it is, it confirms his statement that Moslems who are at all disposed to share in the coming dialogue are at present few and far between.

As for the Buddhist world, with the possible exception of some Japanese, most of the Buddhists I have met are more concerned with putting their own house in order and presenting their own faith to the rest of the world than they are with learning what others have to say. In the countries of Southeast Asia, where resurgent Buddhism is accompanied by newly achieved national independence, there are few Buddhists who conceive that they have anything to learn from any religious tradition other than their own. Most of the Buddhists who have been in residence at Harvard's new Center for the Study of World Religions, of which I have been director for the last few years, have said quite frankly that their interest in other religions is related to their own missionary purpose. By understanding better the outlook of Christians and others, they hope to communicate their own faith more effectively. Nor, on the basis of Buddhist principles, should one expect anything different. If the only reliable word regarding the Way comes from the Enlightened Buddha, from whom else is it possible to learn?

Is such a missionary purpose inimical to the dialogue which is proposed? In a recent discussion held at our Harvard center on this very subject, it was interesting to observe that the representatives from Hindu India held quite firmly that a missionary purpose need not, and should not, stand in the way. Wherever there is sincere and honest conviction and regard for others, they said, there must surely be desire to communicate that conviction. The opinion was the more interesting because Hindus perhaps more than any others in the world today have expressed the need for dialogue, and of all believers they are the most outspoken against any kind of intolerance or prejudice which would hinder such a meeting.

I can imagine quite a number of protests on the part of readers of this anthology as they turn the pages which follow. "But this is not what Christians believe!" I can hear them exclaiming time and again: "Where did the writer get this impression? What has he been reading? Who told him this? Who told him that? This may be true of Christians in the past. It does not apply today. This may be true of some Christians, but it is certainly not true of all."

Such protests may arise even in the case of a writer whose attitude to Christianity is friendly and appreciative. Consider, for example, Professor Fumio Masutani's *Comparative Study of Buddhism and Christianity* (quoted in this anthology). No writer could be more studiously fair and honest in his approach to the subject, and few are more appreciative of the Christian position. He names Christianity as one of the "two most sublime religions mankind has ever had," his own Buddhism being the other. He aims deliberately at "an unbiased comparison." His purpose is a scholarly, objective treatment of the subject. He realizes the extent of the engagement, and he is entirely frank about what he selects for treatment. He is also frank about his own Buddhist loyalties, but he makes the point that his own religious experience should help him rather than hinder him in his effort to understand the Christian position—a point that will be accepted by a good many Christian writers.

Professor Masutani presents a very sympathetic study of Christian and Buddhist answers to such question as, What is the nature of man? But some Christian readers may well raise their eyebrows in surprise when they find him concluding that while the religion of the Buddha is based on ". . . confidence in the reasoning man (*homo sapiens*) that of Jesus is definitely antipodal to the former."[6] In Christianity, says Professor Masutani, the desire for reasoning has to be abandoned.

In support of this conclusion he presents the Buddha's disciples in sharp contrast with Christ's first disciples. The followers of the Buddha were "chiefly young, intelligent men of noble birth." They were able to respond to his appeal to reason. But the disciples of Jesus were "perfect strangers [to] what we call intelligence or

[6] Fumio Masutani, *A Comparative Study of Buddhism and Christianity*, pp. 16-17.

culture in the Greek sense." The rock on which Jesus proposed to build his church was the fisherman, Simon Peter, a fisherman not necessarily of humble birth but representative of the others in his lack of sophisticated intelligence. He was "naive and fragile in mind." Matthew the tax collector was probably accustomed to writing, but he was, all said and done, just a petty official. And it was this Matthew who was thought to have written a document that became the basis of the Gospel! Jesus taught in parables. He addressed himself to simple people who were "full of warm feelings and good faith" but as naïve as they were honest. Paul said as much when he observed that not many that were wise were called.

Professor Masutani's main reference is to the New Testament itself. He observes in his preface that he has deliberately excluded consideration of Buddhist doctrine and Christian theology. Nevertheless, he does make some reference to later Christian writers. He emphasizes Tertullian's statement: "Credo quia absurdum est." He quotes Pascal. It seems pretty clear that while Professor Masutani has made his own examination of Christian texts, his interpretation has been influenced by impressions he has gained from reading or meeting Christian teachers who have presented him with a particular version of the Christian faith. Even those Christians who accept this version would allow that such writers do not speak for all Christians. They know that there are many Christians who interpret the Scriptures to mean a different view of sinful man's rational capacity than that which Professor Masutani conceives. Some would hold that on this issue he has, indeed, misunderstood and therefore misrepresented the total Christian view. He has done so, they might say, because his acquaintance with the Christian tradition has been only partial.

Here we have something which has implications going far beyond the question of how the Christian faith may be seen by others. It is something which may lead Christians, for example, to consider how far their own estimates of Buddhist teachings and other teachings may be similarly inadequate for similar reasons. For a good many in the West today, Buddhism means Zen Buddhism. For earlier students, Buddhism generally meant Theravada Buddhism. In either case, the result has often been statements which some Buddhists would repudiate.

Nor is the issue avoided by saying that Professor Masutani has not presumed to pass judgment on Christianity or even to consider it as a whole, full context of faith and thought. He has only been concerned with Christian answers to certain selected subjects such as the nature of man. But it has conceivably been part of his purpose to learn Christian insights which might be related to his own Buddhist insights. How much more he might have learned if he had studied what other Christians have had to say in the long, persistent debate on the relation between faith and reason which has occupied many of them for a great part of Christian history, a debate which has produced new insights accepted by many of the participants, whatever stand they may have taken!

This consideration is also relevant in the case of Christians who may seek to learn from Buddhists and other believers. One of the major differences between present-day and earlier studies in the field of world religions is the larger respect on the part of modern scholars for the greater diversity of belief and practice to be found, not between one religion and another, but within each of the great traditions. Along with this goes an increasing regard for what has emerged in the course of the consequent dialectic in each case.

A very different view of Christ's disciples from that suggested by Professor Masutani is taken by Dr. Kamel Hussein, the distinguished Moslem author of the *City of Wrong*. He pictures these disciples (in the chapter quoted in this anthology) debating what to do on the eve of their master's crucifixion. Like Professor Masutani he pays tribute to their warmth of heart and piety. "There was no more high-souled or great-hearted group of men on the face of the earth." But as Dr. Hussein goes on to picture these disciples engaged in strenuous argument and long debate, it is evident that he has a very different view of their intelligence than that taken by Professor Masutani. The arguments in which they are said to engage are subtle and sophisticated. These are not simple fishermen! Indeed, Dr. Hussein goes so far in the other direction that again Christians may be surprised by what they read.

But the real cause for wonder here, as Kenneth Cragg observes in his introduction, is that Dr. Hussein, a Moslem, should have discussed these Good Friday events at all. To do so, he has had to overcome certain prejudices which, as a Moslem, he might be expected to share. For Moslems down the centuries have been adamantly disposed to deny that the crucifixion of Jesus ever took place. Their own scripture, the Koran, denies it.

> They [the Jews] say: We killed the Messiah, Jesus, son of Mary, the apostle of God. But they did not kill him, nor did they crucify him [though] it seemed so to them. . . . On the contrary, God raised him to himself, God the strong and the wise. (Koran 4:156)

Many Moslems have believed that another victim was substituted at the last moment. There was a mistake in identity, apparently due to divine ordering and intervention. God "the strong and the wise" could not allow such a thing to happen to Jesus himself, Jesus whom Moslems revere as a great prophet. There is a hint of this view in the statement attributed to one of the disciples in the *City of Wrong:* "Religion has a Lord Who is well able to secure it." Dr. Hussein does not break with Moslem tradition on this point. All that he says about the events of the week and the disciples' perplexity can be said whether one believes that Jesus was actually crucified or not. But he certainly breaks with any Moslem prejudice which might have hindered his interest in the subject, and the result is a treatment of the human situation from which Christians, no less than Moslems, may learn.

Christians should also learn from the fact that Moslem prejudice *might* have prevented such a contribution to the dialogue (for Dr. Hussein has given us a most valuable contribution). Besides the distorted view of other faiths which may result from failure to make full inquiry, distortion may come from inhibitions based on a writer's loyalty to standpoints maintained in his own tradition.

In this respect it is interesting to compare Dr. Hussein's work with that of another writer who is equally sympathetic to the Christian position and equally concerned to promote dialogue. He is, furthermore, equally hindered by his own traditional standpoints from attributing to the crucifixion of Jesus the significance which Christians attach to it. He is in fact more outspoken about this than is Dr. Hussein. I refer to an interesting pamphlet by Swami Ranganathananda of the Ramakrishna Mission, which gives a very reverent treatment of the life of Jesus as told in the Gospels. The pamphlet concludes, however, with the statement that the death of

Jesus on the Cross has no great significance and Christians have indeed made too much of it. One reason for this opinion is that Hindus do not see any special significance in the deaths of their own venerated "spiritual heroes."

> His [Jesus'] life is inspiring. To us in India, however, the end is just tragedy. . . . The deaths of . . . Sri Rama and Sri Krishna were near tragic; but we did not build our religion on them.[7]

Nevertheless the Swami says much from which Christian readers may learn. If his Hindu inhibitions prevent him from seeing any significance in the death of Jesus, they certainly do not prevent some penetrating comments on the life of Jesus. It may indeed be true that Christians, in seeing Jesus as the Man of Sorrows, have failed, as the Swami suggests, to see him as the Man of Joy.

Much the same observations might be made about all of the various views of the Christian faith presented in this anthology. They are statements which may help Christians to see themselves as others see them, and this in itself is certainly worth doing. To realize how the Christian faith has been understood and misunderstood by others is to be alerted to the need to present that faith more effectively. But Christians may also be led to reflect on some of the ways in which they, in turn, may misunderstand and misrepresent the faith of others. Such reflection is indeed urgent if the coming great dialogue between Christians and other believers is to have the rich rewards which may be anticipated.

The approach of the dialogue has taken most of us unawares. The opportunity no less than the challenge presented by the changed world conditions of our day comes at a time when few if any, in East or West, are prepared to meet it. The growing Western interest in Oriental religions may be greater than any Eastern interest in Western religious thought. But such an interest no more constitutes in itself a sufficient preparation for the coming great dialogue than does a narrow concentration on Christian thought and its Western environment, or an indolent tolerance or sentimental preference for what is exotic.

The immediate need is, first, for an intelligent acceptance of the

[7] Swami Ranganathananda, *The Christ We Adore*, Calcutta, 1955.

new conditions which spell the invitation to dialogue and, second, for a clearer understanding of what such dialogue may involve.

As to the first part of this need, it is all too easily assumed that the dialogue may be best undertaken, as it may be more easily accepted, by those who are interested in other religions because they have come to have very little interest in their own. They are supposed to be more open-minded.

They may be. But what is to be learned from them? Often as not, no more than a very jaundiced view of what has ceased to be or has never been for them a living faith. No, if we want to learn from Buddhists, the Buddhists who can teach us most are convinced Buddhists who can speak from the heart of a tradition which they themselves value. Similarly, the Christians who may be able to contribute most in this same engagement are convinced Christians.

Unfortunately, a good many convinced Christians tend to be religious isolationists. They hide behind labels. Professing to be "Biblical theologians" in revolt against the pretensions of "philosophical theology," they make an obsessive interest in the origins of the Christian faith an excuse against dealing with the hard questions which arise today and dealing with them in a way which may convince others besides themselves. Here we touch upon the second part of the immediate need.

Engagement in the dialogue will involve a Christian in something more than flat appeal to his own Biblical revelation. He will need to stand again on the bridge of the philosophy of religion even though he may regard it as a broken and dangerous bridge. Some Western philosophers, it may be observed, appear to dislike this bridge as much as any Christian theologians. There are, however, some signs of a return to the bridge on the part of philosophers. The examination of religious language holds promise of valuable new insights, and there are still some Western philosophers who have not abandoned the metaphysical quest. But it may need the nimble wits and religious interests of Indian logicians to set other Western thinkers free from the spell of inapplicable theories of verification.

Among those who attempt boldly a reconstruction of the philosophical bridge, there are some who look for help from the comparative and historical study of religion. Here again there may be misgiving. Specialists in this field, including those who survey it from such particular standpoints as those of the psychologist and the sociologist, have been going their own separate ways. They often avoid consideration of the issues likely to be raised in the coming dialogue. Engagement in the dialogue, however, may promote a change of outlook. It may mean the overcoming of sibling rivalries and the teamwork which is just as necessary in the science of religion as it is in other sciences. It may also mean a return to something which has all too frequently been ignored in practice: the basic fact that the study of world religions is, whatever else, a study by people of people. The coming dialogue will not be a dialogue between abstractions nor yet a dialogue between religions. It will be a dialogue between believers.

It is believers who confront us in the pages of this present volume. To read their various appraisals of the Christian faith may be a useful introduction to the terms of the coming dialogue. They are appraisals made, for the most part, at some distance from the Christian faith. If they seem to us mistaken or inadequate, our criticism may lead us to reconsider some of our own appraisals of other faiths made at similar distance.

ROBERT LAWSON SLATER

Center for the Study of World Religions
Harvard University.
December 23, 1963.

Sir Sarvepalli Radhakrishnan

Sir Sarvepalli Radhakrishnan was born in 1888. He has been Vice-President of India and before that professor of philosophy for many years at Oxford. He has lectured at the University of Chicago, and is author or coauthor of more than twenty books. His training in philosophy began in the years 1905 to 1909 at the Madras Christian College, with its atmosphere of Christian thought, aspiration, and endeavor.

Radhakrishnan has traveled many times to the West as author, statesman, lecturer, and professor. The following selection is the result of such a visit in 1930, when he delivered the Jowett lecture at the Mary Ward Settlement in London.

EAST AND WEST IN RELIGION *

In the matter of religion, India typifies the East. Geographically it is between the Semitic West and the Mongolian East. The late Mr. Lowes Dickinson in his *Essay on the Civilizations of India, China and Japan* observed that India is the only country that typifies the East. The Semitic spirit is more akin to the Western in its activism and love of power. Having been a close neighbour of Rome, Semitic Asia cultivated the spirit of combat and organization. It is the twilight region between the East and the West. Again, in the Far East the Eastern mysticism glides slowly into love of beauty and order and a spirit of pragmatism. Greece and Rome typify the spirit of the West.

Among living religions, still further, there is none which has a Western origin. They have all been cradled in India, Iran or Palestine. Some of them spread to the West. Thus Christianity is an Eastern religion, transplated into the West where it acquired forms characteristic of the Western mind. Hinduism and Buddhism are confined to the East. Judaism was subjected to pronounced Western influence in the days of the Alexandrian School. In pre-Christian times the Jews of Alexandria came into touch with Greek life and thought. The Judaeo-Alexandrian School of religious philosophy, of which Philo was the last great representative, is the outcome of this contact. Islam grew out of Judaism and is largely indebted to the Greeks and the Spaniards in the West. In the tenth and eleventh centuries which were the golden period of Islamic culture, the

* S. Radhakrishnan, *East and West in Religion*, George Allen & Unwin, Ltd., London, 1933, pp. 46-70.

Greek works of science and philosophy were familiar in Arabic, and the great revolution in thought produced in the twelfth and thirteenth centuries was due to the arrival in Europe of a number of Latin translations of Arabic works. Yet Judaism and Islam remain predominantly oriental. While Hinduism and Buddhism may be regarded as typically Eastern, since they are so both in origin and in development, Christianity may be taken as the type of the Western religion. For it is a law of life that religions like other things take on the nature of the organisms which assimilate them. The distinction between the pure and simple teaching of Jesus and the developments Christianity assumed in the West is a striking illustration of the difference between the Eastern and the Western attitudes to religion.

The Western mind is rationalistic and ethical, positivist and practical, while the Eastern mind is more inclined to inward life and intuitive thinking. Robert Bridges in *The Testament of Beauty* says that in the past the West looked to the East for spiritual wisdom, and the East is now dazzled by the material conquests of the West.

Our fathers travelled eastward to revel in wonders
Where pyramid, pagoda and picturesque attire
Glow in the fading sunset of antiquity;
And now will the orientals make hither in return
Outlandish pilgrimage; their wiseacres have seen
The electric light in the west, and come to worship;
Tasting romance in our unsightly novelties
And scientific tricks; for all things in their day
May have opinion of glory. Glory is opinion,
The vain doxology wherewith man would praise God.[1]

Speaking in general terms we may say that the dominant feature of Eastern thought is its insistence on creative intuition, while the Western systems are characterized by a greater adherence to critical intelligence. The living, the concrete, the individual, is distinct from the merely logical. Logic tends to reduce everything to identity, but there is nothing that remains the same for two successive moments of its existence. Intellect seeks to congeal the flowing stream in blocks of ice. Truth is something that is lived and not

[1] I, 589-598.

merely logically comprehended, and yet we need logic in order to think, prove and communicate our ideas and perceptions. While the East believes that there are realities which cannot be clearly seen, and even assumes that logical attempts to formulate them in communicable propositions do violence to them, the West demands clearness and is shy of mystery. What is expressed and is useful for our immediate ends is real, what is inexpressible and useless is unreal. It has been well said: "The Greeks with all their acuteness and skill had little real religious instinct. In this respect the more practical West and the more mystical East have always diverged."[2] Plato's sympathy with mysticism shows how very far removed he is from the ordinary Greek.

There is an anxiety for definition and form in the Western religions. The Greek spirit is not satisfied with the conception of the supreme as a spiritual reality, or an abstract power or a shadowy force immanent in the world. It must give to its gods concrete natures with definite physical traits. Eros, for example, is a beautiful personal God. The anthropomorphism of the Greek mind is well known.[3] Its "concretizing" nature is responsible for its clothing its gods in as definite forms as the visible and tangible embodiments in the works of plastic art. The great insistence on the personality of God in the Christian religion is an inheritance from Greek intellectualism.

An intelligent religion confuses pictures with proofs, mysteries with dogmas. For it, the objects of knowledge are ever the same, unvarying myth and symbol are only masks. It trades on words and misses their meaning.[4] Absolutism results with its corollary of organ-

[2] Stanley Cook, "Jesus Christ," *Encyclopaedia Britannica,* fourteenth ed., 1929.

[3] Cf. Dr. Farnell: "Of the Hellenic religion no feature is so salient as its anthropomorphism, and throughout its whole development and career the anthropomorphic principle has been more dominating and imperious than it has ever been found to be in other religions." *Greece and Babylon,* 1911, p. 11.

[4] Mephistopheles says of theology: "Generally speaking, stick to words; you will then pass through the safe gate into the temple of certainty." When the student suggests that "there must be some meaning connected with the word," Mephistopheles replies: "Right: only we must not be too anxious about that; for it is precisely where meaning fails that a word comes in most opportunely. Disputes may be admirably carried on with words; a system may be built with words; words form a capital subject for belief; a word admits not an iota being taken from it."

ization on the basis of a creed or a ritual. An organized religion or a church is hostile to every belief which is opposed to its own creed. If new knowledge threatens the old creeds, it is the knowledge that suffers. A church cannot allow liberty of thought within its borders or, for that matter, even without. It is obliged to enforce beliefs and persecute unbelief on principle. If the fair name of Greece is not stained by any religious wars, it was due to its polytheism. The Greeks do not insist that if we call Zeus by some other name, we will suffer eternal perdition.

In the East religion is more the life of spirit. It is the perception of the oneness of man with the spirit of truth, love and beauty in the universe. Such a view does not exaggerate the *rôle* of intellectual propositions. It admits them as timid efforts at simplifying the real. It is convinced of the inexhaustibility of the divine and the infinite number of its possible manifestations. There is a "beyond" of expression into which no expression reaches, though it animates all expressions and lends them substance and significance. Centuries before Israel and the psalms of David we hear the supplication of a nameless Egyptian poet who addresses God not as friend or saviour, not as made in man's image or symbol enshrined in stone. "He is not seen; He hath neither minister nor offerings; He is not worshipped in temples; His dwelling is not known. No shrine of His hath painted images. There is no habitation which may hold Him. Unknown is His name in heaven, and His form is not manifested, for every image of Him is in vain. His home is in the universe, not in any dwelling made by human hands." Religious forms are not so much true as significant. Meaning cannot be measured by external standards. To appreciate the meaning of a religious idea or symbol, we must find out the value it expresses and achieves. The spirit is not tied to any form however adequate. Eastern religions are non-dogmatic and their adherents possess as a rule what may be called spiritual good manners. They do not condemn the good simply because it is not the best. They respect the individual as he is and do not insist on improving him even when he is unwilling. In heaven there are not only many mansions but also many vehicles to reach them. The Hindu and the Buddhist religions recognize every form of faith as a possessor of some degree of truth, with the doubtful result that all sorts of foreign cults and superstitious beliefs are to be found within the pale of these religions.

A natural consequence of this difference in emphasis is that in the East religion is more a matter of spiritual culture than of scholastic learning. We learn the truth not by criticism and discussion but by deepening life and changing the level of consciousness. God is not the highest form to be known but the highest being to be realized. Passive virtues are emphasized, like the meditative calm and the strength of spirit which are the outcome of self-control and waging war on lust, anger and worry. Religion is the dominant thing in life, its light and law. Sheik Abdullah Ansar of Herat used to tell his pupils: "To fly in the air is no miracle, for the dirtiest flies can do it; to cross rivers without bridge or boat is no miracle, for a terrier can do the same; but to help suffering hearts is a miracle performed by holy men." Eastern religions lay stress on the patience of spirit and the gentleness of soul which are born not of fear but of strength which refuses to push its way in a crowd.

Vigorous life and active service appeal to the West. Life is a thing to be possessed and enjoyed. The part of wisdom is to make the most of it and order it to the best purpose, instead of looking vainly beyond to some unknown, unattainable, infinite satisfaction. The life force manifests itself in the visible universe and man is the meaning of the cosmic process. The free power of the individual self and the organized will of the corporate community are the great upbuilding forces. The development of individual personality interpreted humanistically and national efficiency are the ideal ends. Virtue is conformity to custom. It is a sense of fitness or decorum, preserving appearances, respecting public opinion. The golden mean is a Greek contribution to ethical theory. Excess in all things is to be deprecated, whether in the matter of pleasure or power, wealth or wisdom. Rashness is a vice as much as cowardice, asceticism as much as indulgence. To the Greek piety is prudence.

Religion in the East is the cultivation of the interior life. It is the attainment of spiritual freedom, and is essentially the private achievement of the individual won by hard effort in solitude and isolation, on mountain-tops and in monasteries. The calm and compassion of a Buddha victorious over suffering, the meditation of the thinker in communion with the eternal, the rapture of the devotee in love with the transcendent, the dedication of the saint raised above egoistic desires and passions into the selflessness of the divine possess value to the Eastern mind higher than a life of power and enjoyment.

In the West, religion is a social phenomenon, a matter of the ecclesia, of the community. The Greek morality was essentially tribal. The Greek acknowledged duties to those who were bound to him by special ties, but to the rest of mankind, to man as man, he owed only the common obligations that were imposed by the feeling of decency. Religion in the West is a support for social stability and a shield against the innovator. Gods are the promoters of the social customs. Ceremonies which bind the groups are emphasized. Good citizens are good believers and those who break the rules are atheists. Naturally the State becomes a Church and its saviours obtain religious veneration. Hercules and Theseus were deified men. Divine honours were paid to Scipio Africanus and the image of Julius Caesar was carried in the solemn procession of the gods. Roman emperors were admitted to the pantheon after their death. The great funeral speech of Pericles, which may be regarded as the expression of the highest religion of the Greeks, contains no reference to the Greek gods. To fight for Athens is to fight for Athene. In the great battle against the Thebans, Theseus encourages his men, according to Euripides, thus: "O sons of Athens! if ye cannot stay the stubborn spear of the men sprung from the dragon's teeth, the cause of Pallas is overthrown." [5] Dr. Farnell observes: "No other religion of which we have any record was so political as the Hellenic." [6] All cults which favour social harmony are tolerated. Gibbon tells us in his *Decline and Fall of the Roman Empire* that the Roman magistrates "encouraged the public festivals which humanize the manners of the people. They managed the arts of divination as convenient instruments of policy, and they respected as the firmest bond of society the useful persuasion that either in this or a future life the crime of perjury is most assuredly punished by the avenging gods. But whilst they acknowledged the general advantages of religion they were convinced that the various modes of worship contributed alike to the same salutary purposes and that

[5] Farnell, *The Higher Aspects of Greek Religion*, 1912, p. 80.

[6] *Greece and Macedon*, 1911, p. 21.

in every country the form of superstition, which had received the sanction of time and experience, was the best adapted to the climate and its inhabitants." The Greek tolerance is the result of political opportunism and is not a considered conviction. The polytheism of the Greeks and their political sense were their security against intolerance. If a Socrates is persecuted it is because of his danger to the State. Religion in the West becomes confused with a sort of mystical nationalism. The universal element dominates the Eastern religions.

The ahimsā of the Upanisads and the love and compassion of the Buddha enfold even the lowest forms of animal life within their merciful arms. There is a tendency to otherworldliness in Eastern religions, while this worldliness is a characteristic of Western types. Eastern religions aim at producing saints and heroes: Western, men that are sensible and happy. The Eastern religions are directed to the salvation of the individual soul rather than to the maintenance of society. The Western convert religion into a sort of police system for the sake of social order. The great men of the East, Buddha, Jesus, Mohammed, swung the world into a new orbit and wrought inward changes. Their legacy is interwoven into the fabric of men's minds. Caesar, Cromwell and Napoleon are men of the world: they are content to work with the material ready to their hands and reduce it to order and decency. They teach no new way of life and they bring no comfort to the weary and the sick at heart. And yet our social institutions bear the impress of their work. We have in the West the realism of the men of action: in the East the sensitiveness of the artist and imagination of the creative dreamer. The ideal of Western culture, derived from Greek philosophy, is to train men for citizenship that they may be able to realize their full power in the State and for the State. In the East, the good man is one who feels at home in the whole world. Both types are essential, for no spiritual revelation can flourish in an anarchical society.

Emphasis on logical reason, humanist ideals, social solidarity and national efficiency are the characteristic marks of the Western attitude to life. The outstanding epochs of Western culture—the Greek age, the Roman world before Constantine, the period of the Renaissance and our own times—bear witness to the great tradition founded on reason and science, on ordered knowledge of the powers and possibilities of physical nature, and of man conceived as a psycho-physical organism, on an ordered use of that knowledge for a progressive social efficiency and well-being which will make the brief life of man more easy and comfortable.

The difference between the Eastern and the Western approaches and attitudes to religion becomes evident when we compare the life of Jesus, and His teaching as recorded in the Gospels, with the Nicene Creed. It is the difference between a type of personality and a set of dogmas, between a way of life and a scheme of metaphysics. The characteristics of intuitive realization, non-dogmatic toleration, as well as insistence on the non-aggressive virtues and universalist ethics, mark Jesus out as a typical Eastern seer. On the other hand, the emphasis on definite creeds and absolutist dogmatism, with its consequences of intolerance, exclusiveness and confusion of piety with patriotism, are the striking features of Western Christianity.

Jesus' religion was one of love and sympathy, tolerance and inwardness. He founded no organization but enjoined only private prayer. He was utterly indifferent to labels and creeds. He made no distinction between Jew and Gentile, Roman and Greek. He did not profess to teach a new religion but only deepened spiritual life. He formulated no doctrine and did not sacrifice thinking to believing. He learned and taught in the synagogues of the Jews. He observed their ritual so long as it did not blind men to the inner light. He attached no importance to professions of allegiance. There is nothing in common between the simple truths taught by Jesus and the Church militant with its hierarchic constitution and external tests of membership. But the change was inevitable when Christianity went to Rome and took over the traditions of Caesar. When the Greek dialecticians and the Roman lawyers succeeded to the Jewish divines and the prophets, Christian theology became logical in form and based on law. The spirit was the Jew's but the letter or the dogma was the Greek's, and the polity and the organization were the Roman's.[7] Jesus reveals through His life and commends through His teaching the possibility of a life of a higher quality

[7] Dr. Hatch observes: "It shows itself mainly in three ways: (i) The first of them was the tendency to define. The earliest Christians had been content to believe in God and to worship Him without endeavouring to define precisely

than that which is normal to man. He does not discuss intricacies of theology and ritual, but proclaims love of God or insight into the nature of reality, and love of man or oneness with the purpose of the universe, as the central truths of religion. Transplanted into the West, creeds and dogmas took the place of vision and prophecy, and intricate subtleties of scholasticism displaced the simple love of God. The question for the Church is not whether the ideas it represents are spiritually worthy, but what are the ways and means by which the society can be held together. Roman ideas and institutions influenced the ecclesiastical organization.

For Jesus piety is not a matter of knowledge, nor is ignorance the cause of impiety. His simple faith appealed to the uncultured peasants. Celsus sarcastically declared that the law of admission to the Christian communities was: "Let no educated man enter, no wise man, no prudent man, for such things we deem evil; but whoever is ignorant, whoever is unintelligent, whoever is uneducated, whoever is simple, let him come and be welcome." Tertullian asked: "What resemblance is there between a philosopher and a Christian, between a disciple of Greece and a disciple of heaven?" [8] And yet this simple faith, which seems to be so radically opposed to the Greek temperament, when taken over by the Greeks is transformed into a theological scheme.

---

the conception of Him which lay beneath their faith and their worship. They thought of Him as one, as beneficent, and as supreme. But they drew no fence of words round their idea of Him, and still less did they attempt to demonstrate by processes of reason that their idea of Him was true. (ii) The second manifestation of the philosophical habit of mind was the tendency to speculate, that is, to draw inferences from definitions, to weave the inferences into systems and to test assertions by their logical consistency or inconsistency with those systems. The earliest Christians had but little conception of a system. The inconsistency of one apparently true statement with another did not vex their souls. Their beliefs reflected the variety of the world and of men's thoughts about the world. (iii) The holding of approved opinions was elevated to a position at first co-ordinate with, and at last superior to, trust in God and the effort to live a holy life." Hatch, *The Influence of the Greek Ideas and Usages upon the Christian Church,* 1890, pp. 135-137. Cf. Harnack: "Dogma in its conception and development is a work of the Greek spirit on the soil of the gospel." *History of Dogma,* 1896, vol. i, p. 17.

[8] Hatch, *ibid.,* pp. 124, 134

The Greeks and Romans were interested in God as a theoretical explanation of the universe. The relation of the infinite to the finite was the outstanding problem of Greek philosophy, and the solutions offered by Plato and Aristotle were ambiguous and unsatisfactory. The incarnation theory offered a way out. God is no longer separated by a meaningless distance from the human world, but has actually entered into humanity, thus making possible the ultimate unity of the human race with God. In Jesus we have the union of the divine and the human. The spaceless spirit has penetrated the world of sense. The Nicene Creed is an answer to a problem of Greek metaphysics and not of Jewish religion. Since its formulation there have been many doctrinal controversies.

We notice also the gradual transformation of a rigid monotheism into a trinitarian Godhead. The Greeks worshipped not merely Father Zeus but a whole society of gods and goddesses. In Greco-Latin paganism Zeus was conceived as Jupiter and as the head of all the gods and goddesses who shared his divinity. When pagan polytheism and Jewish monotheism became fused together, the Catholic God, a God who is a society, arose. The Roman Emperors, keen on dissolving the distinction between the citizenship of the State and membership of the Church, took up the local deities and converted them into Christian saints.

The Roman Empire failed to destroy Christianity by persecution, but the hour of her victory over Rome signalized the defeat of the gospel of Jesus. Christianity became bound up with the civilization under which it grew. The Church became the depositary of sacred wisdom, a sort of reservoir of theological secrets and not a spring.

Christianity is a syncretistic faith, a blend of various earlier creeds. The Jew, the Greek and the Roman as well as the races of the Mediterranean basin have contributed to it, with the result that, in spite of its anxiety for system, this is lacking. Its ideas about God, to take one example, vary between a loving father, a severe judge, a detective officer, a hard schoolmaster and the head of the clerical profession.

When once religious faith becomes confused with dogmatic creeds, exclusiveness and intolerance become inevitable. Christianity in its early form was quite hospitable to Western thought and beliefs with which it came into contact. The Fourth Gospel adopted the doctrine of the Logos and took up the position that those who worshipped Christ were not setting up a new god. The Fourth Evangelist was not troubled by the fact that the Logos doctrine was Greek in origin and had heathen associations. No canons of orthodoxy bound him to a narrow Jewish faith. Justin Martyr could say: "The teachings of Plato are not alien to those of Christ, though not in all respects similar. For all the writers were able to have a dim vision of realities by means of the indwelling seed of the implanted word." [9] And yet in the fourth century Christianity developed an attitude of intolerance. The great library at Alexandria founded by the first Ptolemy in the third century B.C. and lavishly endowed by his successors was finally destroyed under the orders of the Christian emperor Theodosius the Great in A.D. 389, because it was known to be a hotbed of paganism.[10] A few centuries later, when Christianity came into contact with Islam, it did not adopt the liberal attitude of the earlier stage and try to find out the elements of truth in Islam, but fought it bitterly and bigotedly. Even if we admit that Islam is a militant organization, a fighting brotherhood in which a rigorous discipline is imposed on its followers by means of the scripture of the Koran and the organs of interpretation, we cannot deny that the conception of brotherhood in Islam transcends all barriers of race and nationality, a feature which does not characterize many other religions. To-day when Christianity is faced by the religion of India,[11] it is adopting an attitude of unbending self-sufficiency. It has lost the features of teachability and tolerance which characterized it in its early days.

It has ceased to be a religion of growth and freedom and become one of regimentation. The Church is the bearer of the revelation and only the revelation, not the Church, is authoritative. The prophetic element is authoritative and not its formulations. The Church formulates dogma in terms of the current thought, but she cannot claim absolute intellectual finality for any dogma or formula.

[9] *Apology*, ii, 13.

[10] It is true that it was partly ruined by the army of Julius Caesar during the siege of Alexandria.

[11] "Far more ancient than that of the Greeks, far more enduring, far more spiritual." Hoyland, *The Cross Moves East*, 1931, p. 63.

The thinking of the past in no way renders unnecessary the thinking of the present. The contrast between the free and simple religion of Jesus, and the dogmatic system of the Church, is brought out in the Chapter on "The Grand Inquisitor" in Dostoevsky's book *The Brothers Karamazov.* The Grand Inquisitor explains to Jesus that the Church has undone his work, corrected it and refounded it on the basis of authority. The souls of men were indeed like sheep and could not endure the terrible gift of freedom which Jesus had brought. The Church has been merciful in keeping man from knowledge and free inquiry. It has made mental slaves of its members. Belief is heaven and heresy hell. Consider the repressive legislation of Theodosius, which by heavy penalties forbade the practice of any other religion than Christianity, the closing of the schools of philosophy at Athens by Justinian, the Albigensian Crusades, the Dominican Inquisitions, the Acts of Supremacy and Uniformity in Elizabethan England, the religious wars of the seventeenth century and the cruelties perpetrated upon the anabaptists. Pius IX declared: "Let us most firmly hold that according to Catholic doctrine, there is one God, one Faith, one Baptism, and to go further (in an enquiry as to the fate of souls) were sin." Even those philosophers who profess to be devotees of truth are unable to shake themselves free from the absolutism characteristic of intellectual religions. While they admit that the Christian religion is not the only one, they believe that it is the absolute expression of absolute truth. In it we have the thrusting of the eternal into the temporal. As Hegel says: "It is the Christian religion which is the perfect religion, the religion which represents the Being of Spirit in a realized form or for itself, the religion in which religion has itself become objective in relation to itself." [12] But if we are true to the teaching of Jesus, we shall know that absolute truth goes beyond all forms and creeds, all historic revelations and institutions.

Jesus wants us to make religion the light and law of our life. He substituted an ethical ideal for ceremonial duties. "A broken and contrite heart" counts for more than outer conformity, which is a vain and barren thing without the vitalizing sense of God. Jesus denounced Pharisees who sought to buy peace with heaven a

[12] *Philosophy of Religion,* English Translation, 1895, vol. ii, p. 330.

little too cheaply. The call of God takes precedence of the claims of fathers and mothers, wives and children. But we are unwilling to make religion the shaping power of our lives. We take it with Greek "moderation." The saints are generally creatures set apart, those who flee from the temporal world to seek the reality of God. They live in prayer and devotion. Solitude and isolation are the roots of their existence. Those deeply influenced by the spirit of Jesus even in the West, feed the deer, hold converse with the stars, and if they are men of action they heal the sick and preach the word of God. They are not anxious for popular applause or social approbation.

The practice of the principles of Jesus will mean a society of all mankind, a society in which we bear one another's burdens and sympathize with each other in joy and sorrow. Such a society will be free from national rivalries and industrial competitions, since it will attach little importance to external goods in which one man's gain is another's loss; but we are unwilling to adopt such a view of ethics.

Jesus warns us that it is of no avail if we gain the whole world and lose our soul, if we buy peace with the world at the cost of our convictions. Inward truthfulness and spiritual sincerity are essential. To-day the religious hero is not so much a being near to God as a servant of the nation. St. Joan was clear that he who attacked France attacked God. She announced that France was always right, France was always with God, and to oppose France was to oppose Right and God. Christianity is associated with a religion of nationalism which makes each State an end in itself, an end to which truth and morality, justice and civilization are of necessity subordinated. The Church is in bondage to the State. In the last War the pacifists, with the exception of the Quakers, were outside the official churches. Jesus protested against uniting the gospel to a Jewish nationalism. The Anglican Church is linked up with British Imperialism even as the Greek Church in Russia was bound up with Czardom. The national Churches of Christianity constitute an open revolt against the gospel of Jesus. The teaching of Jesus as professed by the West has not been assimilated by the people. The dignitaries of the Church are alarmed if any of its followers take the gospel of Jesus seriously and put it into practice, though they are quite willing to use Jesus as a decorative symbol in stained glass windows of dimly lit churches. Emerson observed that every Stoic was a Stoic, but it is difficult to find Christians in Christendom. Nietzsche remarked that there was only one Christian in the world and he died on the Cross.

While the course of religion ran from East to West, the course of theology ran in an opposite direction. The intellectual religion of the West with its love of law, order and definition has its striking virtues as well as its defects, even as the intuitive religion of the East has. The one brings to the common stock prudence, knowledge and discipline; the other freedom, originality and courage. The meeting of the two to-day may pave the way for a firm spiritual unity, if mutual appreciation takes the place of cold criticism and patronizing judgment. In the East the exaggerated respect for spiritual life has issued in an indifference to those material conditions in which alone the spiritual intention can be carried out. The Eastern spirituality became petrified in dead forms which are effete and corrupting. Our conservative pandits seem to approach the problem with the mind of the schoolmen, dealing with words and texts rather than with facts and truths. Our radicals, whose minds are barren of initiative and are untouched by vital experience, revel in second-hand imitations of the West. The superiority of Western religion lies in the fact that the individual seeks his salvation in service to others. It is not enough to retire into solitude to seek closer contact with the divine. Religion is not only life-transcending but also life-transforming. True worship is in the service of suffering humanity. Religion *qua* religion affirms the startling doctrine of the immeasurable value of every human soul. The ecstasy of a conscious equality of all souls melts the barriers between man and man. True religion with its intuition of the unity of the human race works for a spiritual community. It dare not stop at nations and continents but must embrace the whole human race. This very love of man requires us to appreciate other peoples' beliefs, a feature in which the Eastern faiths are superior to the Western. It is a common human desire to enforce our own ideas and standards on our fellow men. We all have a sort of sneaking sympathy with this frame of mind. There is nothing more detestable than contempt for honest opinion, especially when that opinion is attached to the spiritual yearnings of mankind. To-day we are not slaves to words as we were. We are able to see the life behind the labels. The time may come sooner than many of us expect when churches, temples and mosques will welcome all men of good will, when faith in God and love of man will be the only requisites for mutual fellowship and service, when the whole of humanity will be bound by one spirit though not by one name. Walter Pater in his book on *The Renaissance* tells the story that when the shipload of sacred earth from the soil of Jerusalem mingled with the common clay of the Campo Santo at Pisa, a new flower grew up from it unlike any that man had seen before—a flower of rarely blended colours and rich complexity of tissues. May it not be that there will flourish through the ages to come, from the mixture and handling of the Eastern and the Western religions, such a flower of exquisite beauty and profusion?

Swami Akhilananda

Swami Akhilananda joined the Ramakrishna Order after completing his formal education at the University of Calcutta in 1919. He came to America in 1926 and shortly thereafter founded the Vedanta Societies at Providence and Boston. Before his death in September, 1962, Swami Akhilananda lectured extensively at various colleges and universities and to many religious groups and cultural lay groups. He was a member of several philosophical organizations in America and a steady contributor to the philosophical journals.

He is the author of "Hindu Psychology and the West," "Mental Health and Hindu Psychology," and "Hindu View of Christ," from which the following essay is taken.

HINDU VIEW OF CHRIST *

> In the beginning was the Word, and the Word was with God and the Word was God.
>
> The same was in the beginning with God.
>
> All things were made by him; and without him was not anything made that was made.
>
> In him was life; and the life was the light of men.
>
> And the light shineth in darkness; and the darkness comprehended it not. (John 1:1-5)

Jesus is recognized by orthodox Christians as God incarnate. Christians usually view Him as the "only begotten son," the only incarnation of God. "For God so loved the world, that he gave his only begotten Son, that whosoever believeth in him should not perish, but have everlasting life" (John 3:16). This makes it clear that Jesus was the life and the light of man, even though "his own received him not" (John 1:10). It is a fact that the advent of an incarnation is not comprehended by his contemporaries or even by some of his followers. As a result, there have been considerable confusion and misunderstanding in the minds of the people throughout the ages. Man also faces pertinent questions about the very advent of an incarnation. Why was Jesus born? Is there any basic difference between Jesus and other human beings in their lives and activities? Did He come to the world as others have come, seemingly

* S. Akhilananda, *Hindu View of Christ*, Philosophical Library, Inc., New York, 1949, pp. 15-43.

impelled by longings, desires, and other such tendencies? These questions often baffle even the most brilliant thinkers.

We want to know if Jesus came to this world with all the ordinary human requirements and tendencies. St. John tells us that "The Word was made flesh and dwelt among us" (John 1:14). There seems to be a marked difference between the personalities known as divine incarnations and other, ordinary people. We are dragged by longings and desires, while the incarnations are free of all earthly inclinations and attachments. They know the purpose for which they came to the world. We are unaware of our purpose in life and do not understand why we were born. We are unsteady like little children when they begin to walk; and we go to and fro, first taking one thing as the goal of life, and the next moment another. However intellectual we may be, we still seem to lack understanding of our purpose in life. Although we are seeking satisfaction in the sense realm, we do not know exactly how to get it, as the various objects of the senses constantly stimulate our desires for more and more gratification. Because of instability of mind, we cannot find satisfaction and we are frustrated time and again. We repeatedly seek new pleasures, thinking that they will satisfy our inner nature. A keen analytical mind easily realizes that our purpose is often defeated by the mad rush for enjoyments of the objective world. We seem to be oblivious of what will really satisfy our inner nature and fulfill the purpose of our lives. Most people are like this. Even great personalities, leaders of human destiny, are disappointed and frustrated toward the end of life.

On the other hand, incarnations of God are fully aware of their purpose, goal, and method of life. They are also fully aware of the opposition they are likely to face as well as the success they will achieve. They give their message and go away peacefully. Jesus likewise came to the world with a definite purpose. From the Hindu point of view, He was fully conscious of His mission as an incarnation and clearly understood the objective of His life and the method that He and His followers must use, whether or not the world accepted His message at that time. He knew that it was bound to be accepted eventually. There was no faltering in His consciousness. He definitely expressed the ideal and left the world cheerfully like a great hero. Swami Vivekananda says:

> But, in the history of mankind, you will find that there come these Messengers, and that from their very birth their mission is found and formed. The whole plan is there, laid down, and you see them swerving not one inch from that. Because, they come with a mission, they come with a message.
>
> . . . .
>
> Do you not remember in your own scriptures the authority with which Jesus speaks: "Go ye, therefore, and teach all nations. . . . Teaching them to observe all things whatsoever I have commanded you." It runs through all His utterances, that tremendous faith in His own message.[1]

Divine incarnations come to fulfill the crying need of the age. It is true that the people of that age do not understand how to stabilize their lives and reach the objective of life. Ordinary people naturally falter as to the goal, as well as to the means of reaching that goal. Even religious personalities often falter in their leadership and guidance of the people. They do not directly follow the method which would lead the human race to a stable society. One of the most important factors in the life of incarnations is that they have a clear vision of the path the mass must follow, even though the mass may remain absolutely ignorant of and indifferent to it. It often happens that their contemporaries misunderstand their motives and criticize and condemn them, even though the incarnations come for the good and happiness of the people. As St. John says: "And the light shineth in darkness; and the darkness comprehended it not" (John 1:5). The light is undaunted in administering its luminous power for the removal of darkness from the world. So the incarnations are undaunted and unperturbed by the antagonistic activities of the people for whom they come.

During the last century about a half dozen books have been written by some psychiatrists and other scholars emphasizing that Jesus was definitely a mental case, that He was a paranoiac with other symptoms of mental disorder. In his book, the *Psychiatric Study of Jesus,* Dr. Albert Schweitzer gives an answer to the

[1] *The Complete Works of Swami Vivekananda,* Advaita Ashrama, Mayavati, Almora, Himalayas, 1931-, IV, 118, 120.

charges levelled against the personality of Jesus. It is not unusual for psychiatrists to evaluate Him from that point of view. They often criticize the religious tendencies of man as disintegrating forces. Freud and others claim that the religious element creates censorship and consequent tension in the mind. Little do they understand that there is a world of difference between the paranoiac and schizophrenic cases and the divine incarnations. Dr. Schweitzer tried to defend Jesus by telling the public that the Fourth Gospel, which is quoted so much by these psychiatrists, is not authentic historically. This seems to us a very weak argument. His arguments regarding the experiences of Jesus do not seem to penetrate to the spiritual depths. However, he rightly establishes the fact that the behavior of Jesus proves that He is not a mental case. It is our contention that divine incarnations are unusual personalities and they are fully aware of their mission, as we shall explain further on in this chapter. Even though occasionally they may use the term "I" in a very exalted sense, below this "I" is the consciousness of "Thou," or the Father, or the Absolute. Their behavior pattern is beyond and above all normality that we can conceive. They are really supernormal beings. In fact, they can transform even subnormal persons to normality and supernormality, as we shall discuss later. It seems that the minds of many psychiatrists are so entangled with abnormal states that they cannot imagine that there is a possibility of a supernormal state. These incarnations soar so high that people who deal with pathological cases cannot even breathe the rarified atmosphere of these heights. It is suffocating to them. We beg to submit to these psychiatrists as well as to Dr. Schweitzer, that a study of the activities of Jesus will clearly reveal that He was a dynamic personality.

One of the most important and unusual characteristics in the lives of all divine incarnations is that they are not only fully conscious of their mission but they are also perfectly satisfied and peaceful. Being aware of the goal of life, they go directly to it without faltering. They reveal joy and bliss in their lives. A survey of their lives shows that their joy knows no bounds. The attraction that the average man and woman feels toward them is due to the joyous atmosphere in them. The blissful nature of God can easily be understood through contact with them. They radiate so much joy that even a disturbed and disgruntled person becomes peaceful and restful after the contact. People are attracted to them like iron to the magnet because of this blissful nature that is revealed in and through their very presence. They have no internal or external conflicts, like ordinary people who have to struggle to overcome their conflicts, even though they are great personalities. The emotions of incarnations are harmoniously integrated; moreover, any person who is trained by them becomes integrated and dynamic. It is apparent that they possess a power which singles them out from the race in which they were born. Thus it is said that they are the "special manifestations of God." Sri Ramakrishna says:

> They are human beings with extraordinary, original powers and entrusted with a Divine commission. Being heirs of Divine powers and glories, they form a class of their own. To this class belong the Incarnations of God like Christ, Krishna, Buddha, and Chaitanya and their devotees of the highest order.[2]

Why was Jesus born? There is an interesting and ennobling statement in the teachings of Sri Krishna:

> Whenever . . . there is decline of Dharma (religion), and rise of Adharma (evil), then I body Myself forth.

Christianity and Hinduism are the two great religions which accept the fact that God incarnates Himself as man. However, the Hindus believe that there have been numerous incarnations (*Avataras*) in the history of the world, of whom Jesus was one, while the Christians take Jesus to be the only one. Here we have a basic resemblance and a basic difference between Hinduism and Christianity. It seems to us that, in spite of the difference, there is a similar attitude toward an incarnation in both the religions, as we shall see in the following pages.

The declaration of the *Gita* has been fulfilled time and again, ever since man began to live on this planet. At critical periods in the history of India, when men and women were extremely materialistic and forgot the spirit of religion, such personalities have

[2] *The Gospel of Ramakrishna,* revised by Swami Abhedananda, The Vedanta Society, New York, 1947, pp. 300-301.

made their appearance every five hundred or thousand years and saved the soul of man from utter degradation and disintegration. It is amazing to note that there is a peculiar sequence in the events of history in which divine incarnations appear. Study of their lives will reveal the selfsame historical reason for every one of them. After observing the facts of history, it seems as if the advent of an incarnation can almost be predicted.

Jesus, the Christ, came to the world to re-establish the spirit of religion in the Jews and other people who then existed in that part of the world. The Jews were extremely ritualistic and many of them had lost the spirit of religion completely. Some Jews twisted the texts of the scriptures to suit their materialistic desires. Temples became business centers for commerce and trade and money changers. It is also an historical fact that the Roman Empire was at the height of its material success, with all the vices of imperialism. The powerful men and women of the empire dominated and exploited the subject groups, keeping them in a state of insecurity, while they, themselves, were addicted to all sorts of vices. Their whole attitude was one of seeking the greatest amount of sense enjoyment and power, and their intellect and other human resources were used for these expressions. The religious side of their lives was completely negated. What little religion they had was used for material success and enjoyment. Although the stoic philosophers like Cicero, Seneca, Epictetus, and Marcus Aurelius were outstanding personalities in the Roman tradition, the major trend in Roman society was not influenced at that time by these great philosophers and religious personalities. It was the most propitious time for the advent of an incarnation to show the then world the way of religion. It is needless to say that the condition of Jewish and Roman life necessitated the coming of an incarnation.

When there are such changes in religious life, the Divine Being out of love and mercy manifests Himself as man to inspire our spiritual ideals and demonstrate that man can realize God. God is not limited to scriptures and philosophies. He is not limited to pulpits and discourses by priests, rabbis, ministers, and swamis. God is a fact of direct and immediate experience. He is a reality. The reality of God is to be demonstrated to mankind by actual verification in life. By His illumination of the soul, He is its redeemer.

Divine incarnations also show us how to be aware of the presence of God and our true nature. As Jesus says: "All things are delivered unto me of my Father: and no man knoweth the Son, but the Father; neither knoweth any man the Father, save the Son, and he to whomsoever the Son will reveal him" (Matthew 11:27). They lead a life which is in itself a demonstration. Human beings require examples and evidence to show the way; otherwise, they cannot understand the abstract ideas and ideals. Incarnations are the very embodiment of the ideals so that we can witness their expression. But for the divine incarnations, human beings could not have understood the real purpose of life and the method of its fulfillment; nor could we have understood the nature of God and the fact that He can be experienced by man. As Sri Ramakrishna tells us, they are the connecting link between God and man.

> The saviours of humanity are those who see God, and being at the same time anxious to share their happiness of divine vision with others . . . willingly undergo the troubles of rebirth in the world in order to teach and lead on struggling humanity to its goal.
>
> An Avatara (incarnation) is a human messenger of God. He is like a viceroy of the mighty Monarch. As when there is any disturbance in some far off province, the king sends the viceroy to quell it, so whenever there is any waning of religion in any part of the world, God sends His Avatara there to guard virtue and foster its growth.
>
> . . . .
>
> When a mighty log of wood floats down the stream, it carries on it hundreds of birds and does not sink. . . . So when a Saviour incarnates, innumerable are the men who find salvation by taking refuge in him.
>
> . . . .
>
> Nothing is problematic to the Avatara. He solves the most difficult and intricate problems of life and the soul as the simplest things in the world, and his expositions are such as even a child can follow. He is the sun of Divine knowledge, whose light dispels the accumulated ignorance of ages.[3]

[3] *Sayings of Sri Ramakrishna,* 3d. ed., Sri Ramakrishna Math, Mylapore, Madras, 1925, chap. IV, 135, 136, 140, 144.

A question may arise in some minds that if an incarnation is fully illumined and is fully aware of his divine nature and if he has no human desires whatsoever, then how can he come again to this world? There may also be a question whether or not an incarnation is completely in God while he is in this world as a human being. Krishna, in the *Bhagavad-Gita*, and Sri Ramakrishna, in His *Sayings*, explain this clearly when they declare that an incarnation willingly imposes on himself some of the human tendencies. St. Paul also says: "Who, being in the form of God, thought it not robbery to be equal with God; But made himself of no reputation, and took upon him the form of a servant, and was made in the likeness of men" (Philippians 2:6-7). Consequently, an incarnation has the power to remove at will this imposition of human nature on Himself. He is always aware of his divine nature; consequently, he is not bound by any limitations whatsoever.

There is a wonderful blending in a divine incarnation of the human and divine. There is a little trace of human characteristics in them, and at the same time their divinity shines forth like the midday sun. The sun is never affected by darkness, even though darkness may be present. Similarly, even though divine incarnations assume human form and live in the midst of human beings who are steeped in ignorance and darkness, who are not aware of their true nature and their relationship with God, they are fully aware of their divinity from the time of their birth. They know that they have a definite purpose to accomplish and that regardless of world conditions it will be fulfilled, no matter what the people do to them or their message. There is no darkness in their consciousness.

As incarnations have no longing or consciousness of permanent multiplicity, people may wonder why they come to this world to help others. Our answer is that, although they are fully aware of the divine presence in all, they know that in the relative state of existence human beings are unaware of their true nature. Most human beings are aware only of diversity; consequently, they are entangled in the consciousness of multiplicity so they act and react emotionally on the basis of their understanding of differences. They become attracted and repelled by others. They seek pleasure and satisfaction in this state of plurality and become more and more entangled in gross worldly desires and their fulfillment, forgetting completely the divine presence within them. In the attempt to satisfy their desires, they become slaves to their passions and adopt means which actually defeat their own purpose. Sri Ramakrishna gives a beautiful example to illustrate this. "Camels are very fond of thorny shrubs: the more they eat them, the more do their mouth bleed, yet they do not refrain from making them their food." [4]

Herein lies the necessity for the advent of a divine incarnation. He comes to show the people that their methods of obtaining joy and satisfaction are wrong and he reveals ways to get them directly by becoming aware of God. This does not mean, however, that divine incarnations prohibit enjoyment of the objective world. They show us that the background of the world is divine, as the eternal subject of experience is also divine. In other words, the subject and object of experience are basically one. They also demonstrate how to live on the basis of this knowledge.

It should be emphasized here that even though ordinary people are born as slaves of ignorance and consequent longings, they have the possibility of becoming free from attachment and bondage. According to the Hindu tradition, ordinary people realize God through their devotional exercises, spiritual practices, and the blessings of divine incarnations of God and great illumined souls. They have to struggle to overcome their inordinate desires through self-discipline. The lives of Christian mystics will illustrate these statements. Sri Krishna also says:

> The turbulent senses . . . do violently snatch away the mind of even a wise man, striving after perfection.
>
> The steadfast, having controlled them all, sits focused on Me as the Supreme. His wisdom is steady, whose senses are under control. (Srimad-Bhagavad-Gita II:60-61)

When they realize God, these aspirants are illumined and become centers of inspiration and enlightenment. Herein lies the difference between ordinary saints and divine incarnations. Saints are at first bound souls and then they become illumined, while incarnations are the veritable embodiment of divine light and power

[4] *Ibid.*, chap. XXXV, 690.

from the very beginning of their lives. The illumined souls are grouped in five classes:

> (1) The *Swapna-Siddhas* are those who attain perfection by means of dream-inspiration.
>
> (2) The *Mantra-Siddhas* are those who attain perfection by means of a sacred *mantra* (name of God, by repeating which, God is realized).
>
> (3) The *Hathat-Siddhas* are those who attain perfection suddenly, like a poor man who at once becomes rich by finding a hidden treasure.
>
> (4) The *Kripa-Siddhas* are those who attain perfection through the grace of God. As a man in clearing a forest may discover some ancient tank or house and need not construct one himself . . . so some fortunately become perfect with very little effort on their own part.
>
> (5) The *Nitya-Siddhas* are those who are ever perfect. As in the gourd or pumpkin creeper, the petals of the flower come out after the appearance of the fruit, so the ever perfect soul is already born a *Siddha*, and all his seeming exertions after perfection are merely for the sake of setting an example to humanity.[5]

India has had the privilege of nurturing various illumined souls at different periods in her history. Many people have pondered over their lives and observed the expression of their power in reforming others, helping and guiding those around them, and lifting them to the divine plane. Some of the illumined souls inspired a few, while others transformed innumerable persons, giving them higher spiritual realization and transporting them to the consciousness of the presence of God. These are the eternally free souls who come to the world with an incarnation to fulfill his mission.

Divine incarnations are, of course, eternally free and they not only transform human beings by giving them illumination but they also start new civilizations. Spiritual power of the greatest magnitude is expressed in their lives through their consciousness of the unity of existence and God; and it is transferred to individuals or even entire groups at the same time. It has been observed that ordinary saints and seers can lift only a few persons, but the eter-

[5] *Ibid.*, chap. XXVII, 558.

nally free souls and incarnations can transform a whole group of persons simultaneously to a higher plane of existence.

Incarnations live an intense life of God-consciousness without any struggle or effort. Their very lives are proof that the superconscious state is to them a normal experience, while the ordinary plane of existence is unnatural. It is an effort for them to bring their minds down to this plane and teach others to reach superconsciousness. It is indeed a struggle for them to force their minds into this realm to help and bless us. Yet willingly and lovingly they sacrifice their consciousness of oneness to re-establish the spirit of religion in human society.

One of the most astounding factors in the lives of these personalities is that they do not utter a word that is not lived by them or that cannot be applied to the lives of all people. That is the very reason that the teachings of divine incarnations are so powerful and enlightening. Whoever hears or reads their words cannot help being inspired and remolded because their words are the dynamics of life. Force is instilled in what they say by the power of their lives. Their words become living; their ideals are translated into action. That is the very reason there is a world of difference between the words of a divine incarnation or illumined soul and the philosopher or theologian. One has dynamic power while the other has only intellectual conception. One has the backing of illumination and the other has only conceptual postulation. One has living force while the other has placid argumentation. One transforms the personality while the other satisfies intellectual curiosity.

The question may arise: If that be the case, then why does not everyone follow the teachings of the incarnations immediately? The reason, according to Hinduism, is that men are steeped in ignorance, inordinate affections and longings, when the incarnations make their appearances. We know what happened to the Roman Empire; it sank to the lowest stage of human existence. The Romans lived such a hedonistic life, it seems that they cared not whether any other man existed. They exploited everyone for their own enjoyment. It takes a long time for spiritual teachings to penetrate the thick veil of ignorance. However, those who are inspired and remolded by the teachings of the incarnations gradually influence the lives of others; and in this way a new dawn of civilization takes place.

It is often considered by some thinkers, who interpret the words of Jesus, that incarnations come merely to destroy the old ways.

> Think not that I am come to send peace on earth: I came not to send peace, but a sword.
>
> For I am come to set a man at variance against his father, and the daughter against her mother, and the daughter in law against her mother in law. (Matthew 10:34-35)

It is our understanding that when divine incarnations come to the world, people who are engrossed in ignorance and the activities thereof become extremely antagonistic to the higher ideals of life which are taught by the incarnations. As the spiritual attitude basically requires self-control and self-discipline, those who are at the lowest ebb of spiritual culture are unwilling to undergo the necessary restraint, fearing they will lose the pleasures of life. They not only dislike any teaching that will require discipline for themselves but they also object to anyone else taking up this method. They seem to suffer from a sense of inferiority in the presence of such persons. This is the very reason that when incarnations come, antagonism and disharmony can be observed in families. When one of the members of a family follows the higher philosophy of life, the other members oppose him because of their selfish attitude of life. They can hardly stand it as they are still in ignorance and consequently do not understand higher values or the primary objective of life. They not only want to give first place to the secondary phases but they want others to do the same. Even well-meaning parents and other relatives, such as husbands or wives, cannot help acting in this manner as they know no better. When incarnations make an appearance in the world, there is discord and dissension and a chaotic condition in society in general.

Unfortunately, the vast majority of the people are used to the hedonistic attitude of life, seeking pleasures in every field of activity. Even scholars and intellectuals use their intellectual achievements for the same purpose. Consequently, contemporary brilliant minds do not understand the higher values which the incarnations come to establish and they are antagonistic and condemn them. Apart from that, well-meaning humanistic persons do not seem to understand the real purpose of incarnations. They seem to criticize them and their immediate followers as otherworldly persons who emphasize the mystic realizations of God and ignore this world. According to Albert Schweitzer, who is a great man and a very practical follower of the social gospel:

> And Christianity also brought European thought into relationship with world and life negation. World and life negation is found in the thought of Jesus in so far as He did not assume that the Kingdom of God would be realised in this natural world. He expected that this natural world would very speedily come to an end and be superseded by a supernatural world in which all that is imperfect and evil would be overcome by the power of God.[6]

Then he confuses the reader by saying that the idea of world and life negation in the teachings of Jesus is different from that found in the Orient. However, he admits that:

> It is characteristic of the unique type of the world and life negation of Jesus that His ethics are not confined within the bounds of that conception. He does not preach the inactive ethic of perfecting the self alone, but active, enthusiastic love of one's neighbor. It is because His ethic contains the principle of activity that it has affinity with world and life affirmation.[7]

So it is that different members of society, the intellectualists, and, unfortunately, even the humanists, misunderstand divine incarnations. Consequently, there arise various types of conflicts at the time of their advent, even though they come to establish harmony in the world. ". . . I am not come to destroy, but to fulfill" (Matthew 5:17).

Their only desire, if it can be called desire, is to establish a spirit of religion and rescue the souls of men from utter degradation. They do not come to create any confusion in the existing conception of religion; on the contrary, they give a new spirit and

[6] Albert Schweitzer, *Indian Thought and Its Development,* Henry Holt and Company, Inc., 1936, p. 4.
[7] *Ibid.,* pp. 4-5.

power to the existing real religious attitude. From a study of their lives it is evident that their practices and words are meant to push the people forward from where they stand in spiritual development. In the reconstruction of human life and society they always use constructive and evolutionary methods rather than those which are destructive and dissipative. No doubt their message is meant to a great extent for the stabilization of individuals; yet this very process on an individual basis leads to the reconstruction of society at large. The influence of the incarnations is felt like the dewdrops of a tropical spring which nourish the blossoms of the flowers. Likewise society feels their influence in the reconstruction and stabilization of the new structure. That is the very reason all incarnations express practically the sentiment of Jesus: ". . . I am not come to destroy, but to fulfill." Sri Krishna says: ". . . for the establishment of Dharma (religion), I come into being in every age" (Seiman-Bhagavad-Gita IV: 8). The same idea is expressed in the *Bhagavatam.*

This again brings up the question of whether or not divine incarnations have desire as we understand it. True, there is a kind of desire or longing in them, because of what we have already mentioned, the little touch of the human element. But at any moment they can give it up as they are not bound by it, being free souls. Of their own volition they assume the desire to alleviate the sufferings of humanity.

On the other hand, how much we human beings suffer if we cannot fulfill our objectives and desires! How restless and miserable we are! For such desires are based on an egocentric attitude of life. Divine incarnations have no such attitude. They are not selfish. On the contrary, they are completely established in the higher self; and, consequently, their desire is only for the good of the world.

When they depart from the world, they feel no pain or agony because they are leaving it; there is no feeling of separation. They are free from attachment to the world and are established in their divine nature. According to Indian or Hindu philosophy, they are called the rulers of *maya* (*mayadhisa*), while we are the slaves of *maya* (*mayadhina*). In other words, incarnations are masters of ignorance, while human beings are its slaves.

Many persons question whether or not Jesus fulfilled His purpose during His lifetime. If He did not, then we would assume that He must have been disappointed. We feel disappointed when we do not obtain the objects of our desires. When we suffer misfortune, we are extremely disturbed and many times go to pieces. Observe human life and you will find that most people behave in that way. They act recklessly when threatened with failure or disappointment. Therefore, we naturally suppose that Jesus was disappointed in His mission, as it did not seem at that time that He established the Kingdom of God as He professed. If it can be accepted as true that He was disappointed, it is logical to assume that He was on the same plane as any other human being. Under such conditions, He would have had noble ideas of doing good to the world but would think that He could not give the world the Kingdom of God. So He would have been disappointed just as any ordinary man would be.

There is, however, actually a vast difference between an incarnation and the ordinary person whose expectations are defeated when he cannot do something for himself, his family, or society. Take, for instance, political leaders or social reformers; many are pessimistic and heartbroken when they approach the evening of life. Yet divine incarnations, such as Jesus, are not frustrated when they see no immediate results of their work. They understand human nature and realize that time is needed for the world to absorb their message.

A man once went to Sri Ramakrishna for advice concerning his daily life. Sri Ramakrishna talked with him and gave the advice. Afterwards, He told one of His disciples: "This man will not heed my words nor do what I suggested; he will do exactly as he wishes. Just the same, I have told him what is the right thing to do." Now, if we know that a man will not do what we advise, we become furious, even in routine matters. Some of us would say: "I am not going to waste my time; he will not do it anyhow. I intend to sit tight and mind my own business." Others would express hatred and anger. However, Sri Ramakrishna did not utter a word of disappointment although He well knew that the man would not accept His suggestions. His love impelled him to give advice to erring humanity.

Divine incarnations understand human frailties and the nature of the human mind. They are the real psychologists. Although it takes a long time for the mind to change its pattern and old ways of thinking, Jesus still gave His message of love. He declared: "Thou shalt love thy neighbor . . ." when He knew full well the Jews and Gentiles would not immediately accept that as a principle and method of life. He was also aware that His disciple, Judas, would betray Him for thirty pieces of silver. He knew it during the Last Supper when He said: "He that dippeth his hand with me in the dish, the same shall betray me." Yet He did not withdraw His blessings, His love, or His grace from Judas. Can an ordinary man be found who will behave in this manner when he knows that an avowed friend and follower is going to betray him and be the cause of his crucifixion? Anyone else would have hated and killed Judas. But Jesus allowed him to carry out his destructive plans.

Buddha declared: "Let a man overcome anger by love, let him overcome evil by good. . . ." (Dhammapada XLVIII: 36) But He knew that the people would not immediately practice the gospel of love. Similarly, Jesus said: "But I say unto you, Love your enemies, bless them that curse you, do good to them that hate you, and pray for them which despitefully use you, and persecute you" (Matthew 5:44). As an incarnation of God, Jesus also knew that it would perhaps be a few centuries before His message of love would be accepted, that the Romans would not assimilate His ideas at once nor would the Jews put them into practice. But it was not His failure when only a handful of Jews and Gentiles became His followers.

As an incarnation, God sees the past, present, and future. In the Indian language, He is called *Trikalajnas,* a knower of time in three periods—past, present, and future. As He is fully enlightened, He knows the whole world's history for centuries. We know from the life of Sri Ramakrishna that He was fully aware of what was going to happen in the world. On one occasion, Swami Vivekananda privately discussed the future of India and definitely stated when the Indian situation would change in an "unprecedented way," years later. Does anyone think that Jesus did not know the world's future? According to the Hindu viewpoint, Jesus as an incarnation must have understood what was going to happen and with this knowledge He gave His message. He was not at all disappointed, as some persons seem to conclude.

Human beings are slow to change habits and ways of life. For instance, we often realize that we have been guilty of anger; we know that hatred is not right; and we are aware that we should not have behaved in certain ways toward our friends and relatives. Yet we repeatedly have the same feelings and express the same behavior; because, in spite of our knowledge, understanding, and historically religious background, we do not take the time to change our thought forms and ways of life. Psychologically speaking, it is evident that when certain emotional reactions are created by persons and objects our conscious as well as unconscious mind retains those impressions. Whenever similar occasions arise, we react almost automatically, due to our previous reactions which are preserved in the unconscious. In order to transform these thought patterns created by inordinate tendencies, disagreeable as they may be from the conscious point of view, considerable time is required to reconstruct new types of reactions. But new sets of unconscious impressions must be built in order to overcome the old impressions.

The divine incarnations intensely love their disciples and followers; love is the connecting link between them. It is this love that attracts the disciples to the incarnations, as the magnet attracts base metal. We have seen time and again in history as well as in our personal experience that illumined souls have intense love for human beings. They can inspire and transform the people because of their love for them. In fact, it is love that becomes the dynamic power in their influence over others. It is very interesting to note that the modern psychoanalysts think in different terms, even though they are often helpful to their patients and clients. Many of their techniques seem to be quite different from what we observe in the lives of divine incarnations and other illumined souls or saints.

The analyst, teacher, or spiritual leader must also have an infinite amount of patience. He is not a true leader if he has not infinite patience, sympathy, and above all, infinite love. The analyst will be a failure in the long run, in spite of technical knowledge, if he has not sympathy for human suffering and patience with man's inability to change himself overnight. An impatient person cannot have the confidence of anyone. On the other hand, a person with patience, who knows human nature as it is, persistently sympathizes with the weaknesses of individuals. This gradually creates confidence in them. This confidence of the client, patient, follower, or disciple is of vital importance in the reconstruction of human personality. Love between the teacher and disciple is the most important factor in the transformation of an individual. Divine incarnations are veritable embodiments of patience and forgiveness, love and sympathy. The love that we find in them cannot be duplicated anywhere else in the world.

I remember a statement which was made by our master, Swami Brahmananda. He said: "What love have we seen in Sri Ramakrishna! If one can have just a little glimpse of that love, one gets intoxicated by it." Then he added: "Do you know, we were boys when we went to Sri Ramakrishna. What fullness of love He had for us! We could not stay away from Him. His love was so intense that we left everything and went to Him."

When we study the lives of other divine incarnations like Sri Krishna and Buddha, we find the same intense love in Them. In fact, the people who went to any of the incarnations were irresistibly drawn to them by their all-consuming love which was showered on all without any differentiation or expectation. It was supremely unselfish.

It seems as if a tidal wave of love flows from them. This is a distinctive mark which separates incarnations from all others. They forgive the weaknesses and inordinate tendencies of human beings. Jesus forgave Judas and blessed him. He forgave those who crucified Him, saying: "Father, forgive them, for they know not what they do," because He had infinite love for human beings and infinite sympathy for their weakness. Ordinary people become disappointed and angry if their friends and relatives misbehave and do not act as they wish. Swami Brahmananda told us one day: "Even if you do all the good things you can for a person all your life and do one thing that is not wished or liked by him, all your good deeds are in vain. You are no good to him. God is just the opposite. You do everything wrong all your life and then one day you think of Him with love and devotion and you do the right thing. At once He forgives your entire past and lifts you to the higher plane." The parable of the prodigal son as told by Jesus is well known, in this connection (Luke 15:11-32).

A question may arise in the minds of many thinkers that if God, as the great Swami said, forgives and showers His grace and blessings even on persons of misdeeds, then where is the place of the law of *karma* (cause and effect)? Naturally, one would think that the Hindu-Buddhistic idea of the law of *karma* cannot justify the grace of God. If the law of *karma*, or, as Emerson calls it, the law of compensation and retribution, is exact, then how can the Hindus justify the Christian idea of the grace of God? This idea is not exclusively a Christian idea in the first place. It is accepted by the Hindus, even though they firmly believe in the law of causation. Sri Krishna says in the *Gita:* "Fixing thy mind on Me, thou shalt, by My grace overcome all obstacles. . . ." (Srimad-Bhagavad-Gita XVIII:58)

Sri Ramakrishna says that God is beyond any law although all laws are according to His will. If He chooses, He can wipe away all effect of laws. It may seem arbitrary, yet the lawmaker is greater than the law itself. When anything functions on the relative plane, it is, no doubt, within the realm of the law of causation; but God, as the maker of law, can also suspend its functioning. This is not only the Christian view; it is also accepted by the Hindus.

A divine incarnation, being a manifestation of God, has the power of grace. That is the very reason that our prayers, supplications, and such other devotional practices become effective, provided, however, there is a desire to depend on God. The breeze of God's grace blows constantly, but only the person who is energetic enough to keep his sails unfurled can enjoy it.[8] To use a Christian expression: When a man is "repentant," he gets the grace of God. According to the Hindu view, the divine incarnation has the power of dispensing all limitations and weaknesses of a man and giving direct illumination to a saint as well as a sinner.

It is very interesting to note that Professor Rudolph Otto, a great German thinker, finds the doctrine of redemption and grace fully developed in Hinduism as it is in Christianity. In his book, *India's*

[8] *Sayings of Sri Ramakrishna,* chap. XXVI:538.

Religion of Grace and Christianity, he gives a very clear account of the grace of God, as advocated by the Hindus. He writes:

> Beginning in the profound verses of the pre-Christian *Bhagavad-Gita,* the book most loved and honoured by millions of Hindus, passing through times of obscuration and reformation, as with us, this doctrine of grace rises till it gains at last positions which dumbfound us Protestants by their analogy to our fundamental ideas. . . .

When an incarnation comes to the world, the path of religion seems to be very easy. Men and women of every station in life and development and even lower beings and those on other planes of existence are redeemed. His presence makes the path easy and simple. Thus Jesus says:

> Come unto me, all ye that labour and are heavy laden, and I will give you rest.
>
> Take my yoke upon you, and learn of me; for I am meek and lowly in heart: and ye shall find rest unto your souls.
>
> For my yoke is easy, and my burden is light. (Matthew 11:28-30)

Similarly, Sri Krishna tells us: "Relinquishing all Dharmas (laws) take refuge in Me alone, I will liberate thee from all sins; grieve not" (Srimad-Bhagavad-Gita XVIII:66). And again Sri Ramakrishna says: "As a large and powerful steamer moves swiftly over the waters, towing rafts and barges in its wake—so when a Saviour descends, He easily carries thousands to the haven of safety across the ocean of *Maya.*"[9] When we study the lives of divine incarnations, we find an extraordinary display of power of spiritual illumination. It seems they can transform any person instantaneously and lift him to the radiant presence of God, with no personal effort on the part of the individual. This is what Christians call grace and redemption.

Incarnations are never disappointed. Jesus was never disappointed because of the iniquities and weaknesses of human beings, as we know from the many incidents of His life. He came to demonstrate how man can become God-conscious. His purpose was fulfilled when He inspired a few persons, however small the number

[9] *Ibid.,* chap. IV:138.

might be. He knew that this group would perpetuate and transmit His message through successive links of teachers and disciples, and that the spirit He awakened in the souls of men would operate for centuries until mankind would again become materialistic and selfish. He was also aware that His message would be diluted by His followers in the course of time and that they would act against His ideals; that the reforms He introduced would be misunderstood by them in a few centuries; that they would twist the meaning of His teachings to suit their own desires and ambitions. How beautifully St. John said: "And the light shineth in darkness; and the darkness comprehended it not" (John 1:5).

Swami Vivekananda tells us that civilizations move in wavelike motion, up and down.

> The wave rises on the ocean, and there is a hollow. Again another wave rises, perhaps bigger than the former, to fall down again; similarly, again to rise—driving onward. . . . This is the nature of the universe. Whether in the world of our thoughts, the world of our relations in society, or in our spiritual affairs, the same movement of succession, of rises and falls, is going on.[10]

Jesus was aware of this fact. Yet, because of His infinite mercy, His infinite love, He took human beings as they were. He introduced reforms to inspire people.

When an incarnation comes, the world is blessed, even though, as St. John tells us: "He came unto his own, and his own received him not" (John 1:11). The souls of many are inspired and they are irresistibly drawn to that center of spiritual and magnetic power. Those who come to the world during the lifetime of an incarnation or a little after are thrice blessed. God is manifested to the fullest extent in Him; nay, He is God. Swami Vivekananda understood this when he said of Christ: "If I, as an Oriental, have to worship Jesus of Nazareth, there is only one way left to me, that is, to worship Him as God and nothing else." This shows how an Oriental spiritual personality considers Jesus. Naturally, a thinking man would like to know if the ideal lived and taught by Jesus is in harmony with the ideals of the so-called Oriental people.

[10] *The Complete Works of Swami Vivekananda,* Advaita Ashrama, Mayavah, Almora, Himalayas, 1931-, 134.

We may say that it is evident that the Hindu view is closer to Christian orthodoxy than to "liberalism." The Hindu will agree with the orthodox in regarding Christ as unique in comparison with ordinary men; yet he will differ in holding that there have been and will be numerous incarnations of God. The Hindu would reject the view of those Christian liberals who regard all men as equally divine, Christ no more than anyone else. The Hindu accepts many special revelations and special manifestations in the form of divine incarnations.

Ananda Kentish Coomaraswamy

Ananda Coomaraswamy was born in Colombo, Ceylon, in 1877 of an English mother and a Ceylonese father. At the age of two he was taken to England and remained there until he had completed his formal education, receiving his Doctor of Science from the University of London at the age of twenty-five. From mineralogy and geology his interests turned to theology and art, and he came to America to join the Boston Museum of Fine Arts in 1917.

As a believing Hindu, he has asserted that a faithful account of Hinduism might be attained by categorically denying most statements ever made about it. Coomaraswamy's principal publications include "The Transformation of Nature in Art," "Hinduism and Buddhism," and "History of Indian and Indonesian Art." The following essay, which was entitled "Two Paths to the Same Summit," appeared in the book "Am I My Brother's Keeper?"

AM I MY BROTHER'S KEEPER? *

"There is no Natural Religion. . . . As all men are alike (though infinitely various), so all Religions, as all similars, have one source."
—William Blake

"There is but one salvation for all mankind, and that is the life of God in the soul."—William Law

The constant increase of contacts between ourselves, who for the purposes of the present essay may be assumed to be Christians, and other peoples who belong to the great non-Christian majority has made it more than ever before an urgent necessity for us to understand the faiths by which they live. Such an understanding is at the same time intrinsically to be desired, and indispensable for the solution by agreement of the economic and political problems by which the peoples of the world are at present more divided than united. We cannot establish human relationships with other peoples if we are convinced of our own superiority or superior wisdom, and only want to convert them to our way of thinking. The modern Christian, who thinks of the world as his parish, is faced with the painful necessity of becoming himself a citizen of the world; he is invited to participate in a symposium and a *convivium;* not to preside—for there is Another who presides unseen—but as one of many guests.

* A. Coomaraswamy, *Am I My Brother's Keeper?*, The John Day Company, Inc., New York, and Dennis Dobson, Ltd., London, 1947, pp. 36-50.

It is no longer only for the professed missionary that a study of other religions than his own is required. This very essay, for example, is based upon an address given to a large group of schoolteachers in a series entitled "How to Teach about Other Peoples," sponsored by the New York School Board and the East and West Association. It has, too, been proposed that in all the schools and universities of the postwar world stress should be laid on the teaching of the basic principles of the great world religions as a means of promoting international understanding and developing a concept of world citizenship.

The question next arises, By whom can such teaching be properly given? It will be self-evident that no one can have understood, and so be qualified to teach, a religion, who is opposed to all religion; this will rule out the rationalist and scientific humanist, and ultimately all those whose conception of religion is not theological, but merely ethical. The obvious ideal would be for the great religions to be taught only by those who confess them; but this is an ideal that could only be realized, for the present, in our larger universities. It has been proposed to establish a school of this kind at Oxford.

As things are, a teaching about other than Christian faiths is mainly given in theological seminaries and missionary colleges by men who do believe that Christianity is the only true faith, who approve of foreign missions, and who wish to prepare the missionary for his work. Under these conditions, the study of comparative religion necessarily assumes a character quite different from that of other disciplines; it cannot but be biased. It is obvious that if we are to teach at all it should be our intention to communicate only truth: but where a teaching takes for granted that the subject matter to be dealt with is intrinsically of inferior significance, and the subject is taught, not *con amore,* but only to instruct the future schoolmaster in the problems that he will have to cope with, one cannot but suspect that at least a part of the truth will be suppressed, if not intentionally, at least unknowingly.

If comparative religion is to be taught as other sciences are taught, the teacher must surely have recognized that his own religion is only one of those that are to be "compared"; he may not expound any "pet theories" of his own, but is to present the truth without bias, to the extent that it lies in his power. In other words, it will be "necessary to recognize that those institutions which are based on the same premises, let us say the supernatural, must be considered together, our own amongst the rest," whereas "today, whether it is a question of imperialism, or of race prejudice, or of a comparison between Christianity and paganism, we are still preoccupied with the uniqueness . . . of our own institutions and achievements, our own civilization." [1] One cannot but ask whether the Christian whose conviction is ineradicable that his is the only true faith can conscientiously permit himself to expound another religion, knowing that he cannot do so honestly.

We are, then, in proposing to teach about other peoples, faced with the problem of tolerance. The word is not a pretty one; to tolerate is to put up with, endure, or suffer the existence of what are or appear to be other ways of thinking than our own; and it is neither very pleasant merely "to put up with" our neighbors and fellow guests, nor very pleasant to feel that one's own deepest institutions and beliefs are being patiently "endured." Moreover, if the Western world is actually more tolerant today than it was some centuries ago, or has been since the fall of Rome, it is largely because men are no longer sure that there is any truth of which we can be certain, and are inclined to the "democratic" belief that one man's opinion is as good as another's, especially in the fields of politics, art, and religion. Tolerance, then, is a merely negative virtue, demanding no sacrifice of spiritual pride and involving no abrogation of our sense of superiority; it can be commended only in so far as it means that we shall refrain from hating or persecuting others who differ or seem to differ from ourselves in habit or belief. Tolerance still allows us to pity those who differ from ourselves, and are consequently to be pitied!

Tolerance, carried further, implies indifference, and becomes intolerable. Our proposal is not that we should tolerate heresies, but rather come to some agreement about the truth. Our proposition is that the proper objective of an education in comparative religion should be to enable the pupil to discuss with other believers the validity of particular doctrines, leaving the problem of

[1] Ruth Benedict, *Patterns of Culture,* New York, 1934, p. 5.

the truth or falsity, superiority or inferiority, of whole bodies of doctrine in abeyance until we have had at least an opportunity to know in what respects they really differ from one another, and whether in essentials or in accidentals. We take it for granted, of course, that they will inevitably differ accidentally, since "nothing can be known except in the mode of the knower." One must at least have been taught to recognize equivalent symbols, e.g., rose and lotus (Rosa Mundi and Padmāvatī); that Soma is the "bread and water of life"; or that the Maker of all things is by no means accidentally, but necessarily a "carpenter" wherever the material of which the world is made is *hylic*. The proposed objective has this further and immediate advantage, that it is not in conflict with even the most rigid Christian orthodoxy; it has never been denied that some truths are embodied in the pagan beliefs, and even St. Thomas Aquinas was ready and willing to find in the works of the pagan philosophers "extrinsic and probable proofs" of the truths of Christianity. He was, indeed, acquainted only with the ancients and with the Jews and some Arabians; but there is no reason why the modern Christian, if his mental equipment is adequate, should not learn to recognize or be delighted to find in, let us say, Vedāntic, Sūfī, Taoist, or American Indian formulations extrinsic and probable proofs of the truth as he knows it. It is more than probable, indeed, that his contacts with other believers will be of very great advantage to the Christian student in his exegesis and understanding of Christian doctrine; for though himself a believer, this is in spite of the nominalist intellectual environment in which he was born and bred, and by which he cannot but be to some degree affected; while the Oriental (to whom the miracles attributed to Christ present no problem) is still a realist, born and bred in a realistic environment, and is therefore in a position to approach Plato or St. John, Dante or Meister Eckhart more simply and directly than the Western scholar who cannot but have been affected to some extent by the doubts and difficulties that force themselves upon those whose education and environment have been for the greater part profane.

Such a procedure as we have suggested provides us immediately with a basis for a common understanding and for co-operation. What we have in view is an ultimate "reunion of the churches" in a far wider sense than that in which this expression is commonly employed: the substitution of active alliances—let us say of Christianity and Hinduism or Islam, on the basis of commonly recognized first principles, and with a view to an effective co-operation in the application of these principles to the contingent fields of art (manufacture) and prudence—for what is at present nothing better than a civil war between the members of one human family, children of one and the same God, "whom," as Philo said, "*with one accord* all Greeks and Barbarians acknowledge together."[2] It is with reference to this statement that Professor Goodenough remarks, "So far as I can see Philo was telling the simple truth about paganism as he saw it, not as Christian propaganda has ever since misrepresented it."

It need not be concealed that such alliances will necessarily involve an abandonment of all missionary enterprises such as they are now; interdenominational conferences will take the place of those proselytizing expeditions of which the only permanent result is the secularization and destruction of existing cultures and the pulling up of individuals by their roots. *You* have already reached the point at which culture and religion, utility and meaning, have been divorced and can be considered apart, but this is not true of those peoples whom you propose to convert, whose religion and culture *are one and the same thing* and none of the functions of whose life are necessarily profane or unprincipled. If ever you should succeed in persuading the Hindus that their revealed scriptures are valid only "as literature," you will have reduced them to the level of your own college men who read the Bible, if at all, only as literature. Christianity in India, as Sister Nivedita (Patrick Geddes' distinguished pupil, and author of *The Web of Indian Life*) once remarked, "carries drunkenness in its wake"—for if you teach a man that what he has thought right is wrong, he will be apt to think that what he has thought wrong is right.

We are all alike in need of repentance and conversion, a "change of mind" and a "turning round": not, however, from one *form* of belief to another, but from unbelief to belief. There can be no more vicious kind of tolerance than to approach another man, to tell

[2] E. R. Goodenough, *Introduction to Philo Judaeus*, New York, 1940, pp. 105, 108.

him, "We are both serving the same God, you in your way and I in His!" The "compassing of sea and land to make one proselyte" can be carried on as an institution only for so long as our ignorance of other peoples' faiths persists. The subsidizing of educational or medical services accessory to the primary purpose of conversion is a form of simony and an infringement of the instruction, "Heal the sick . . . provide neither gold nor silver nor brass in your purses, nor scrip for your journey . . . [but go] forth as sheep in the midst of wolves." Wherever you go, it must be not as masters or superiors but as guests, or as we might say nowadays, "exchange professors"; you must not return to betray the confidences of your hosts by any libel. Your vocation must be purged of any notion of a "civilizing mission"; for what you think of as "the white man's burden" here is a matter of "white shadows in the South Seas" there. Your "Christian" civilization is ending in disaster—and you are bold enough to offer it to others! Realize that, as Professor Plumer has said, "the surest way to betray our Chinese allies is to sell, give or lend-lease them our [American] standard of living,"[3] and that the hardest task you could undertake for the present and immediate future is to convince the Orient that the civilization of Europe is in any sense a Christian civilization, or that there really are reasonable, just, and tolerable Europeans amongst the "barbarians" of whom the Orient lives in terror.

The word "heresy" means choice, the having opinions of one's own, and thinking what we *like* to think: we can only grasp its real meaning today, when "thinking for oneself" is so highly recommended (with the proviso that the thinking must be "100 per cent"), if we realize that the modern equivalent of heresy is "treason." The one outstanding, and perhaps the only, real heresy of modern Christianity in the eyes of other believers is its claim to exclusive truth; for this is treason against Him who "never left himself without a witness," and can only be paralleled by Peter's denial of Christ; and whoever says to his pagan friends that "the light that is in you is darkness," in offending these is offending the Father of lights. In view of St. Ambrose's well-known gloss on I Corinthians

[3] J. M. Plumer, "China's High Standard of Living," *Asia and the Americas*, February, 1944.

12:2, "all that is true, *by whomsoever it has been said,* is from the Holy Ghost" (a dictum endorsed by St. Thomas Aquinas), you may be asked, "On what grounds do you propose to distinguish between your own 'revealed' religion and our 'natural' religion, for which, in fact, we also claim a supernatural origin?" You may find this question hard to answer.

The claim to an exclusive validity is by no means calculated to make for the survival of Christianity in a world prepared to prove all things. On the contrary, it may weaken enormously its prestige in relation to other traditions in which a very different attitude prevails, and which are under no necessity of engaging in any polemic. As a great German theologian has said, ". . . human culture [*Menschheitsbildung*] is a unitary whole, and its separate cultures are the dialects of one and the same language of the spirit."[4] The quarrel of Christianity with other religions seems to an Oriental as much a tactical error in the conflict of ideal with sensate motivations as it would have been for the Allies to turn against the Chinese on the battlefield. Nor will he participate in such a quarrel; much rather he will say, what I have often said to Christian friends, "Even if you are not on our side, we are on yours." The converse attitude is rarely expressed; but twice in my life I have met a Roman Catholic who could freely admit that for a Hindu to become a professing Christian was not essential to salvation. Yet, could we believe it, the Truth or Justice with which we are all alike and unconditionally concerned is like the Round Table to which "al the worlde crysten and hethen repayren" to eat of one and the same bread and drink the same wine, and at which "all are equal, the high and the low." A very learned Roman Catholic friend of mine, in correspondence, speaks of Srī Rāmakrishna as "another Christ . . . Christ's own self."

Let us now, for a moment, consider the points of view that have been expressed by the ancients and other non-Christians when they speak of religions other than their own. We have already quoted Philo. Plutarch, first with bitter irony disposing of the Greek euhemerists "who spread atheism all over the world by obliterating

[4] Alfred Jeremias, *Altorientalische Geisteskultur,* Vorwort.

the Gods of our belief and turning them all alike into the names of generals, admirals and kings," and of the Greeks who could no longer distinguish Apollo (the intelligible Sun) from Helios (the sensible sun), goes on to say, "Nor do we speak of the 'different Gods' of different peoples, or of the Gods as 'Barbarian' and 'Greek,' but as common to all, though differently named by different peoples, so that for the One Reason (Logos) that orders all these things, and the One Providence that oversees them, and for the minor powers [i.e., gods, angels] that are appointed to care for all things, there have arisen among different peoples different epithets and services, according to their different manners and customs." [5] Apuleius recognizes that the Egyptian Isis (our Mother Nature and Madonna, Natura Naturans, Creatrix, Deus) "is adored throughout the world in divers manners, in variable customs and by many names" (*The Golden Ass of Apuleius*).

The Mussulman Emperor of India, Jahāngīr, writing of his friend and teacher, the Hindu hermit Jadrūp, says that "his Vedānta is the same as our Tasawwulf": and, in fact, Northern India abounds in a type of religious literature in which it is often difficult, if not impossible, to distinguish Mussulman from Hindu factors. The indifference of religious forms is indeed, as Professor Nicholson remarks, "a cardinal Sūfī doctrine." So we find ibn-ul-'Arabī saying:

> *My heart is capable of every form: it is a pasture for gazelles and a convent for Christian monks,*
> *And idol-temple and the pilgrim's Ka'ba* [*Mecca*], *and the tables of the Torah and the book of the Koran;*

[5] Plutarch, *Isis and Osiris,* 67 (*Moralia,* 377). So William Law, in continuation of the citation above: "There is not one [salvation] for the Jew, another for the Christian, and a third for the heathen. No, God is one, human nature is one, and the way to it is one; and that is, the desire of the soul turned to God." Actually, this refers to "the baptism of desire" or "of the Spirit" (as distinguished from baptism by water, which involves an actual membership in the Christian community) and only modifies the Christian dogma *extra Ecclesiam nulla salus.* The real problem is that of the proper meaning of the words "Catholic Church"; we say that this should mean not any one religion as such, but the community, or universe of experience, of all those who love God. As William Law says also, "The chief hurt of a sect is this, that it takes itself to be necessary to the truth, whereas the truth is only then found when it is known to be of no sect but as free and universal as the goodness of God and as common to all names and nations as the air and light of this world."

I follow the religion of Love, whichever way his camels take; my religion and my faith is the true religion.[6]

That is to say that you and I, whose religions are distinguishable, can each of us say that "mine is the true religion," *and* to one another that "yours is the true religion"—whether or not either or both of us be truly religious depending not upon the form of our religion but upon ourselves and on grace. So, too, Shams-i-Tabriz:

If the notion of my Beloved is to be found in an idol-temple,
'Twere mortal sin to circumscribe the Ka'ba!
The Ka'ba is but a church if there His trace be lost:
My *Ka'ba is whatever "church" in which His trace is found!*[7]

Similarly in Hinduism; the Tamil poet-saint Tāyumānavar, for example, says in a hymn to Siva:

Thou didst fittingly . . . inspire as Teacher millions of religions.
Thou didst in each religion, while it like the rest showed in splendid fulness of treatises, disputations, sciences, [make] each its tenet to be the truth, the final goal.[8]

The *Bhaktakalpadruma* of Pratāpa Simha maintains that "every man should, as far as in him lieth, help the reading of the Scriptures, whether those of his own church or those of another." [9]

[6] R. A. Nicholson, *Mystics of Islam*, 1914, p. 105. Similarly, "If he [the follower of any particular religion] understood the saying of Junayd, 'The color of the water is the color of the water containing it,' he would not interfere with the beliefs of others, but would perceive God in every form and in every belief" (ibn-ul-'Arabī, Nicholson, *Studies in Islamic Mysticism*, 1921, p. 159). And, "Henceforth I knew that there were not many gods of human worship, but one God only, who was polyonomous and polymorphous, being figured and named according to the variety of the outward condition of things" (Sir George Birdwood, *Sva*, 1915, p. 28).

[7] R. A. Nicholson, *Diwani Shams-i-Tabriz*, 1898, p. 238; cf. p. 221. Cf. Faridu'd Din 'Attar, in the *Mantiqu't Tayr*: "Since, then, there are different ways of making the journey, no two [soul-] birds will fly alike. Each finds a way of his own, on this road of mystic knowledge, one by means of the Mihrab, and another through the Idol."

[8] Sir P. Arunachalam, *Studies and Translations*, Colombo, 1937, p. 201.

[9] Translation by Sir George Grierson, *Jras*, 1908, p. 347.

In the *Bhagavad Gītā* (VII:21) Srī Krishna proclaims, "If any lover whatsoever seeks with faith to worship any form [of God] whatever, it is I who am the founder of his faith," and (IV:11), "However men approach Me, even do I reward them, for the path men take from every side is Mine."

We have the word of Christ himself that he came to call, not the just, but sinners (Matthew 9:13). What can we make out of that, but that, as St. Justin said, "God is the Word of whom the whole human race are partakers, and those who lived according to Reason are Christians even though accounted atheists. . . . Socrates and Heracleitus, and of the barbarians Abraham and many others." So, too, Meister Eckhart, greatest of the Christian mystics, speaks of Plato (whom the Moslem Jīlī saw in a vision, "filling the world with light") as "that great priest," and as having "found the way ere ever Christ was born." Was St. Augustine wrong when he affirmed that "the very thing that is now called the Christian religion was not wanting amongst the ancients from the beginning of the human race, until Christ came in the flesh, after which the true religion, which already existed, began to be called 'Christian' "? Had he not retracted these brave words, the blood-stained history of Christianity might have been otherwise written!

We have come to think of religion more as a set of rules of conduct than as a doctrine about God; less as a doctrine about what we should *be*, than one of what we ought to *do;* and because there is necessarily an element of contingency in every application of principles to particular cases, we have come to believe that theory differs as practice must. This confusion of necessary means with transcendent ends (as if the vision of God could be earned by works) has had unfortunate results for Christianity, both at home and abroad. The more the Church has devoted herself to "social service," the more her influence has declined; an age that regards monasticism as an almost immoral retreat is itself unarmed. It is mainly because religion has been offered to modern men in nauseatingly sentimental terms ("Be good, sweet child," etc.), and no longer as an intellectual challenge, that so many have been revolted, thinking that *that* "is all there is to" religion. Such an emphasis on ethics (and, incidentally, forgetfulness that Christian doctrine has as much to do with art, i.e., manufacture, making, what and how, as it has to do with behavior) plays into the skeptic's hands; for the desirability and convenience of the social virtues is such and so evident that it is felt that if that *is* all that religion means, why bring in a God to sanction forms of conduct of which no one denies the propriety? Why indeed? At the same time this excessive emphasis upon the moral, and neglect of the intellectual virtues (which last alone, in orthodox Christian teaching, are held to survive our dissolution) invite the retorts of the rationalists who maintain that religion has never been anything but a means of drugging the lower classes and keeping them quiet.

Against all that, the severe intellectual discipline that any serious study of Eastern, or even "primitive," religion and philosophy demands can serve as a useful corrective. The task of co-operation in the field of comparative religion is one that demands the highest possible qualifications; if we cannot give our best to the task, it would be safer not to undertake it. The time is fast coming when it will be as necessary for the man who is to be called "educated" to know either Arabic, Sanskrit, or Chinese as it is now for him to read Latin, Greek, or Hebrew. And this, above all, in the case of those who are to teach about other peoples' faiths; for existing translations are often in many different ways inadequate, and if we are to know whether or not it is true that all believing men have hitherto worshiped and still worship one and the same God, whether by his English, Latin, Arabic, Chinese, or Navajo names, one must have searched the scriptures of the world—never forgetting that *sine desiderio mens non intelligit.*

Nor may we undertake these activities of instruction with ulterior motives: as in all other educational activities, so here the teacher's effort must be directed to the interest and advantage of the pupil himself, not that he may do good, but that he may be good. The dictum that "charity begins at home" is by no means necessarily a cynicism: it rather takes for granted that to do good is only possible when we are good, and that if we are good we shall do good, whether by action or inaction, speech or silence. It is sound Christian doctrine that a man must first have known and loved himself, his inner man, before he loves his neighbor.

It is, then, the pupil who comes first in our conception of the teaching of comparative religion. He will be astounded by the effect upon his understanding of Christian doctrine that can be induced by the recognition of similar doctrines stated in another language and by means of what are to him strange or even grotesque figures of thought. In the following of the *vestigia pedis,* the soul "in hot pursuit of her quarry, Christ," he will recognize an idiom of the language of the spirit that has come down to us from the hunting cultures of the Stone Age; a cannibal philosophy in that of the Eucharist and the Soma sacrifice; and the doctrine of the "seven rays" of the intelligible Sun in that of the Seven Gifts of the Spirit and in the "seven eyes" of the Apocalyptic Lamb and of Cuchulainn. He may find himself far less inclined than he is now to recoil from Christ's harder sayings, or those of St. Paul on the "sundering of soul from spirit." If he balks at the command to hate, not merely his earthly relatives, but "yea, and his own soul also," and prefers the milder wording of the Authorized Version, where "life" replaces "soul," or if he would like to interpret in a merely ethical sense the command to "deny himself," although the word that is rendered by "deny" means "utterly reject"; if he now begins to realize that the "soul" is of the dust that returns to the dust when the spirit returns to God who gave it, and that equally for Hebrew and Arabic theologians this "soul" (*nefesh, nafs*) imports that carnal "individuality" of which the Christian mystics are thinking when they say that "the soul must put itself to death," or that our existence (distinguishing *esse* from *essentia,* γένεσις from οὐσία, *bhū* from *as*) is a crime; and if he correlates all these ideas with the Islamic and Indian exhortation to "die before you die" and with St. Paul's "I live, yet *not I,*" then he may be less inclined to read into Christian doctrine any promise of eternal life for any "soul" that has been concreated with the body—and better equipped to show that the spiritualists' "proofs" of the survival of human personality, however valid, have no religious bearings whatever.

The mind of the democratic student to whom the very name of the concept of a "divine right" may be unintelligible is likely to be roughly awakened if he ever realizes that, as Professor Buckler often reminds us, the very notion of a *kingdom* of God on earth "depends for its revelation on the inner meaning of eastern kingship," for he may have forgotten in his righteous detestation of all dictatorships, that the classical definition of "tyranny" is that of "a king ruling in his own interests."

Nor is this a one-sided transaction; it would not be easy to exaggerate the alteration that can be brought about in the Hindu's or Buddhist's estimate of Christianity when the opportunity is given him to come into closer contact with the quality of thought that led Vincent of Beauvais to speak of Christ's "ferocity" and Dante to marvel at "the multitude of teeth with which this Love bites."

"Some contemplate one Name, and some another? Which of these is the best? All are eminent clues to the transcendent, immortal, unembodied Brahma: these Names are to be contemplated, lauded, and at last denied. For by them one rises higher and higher in these worlds; but where all comes to its end, there he attains to the Unity of the Person" (*Maitri Upanishad*). Whoever knows this text, but nothing of Western technique, will assuredly be moved by a sympathetic understanding when he learns that the Christian also follows a *via affimativa* and a *via remotionis!* Whoever has been taught a doctrine of "liberation from the pairs of opposites" (past and future, pleasure and pain, etc., the Symplegades of "folk-lore") will be stirred by Nicholas of Cusa's description of the wall of Paradise wherein God dwells as "built of contradictories," and by Dante's of what lies beyond this wall as "not in space, nor hath it poles," but "where every where and every when is focussed." We all need to realize, with Xenophon, that "when God is our teacher, we come to think alike."

For there are as many of these Hindus and Buddhists whose knowledge of Christianity and of the greatest Christian writers is virtually nil, as there are Christians, equally learned, whose real knowledge of any other religion but their own is virtually nil, because they have never imagined what it might be to *live* these other faiths. Just as there can be no real knowledge of a language if we have never even imaginatively participated in the activities to which the language refers, so there can be no real knowledge of any "life" that one has not in some measure lived. The greatest of modern Indian saints actually practiced Christian and Islamic disciplines, that is, worshiped Christ and Allah, and found that all led to the same goal: he could speak from experience of the equal validity of all these "ways," and feel the same respect for each, while still preferring for himself the one to which his whole being was naturally attuned by nativity, temperament, and training. What a loss it would have been to his countrymen and to the world, and even to Christianity, if he had "become a Christian"! There are many paths that lead to the summit of one and the same mountain; their differences will be the more apparent the lower down we are, but they vanish at the peak; each will naturally take the one that starts from the point at which he finds himself; he who goes round about the mountain looking for another is not climbing. Never let us approach another believer to ask him to become "one of *us*," but approach him with respect as one who is already "one of *His*," who *is*, and from whose invariable beauty all contingent being depends!

Mohandas Karamchand Gandhi

Mohandas Karamchand Gandhi was born October 2, 1869, and was assassinated January 29, 1948. Gandhi's philosophy was his life: "I have nothing new to teach the world. Truth and non-violence are as old as the hills." His contact with Christianity was long and disappointing. Sundhar Singh said of both Gandhi and Rabindranath Tagore that they ". . . would have become Christians had they never visited Europe."

The following selection is from a series of brief essays which first appeared in a Navajivan Press publication entitled "Christian Missions"; they have since been grouped and edited by Clifford Manshardt and published as "The Mahatma and the Mission." This highly autobiographical excerpt from Manshardt's edition reflects both Gandhi's love for Christianity and his discontent with the Christian mission.

THE MAHATMA AND THE MISSIONARY *

I saw no reason for changing my belief—my religion.[1] It was impossible for me to believe that I could go to heaven or attain salvation only by becoming a Christian. When I frankly said so to some of the good Christian friends, they were shocked. But there was no help for it.

My difficulties lay deeper. It was more than I could believe that Jesus was the only incarnate son of God, and that only he who believed in Him would have everlasting life. If God could have sons, all of us were His sons. If Jesus was like God, or God Himself, then all men were like God and could be God Himself. My reason was not ready to believe literally that Jesus by his death and by his blood redeemed the sins of the world. Metaphorically there might be some truth in it. Again, according to Christianity only human beings had souls, and not other living beings, for whom death meant complete extinction; while I held a contrary belief. I could accept Jesus as a martyr, an embodiment of sacrifice, and a divine teacher, but not as the most perfect man ever born. His death on the Cross was a great example to the world, but that there was anything like a mysterious or miraculous virtue in it, my heart could not accept. The pious lives of Christians did not give

* M. Gandhi, *The Mahatma and the Mission* (C. Manshardt, ed.), Navajivan Trust, Navajivan, India, 1941, pp. 38-45, 114-131.

[1] Shortly after Gandhi's adult introduction to Christianity, he was taken to a Christian convention by some of his friends. What follows is his reaction to that convention and to Christianity in general. Editor.

me anything that the lives of men of other faiths had failed to give. I had seen in other lives just the same reformation that I had heard of among Christians. Philosophically there was nothing extraordinary in Christian principles. From the point of view of sacrifice it seemed to me that the Hindus greatly surpassed the Christians. It was impossible for me to regard Christianity as a perfect religion or the greatest of all religions.

I shared this mental churning with my Christian friends whenever there was an opportunity, but their answers could not satisfy me.

Thus if I could not accept Christianity either as a perfect, or the greatest religion, neither was I then convinced of Hinduism being such. Hindu defects were pressingly visible to me. If untouchability could be a part of Hinduism, it could be but a rotten part or an excrescence. I could not understand the *raison d'être* of a multitude of sects and castes. What was the meaning of saying that the Vedas were the inspired Word of God? If they were inspired, why not also the Bible and the Koran?

As Christian friends were endeavouring to convert me, even so were Mussalman friends. Abdulla Sheth had kept on inducing me to study Islam, and of course he had always something to say regarding its beauty.

I expressed my difficulties in a letter to Raychandbhai. I also corresponded with other religious authorities in India and received answers from them. Raychandbhai's letter somewhat pacified me. He asked me to be patient and to study Hinduism more deeply. One of his sentences was to this effect: "On a dispassionate view of the question, I am convinced that no other religion has the subtle and profound thought of Hinduism, its vision of the soul, or its charity."

I purchased Sale's translation of the Koran and began reading it. I also obtained other books on Islam. I communicated with Christian friends in England. One of them introduced me to Edward Maitland, with whom I opened correspondence. He sent me *The Perfect Way*, a book he had written in collaboration with Anna Kingsford. The book was a repudiation of the current Christian belief. He also sent me another book, *The New Interpretation of the Bible*. I liked both. They seemed to support Hinduism. Tolstoy's *The Kingdom of God Is within You* overwhelmed me. It left an abiding impression on me. Before the independent thinking, profound morality, and the truthfulness of this book, all the books given me by Mr. Coates seemed to pale into insignificance.

My studies thus carried me in a direction unthought of by the Christian friends. My correspondence with Edward Maitland was fairly prolonged, and that with Raychandbhai continued until his death. I read some of the books he sent me. These included *Panchikaran, Maniratnamala, Mumukshu Prakaran of Yogavasishtha, Haribhadra Suri's Shaddarshana Samuchchaya* and others.

Though I took a path my Christian friends had not intended for me, I have remained forever indebted to them for the religious quest that they awakened in me. I shall always cherish the memory of their contact. The years that followed had more, not less, of such sweet and sacred contacts in store for me. . . .

If, in South Africa, I found myself entirely absorbed in the service of the community, the reason behind it was my desire for self-realization. I had made the religion of service my own, as I felt that God could be realized only through service. And service for me was the service of India, because it came to me without my seeking, because I had an aptitude for it. I had gone to South Africa for travel, for finding an escape from Kathiawad intrigues and for gaining my own livelihood. But as I have said, I found myself in search of God and striving for self-realization.

Christian friends had whetted my appetite for knowledge which had become almost insatiable, and they would not leave me in peace, even if I had desired to be indifferent. In Durban Mr. Spencer Walton, the head of the South African General Mission, found me out. I became almost a member of his family. At the back of this acquaintance was of course my contact with Christians in Pretoria. Mr. Walton had a manner all his own. I do not recollect his ever having invited me to embrace Christianity. But he placed his life as an open book before me, and let me watch all his movements. Mrs. Walton was a very gentle and talented woman. I liked the attitude of this couple. We knew the fundamental differences between us. Any amount of discussion could not efface them. Yet even differences prove helpful, where there are tolerance, charity and truth. I liked Mr. and Mrs. Walton's humility, perseverance and devotion to work, and we met very frequently.

This friendship kept alive my interest in religion. It was impossible now to get the leisure that I used to have in Pretoria for my religious studies. But what little time I could spare I turned to good account. My religious correspondence continued. Raychandbhai was guiding me. Some friend sent me Narmadshankar's book *Dharma Vichar*. Its preface proved very helpful. I had heard about the Bohemian way in which the poet had lived, and a description, in the preface, of the revolution effected in his life by his religious studies captivated me. I came to like the book, and read it from cover to cover with attention. I read with interest Max Muller's book, *India—What Can It Teach Us?* and the translation of the *Upanishads* published by the Theosophical Society. All this enhanced my regard for Hinduism, and its beauties began to grow upon me. It did not, however, prejudice me against other religions. I read Washington Irving's *Life of Mahomet and His Successors* and Carlyle's panegyric on the Prophet. These books raised Muhammad in my estimation. I also read a book called *The Sayings of Zarathustra.*

Thus I gained more knowledge of the different religions. The study stimulated my self-introspection, and fostered in me the habit of putting into practice whatever appealed to me in my studies. Thus I began some of the Yogic practices, as well as I could understand them from a reading of the Hindu books. But I could not get on very far, and decided to follow them with the help of some expert when I returned to India. The desire has never been fulfilled.

I made too an extensive study of Tolstoy's books. *The Gospels in Brief, What to Do?* and other books made a deep impression on me. I began to realize more and more the infinite possibilities of universal love.

About the same time I came in contact with another Christian family. At their suggestion, I attended the Wesleyan Church every Sunday. For these days I also had their standing invitation to dinner. The church did not make a favourable impression on me. The sermons seemed to be uninspiring. The congregation did not strike me as being particularly religious. They were not an assembly of devout souls; they appeared rather to be worldly-minded people going to church for recreation and in conformity to custom. Here, at times, I would involuntarily doze. I was ashamed, but some of my neighbours, who were in no better case, lightened the shame. I could not go on long like this, and soon gave up attending the service. . . .

My final deliberate striving to realize Christianity as it was presented to me was in 1901, when in answer to promises made to one of my Christian friends, I thought it my duty to see one of the biggest of Indian Christians, as I was told he was—the late Kali Charan Banerjee. I went over to him—I am telling you of the deep search that I have undergone in order that I might leave no stone unturned to find out the true path—I went to him with an absolutely open mind and in a receptive mood, and I met him also under circumstances which were most affecting. I found that there was much in common between Mr. Banerjee and myself. His simplicity, his humility, his courage, his truthfulness, all these things I have all along admired. He met me when his wife was on her death-bed. You cannot imagine a more impressive scene, a more ennobling circumstance. I told Mr. Banerjee, "I have come to you as a seeker. I have come to you in fulfillment of a sacred promise I have made to some of my dearest Christian friends that I will leave no stone unturned to find out the true light." I told him that I had given my friends the assurance that no worldly gain would keep me away from the light, if I could but see it. Well, I am not going to engage you in giving a description of the little discussion that we had between us. It was very good, very noble. I came away, not sorry, not dejected, not disappointed, but I felt sad that even Mr. Banerjee could not convince me. . . .

Through the years Christian missionaries have made many attempts to convert me. I was favoured with some literature even at Yeravda prison by well-meaning missionaries, which seemed to be written as if merely to belittle Hinduism. . . . But it is a matter of pleasure to me to be able to say that, if I have had painful experiences of Christians and Christian missionaries, I have had pleasant ones also which I treasure. There is no doubt that among them the spirit of toleration is growing. Among individuals there is also a deeper study of Hinduism and other faiths and an appreciation of their beauties, and among some even an admission that the other great faiths of the world are not false. One is thankful for the growing liberal spirit, but I have the conviction that much still remains to be done in that direction.

My acquaintance with missionaries is by no means a new thing. In South Africa, where I found myself in the midst of inhospitable surroundings, I was able to make hundreds of Christian friends. I came in touch with the late Mr. Spencer Walton, Director of the South Africa General Mission, and later with the great divine, Reverend Mr. A. Murray, and several others. . . .

There was even a time in my life when a very sincere and intimate friend of mine, a great and good Quaker, had designs on me. He thought that I was too good not to become a Christian. I was sorry to have disappointed him. One missionary friend of mine in South Africa still writes to me and asks me, "How is it with you?" I have always told this friend that so far as I know it is all well with me. If it was prayer that these friends expected me to make, I was able to tell them that every day the heart-felt prayer within the closed door of my closet went to the Almighty to show me light and give me wisdom and courage to follow that light.

An English friend has been at me for the past thirty years trying to persuade me that there is nothing but damnation in Hinduism and that I must accept Christianity. When I was in jail I got, from separate sources, no less than three copies of *The Life of Sister Thérèse*, in the hope that I should follow her example and accept Jesus as the only begotten son of God and my Saviour. I read the book prayerfully but I could not accept even Saint Thérèse's testimony for myself. I must say, however, I have an open mind, if indeed at this stage and age of my life I can be said to have an open mind on this question.

Though I have been a friend of missions for years, I have always been a critic, not from any desire to be critical, but because I have felt that I would be a better friend if I opened out my heart, even at the risk of wounding feelings. . . . The first distinction I would like to make, after these prefatory remarks, between Christian missionary work and mine, is that while I am strengthening the faith of the people, missions are undermining it. I have always felt that mission work will be the richer if missionaries accept as settled facts the faiths of the people they come to serve—faiths which, however crude, are valuable to them. And in order to appreciate my point of view, it becomes perhaps necessary to re-read the message of the Bible in terms of what is happening around us. The word is the same, but the spirit ever broadens intensively and extensively, and it might be that many things in the Bible will have to be re-interpreted in the light of discoveries—not of modern science—but in the spiritual world in the shape of direct experiences common to all faiths. The fundamental verses of St. John do require to be re-read and re-interpreted. I have come to feel that like us human beings words have their evolution from stage to stage in the contents they hold. For instance the contents of the richest word—God—are not the same to every one of us. They will vary with experiences of each. They will mean one thing to the Santhal and another to his next door neighbor Rabindranath Tagore. The Sanatanist may reject my interpretation of God and Hinduism. But God Himself is a long-suffering God who puts up with any amount of abuse and misinterpretations. If we were to put the spiritual experiences together, we would find a result that would answer the cravings of human nature. Christianity is 1900 years old, Islam is 1300 years old; who knows the possibility of either? I have not read the Vedas in the original, but I have tried to assimilate their spirit and have not hesitated to say that, though the Vedas may be 13,000 years old—or even a million years old—as they well may be, for the word of God is as old as God Himself, even the Vedas must be interpreted in the light of our experience. The powers of God should not be limited by the limitations of our understanding. To those who have come to teach India, I therefore say, you cannot give without taking. If you have come to give rich treasures of experience, open your hearts out to receive the treasures of this land, and you will not be disappointed, neither will you have misread the message of the Bible.

But unfortunately, missionaries come to India thinking they come to a land of heathens, of idolaters, of men who do not know God. One of the greatest of Christian divines, Bishop Heber, wrote the two lines which have always left a sting with me: "Where every prospect pleases, and only man is vile." I wish he had not written them. My own experience in my travels throughout India has been to the contrary. I have gone from one end of the country to the other, without any prejudice, in a relentless search after truth, and I am not able to say that here in this fair land, watered by the great Ganges, the Brahmaputra and the Jumna, man is vile. He is not vile. He is as much a seeker after truth as you and I are, possibly more so. This reminds me of a French book translated for me by a French friend. It is an account of an imaginary expedition in search of knowledge. One party landed in India and found Truth and God personified, in a little pariah's hut. I tell you there are many such huts belonging to the untouchables where you will certainly find God. They do not reason, but they persist in their belief that God is. They depend upon God for His assistance and find it too. There are many stories told throughout the length and breadth of India about these noble untouchables. Vile as some of them may be there are noblest specimens of humanity in their midst. But does my experience exhaust itself merely with the untouchables? No, I can say that there are non-Brahmins, there are Brahmins who are as fine specimens of humanity as you will find in any place on the earth. There are Brahmins, today in India, who are embodiments of self-sacrifice, godliness and humility. There are Brahmins who are devoting themselves body and soul to the service of untouchables, with no expectation of reward from the untouchables, but with execration from orthodoxy. They do not mind it, because in serving pariahs they are serving God. I can quote chapter and verse from my experience. I place these facts before my missionary friends in all humility for the simple reason that they may know this land better—the land which they have come to serve. The missionaries are here to find out the distress of the people of India and remove it. But I hope that they are also here in a receptive mood, and if there is anything that India has to give, they will not stop their ears, they will not close their eyes, and steel their hearts, but open up their ears, eyes and most of all their hearts to receive all that may be good in this land. I give my assurance that there is a great deal of good in India. Missionaries must not flatter themselves with the belief that a mere recital of that celebrated verse in St. John makes a man a Christian. If I have read the Bible correctly, I know many men who have never heard the name of Jesus Christ or have even rejected the official interpretation of Christianity will, probably, if Jesus came in our midst today in the flesh, be owned by him more than many of us. I therefore ask you to approach the problem before you with open-heartedness and humility.

I recently engaged in a friendly conversation with some missionaries. I do not want to relate that conversation. But I do want to say that they were fine specimens of humanity. They did not want to misunderstand me, but I had to pass nearly one hour and a half in my attempt to explain to them that in writing what I had written I had not written anything in a spirit of ill will or hatred towards Englishmen. I was hard put to it to carry that conviction. In fact I do not know whether I carried that conviction to them at all. If salt loseth its savour, wherewith shall it be salted? If I could not drive home the truth that was in me to the three friends who certainly came with open minds, how should I fare with others? It has often occurred to me that a seeker after truth has to be silent. I know the wonderful efficacy of silence. I visited a Trappist monastery in South Africa. A beautiful place it was. Most of the inmates of that place were under a vow of silence. I enquired of the Father the motive of it, and he said that the motive was apparent. "We are frail human beings. We do not know very often what we say. If we want to listen to the still small voice that is always speaking within us, it will not be heard if we continually speak." I understood that precious lesson. I know the secret of silence. I do not know just now whether it would not have been wise if I had said nothing to those friends beyond saying, "We shall know each other better when the mists have rolled away." Just now I feel humiliated. Why did I argue with these friends? But I say these things, first of service. I have told my misionary friends, "Noble as you are, you have isolated yourselves from the people you want to serve." I cannot help recalling the conversation I related in Darjeeling at the missionary Language School. Lord Salisbury was waited upon by a deputation of missionaries in connection with China and this deputation wanted protection. I cannot recall the exact words but give the purport of the answer Lord Salisbury gave.

He said, "Gentlemen, if you want to go to China to preach the message of Christianity, then do not ask for the assistance of the temporal power. Go with your lives in your hands and, if the people of China want to kill you, imagine that you have been killed in the service of God." Lord Salisbury was right. Christian missionaries come to India under the shadow, or, if you like, under the protection of a temporal power, and it creates an impassable bar.

If you give me statistics that so many orphans have been reclaimed and brought to the Christian faith, I would accept them but I do not feel convinced thereby that it is the Christian mission. In my opinion the missionary purpose is infinitely superior to that. You want to find men in India and, if you want to do that, you will have to go to the lowly cottages, not to give them something but perhaps to take something from them. . . . I miss receptiveness, humility, and willingness on the part of the missionaries to identify themselves with the masses of India.

By taking the position that he is going to *give* his spiritual goods, the missionary labels himself as belonging to a different and higher species, which makes him inaccessible to others. There certainly is plenty of good work for American missionaries to do in America. They are not a superfluity there. If it was not for the curious position that their Church has taken, they would not be here. The missionary cannot claim infallibility. He assumes knowledge of all people, which he could do only if he were God. Missionaries in India are laboring under a double fallacy: that what they think best for another person is really so; and that what they regard as the best for themselves is the best for the whole world. I am pleading for a little humility.

Missionaries should alter their attitude. Today they tell people that there is no salvation for them except through the Bible and through Christianity. It is customary to decry other religions and to offer their own as the only one that can bring deliverance. That attitude should be radically changed. Let them appear before the people as they are, and try to rejoice in seeing Hindus become better Hindus and Mussalmans better Mussalmans. Let them start work at the bottom, let them enter into what is best in their life and offer nothing inconsistent with it. That will make their work far more efficacious, and what they will say and offer to the people will be appreciated without suspicion and hostility. In a word, let them go to the people not as patrons, but as one of them, and not to oblige them but to serve them and to work among them.

To the missionary I would say: Just forget that you have come to a country of heathens, and think that they are as much in search of God as you are; just feel that you are not attempting to give your spiritual goods to the people, but share your worldly goods, of which you have a good stock. You will then do your work without a mental reservation and thereby you will share your spiritual treasures. . . . It is not wrong that a Christian missionary should rely on his own experience, but [wrong] that he should dispute the evidence of a Hindu devotee's life. Just as he has his spiritual experience and the joy of communion, even so has a Hindu.

Christian missionaries quite unconsciously do harm to themselves and so to us. It is perhaps impertinent for me to say that they do harm to themselves, but quite pertinent to say that they do harm to us. They do harm to those amongst whom they work and those amongst whom they do not work, i.e., the harm is done to the whole of India. They present a Christianity of their belief but not the message of Jesus as I understand it. The more I study their activities the more sorry I become. There is such a gross misunderstanding of religion on the part of those who are intelligent, very far advanced, and whose motives need not be questioned. It is a tragedy that such a thing should happen in the human family.

Missionaries should cease to think that they must convert the whole world to their interpretation of Christianity. At the end of reading the Bible, let me tell you, it did not leave on my mind the impression that Jesus ever meant Christians to do what the bulk of those who take his name do. The moment you give up the attitude of religious imperialism the field of service becomes limitless. You limit your own capacity by thinking and saying that you must proselytize. Let Christian missionaries literally follow the words of Jesus—"Not he that sayeth 'Lord, Lord,' but he that doeth His will. . . ." That brings me to the duty of tolerance. If you cannot feel that the other faith is as true as yours, you should feel at least that the men are as true as you.

I want missionaries to complement the faith of the people instead of undermining it. As the Dewan of Mysore said in his address to the Assembly, the Adi Karnatakas should be made better Hindus, as they belong to Hinduism. I would similarly say to you make us better Hindus, i.e., better men or women. Why should a man, even if he becomes a Christian, be torn from his surroundings? Whilst a boy I heard it being said that to become a Christian was to have a brandy bottle in one hand and beef in the other. Things are better now, but it is not unusual to find Christianity synonymous with denationalization and Europeanization. Must we give up our simplicity to become better people? Do not lay the axe at our simplicity.

The teaching of Jesus should not be confused with what passes for modern civilization. It is no part of the missionary call to tear the life of the people of the East by its roots. Tolerate whatever is good in that life and do not hastily, with preconceived notions, judge it. In spite of your belief in the greatness of Western civilization and in spite of your pride in all your achievements, I plead with you for humility, and ask you to leave some little room for doubt in which, as Tennyson sang, there was more truth, though by "doubt" he no doubt meant a different thing. Let each one live his life, and if ours is the right life, where is the cause for hurry? It will react of itself.

A time is coming when those who are in the mad rush today of multiplying their wants, vainly thinking that they add to the real substance, real knowledge of the world, will retrace their steps and say, "What have we done?" Civilizations have come and gone, and in spite of all our vaunted progress I am tempted to ask again and again, "To what purpose?" . . . Let us by all means drink deep of the fountains that are given to us in the Sermon on the Mount, but then we shall have to take to sackcloth and ashes. The teaching of the Sermon was meant for each and every one of us. You cannot serve both God and Mammon.

The ability of missionaries is unquestioned. All of these abilities can be used for the service of India, and India will appreciate them. But that can only happen if there are no mental reservations. If you come to give education, you must give it after the Indian pattern. You should sympathetically study our institutions and suggest changes. But you come with preconceived notions and seek to destroy. If people from the West came on Indian terms, they would supply a felt want. When Americans come and ask me what service they can render, I tell them: If you dangle your millions before us, you will make beggars of us and demoralize us. But in one thing I do not mind being a beggar. I would beg of you your scientific talent. You can ask your engineers and agricultural experts to place their services at our disposal. They must not come to us as our lords and masters but as volunteer workers. . . . A Mysore engineer (who is a Pole) has sent me a box of handmade tools made to suit village requirements. Supposing an engineer of that character comes and studies our tools and our cottage machines and suggests improvements in them, he would be of great service. If you do this kind of work in a religious spirit, you will have delivered the message of Jesus.

Service, which has not the slightest touch of self in it, is itself the highest religion. . . . Conversion and service go ill together. My complaint with my missionary friends is that they do not bring to bear on their work a purely humanitarian spirit. Their object is to add more members to their fold. . . . Some of the friends of a Mission were the other day in high glee over the conversion to Christianity of a learned pandit. They have been dear friends, and so I told them that it was hardly proper to go into ecstasies over a man forsaking his religion. Today it is the case of a learned Hindu, tomorrow it may be that of an ignorant villager not knowing the principles of his religion. . . . Certainly I would feel no joy if a Christian should embrace Hinduism. Here is Miraben. I would have her find all the spiritual comfort she needs from Christianity, and I should not dream of converting her to Hinduism, even if she wanted to do so. Today it is the case of a grown-up woman like her, tomorrow it may be that of a European child trusted to my care by a friend. Take the case of Khan Saheb's daughter entrusted to my care by her father. I should jealously educate her in her own faith and should strive my utmost against her being lured away from it, if ever she was so inclined. I have had the privilege of having children and grown-up persons of other faiths with me. I was thankful to find them better Christians, Mussalmans, Parsis or Jews by their contact with me. . . . Let my missionary friends remember that it was none but that most Christlike of all Christians, Albert Schweitzer, who gave Christianity a unique interpretation when he himself resolved "not to preach any more, not to lecture any more," but to bury himself in Equatorial Africa simply with a view to fulfill somewhat the debt that Europe owes to Africa.

Let us consider the matter of missionary hospitals in this connection. When missionaries give medical help they expect a reward in the shape of some of their patients becoming Christians. At the back of their minds is not pure service for its sake, but the result of service in the shape of many people coming to the Christian fold. . . . The kink is in the Church thinking that there are people in whom certain things are lacking, and that you must supply them whether they want them or not. If you simply say to your patients, "You have taken the medicine I gave you. Thank God, He has healed you. Don't come again," you have done your duty. But if you also say, "How nice it would be if you had the same faith in Christianity as I have," you do not make of your medicine a free gift. . . . The way out of the difficulty, as I see it, is for you to feel that what you possess, your patient also can possess, but through a different route. . . . Because you adore your mother, you cannot wish that all other children were your mother's children. That would be a physical impossibility. In like manner, your position is a spiritual impossibility. God has the whole of humanity as His children. How can I limit His grace by my little mind and say that mine is the only way?

That which is true of the medical work of Christian missions is also true of the educational and social work. These activities are undertaken, not for their own sake, but as an aid to the salvation of those who receive such service. The history of India would have been written differently if the Christians had come to India to live their lives in our midst and permeate ours with their aroma, if there was any. There would then have been mutual good will and utter absence of suspicion. "But," say some of you, "if what you say had held good with Jesus, there would have been no Christians." To answer this would land me in a controversy in which I have no desire to engage. But I may be permitted to say that Jesus preached not a new religion but a new life. He called men to repentance. It was he who said, "Not every one that saith unto me, 'Lord, Lord,' shall enter into the kingdom of heaven; but he that doeth the will of my Father which is in heaven."

Much good work is being done by missions, but give up that which makes you objects of suspicion and demoralizes us also. We go to your hospitals with the mercenary motive of having an operation performed, but with no object of responding to what is at the back of your mind, even as our children do when they go to Bible classes in their colleges and then laugh at what they read there. I tell you our conversation at home about these missionary colleges is not at all edifying. Why then spoil your good work with other motives?

I am convinced that the American and British money which has been voted for Missionary Societies has done more harm than good. You cannot serve God and Mammon both. And my fear is that Mammon has been sent to serve India and God has remained behind, with the result that He will one day have His vengeance.

I would say to Christian leaders that there should be less of theology and more of truth in all that you say and do. . . . Amongst agents of the many untruths that are propounded in the world one of the foremost is theology. I do not say there is no demand for it. There is a demand in the world for many a questionable thing. But even those who have to do with theology as part of their work have to survive their theology. I have two good Christian friends who gave up theology and decided to live the gospel of Christ. I have profited from my study of Jesus, but not, let me tell you, through theology or through the ordinary interpretation of theologists.

There is a proper evangelization. When you feel that you have received peace from your particular interpretation of the Bible, you share it with others. But you do not need to give vocal expression to it. Your whole life is more eloquent than your lips. Language is always an obstacle to the full expression of thought. How, for instance, will you tell a man to read the Bible as you read it, how by word of mouth will you transfer to him the light as you receive it from day to day and moment to moment? Therefore all religions say, "Your life is your speech." If you are humble enough, you will say you cannot adequately represent your religion by speech or pen. . . . Language is a limitation of the truth which can only be represented by life.

Life is its own expression. I take the simile of the rose I used years ago. The rose does not need to write a book or deliver a sermon on the scent it sheds all around, or on the beauty which everyone who has eyes can see. Well, spiritual life is infinitely superior to the beautiful and fragrant rose, and I make bold to say that the moment there is a spiritual expression in life, the surroundings will readily respond. There are passages in the Bible, the *Gita*, the *Bhagawat*, the Koran, which eloquently show this. "Wherever," we read, "Krishna appeared, people acted like those possessed." The same thing about Jesus. But to come nearer home, why are people touched as if by magic wherever Jawaharlal goes? They sometimes do not even know he has come, and yet they take sudden fire from the very thought that he is coming. Now there it may not be described as a spiritual influence, but there is a subtle influence and it is unquestionably there, call it by what name you like. They do not want to hear him, they simply want to see him. And that is natural. You cannot deal with millions in any other way. Spiritual life has greater potency than Marconi waves. When there is no medium between me and my Lord, and I simply become a willing vessel for His influences to flow into it, then I overflow as the water of the Ganges at its source. There is no desire to speak when one lives the truth. Truth is most economical of words. There is thus no truer or other evangelism than life.

I should like to see all men, not only in India but in the world, belonging to different faiths, become better people by contact with one another and, if that happens, the world will be a much better place to live in than it is today. I plead for the broadest toleration, and I am working to that end. I ask people to examine every religion from the point of the religionists themselves. I do not expect the India of my dream to develop one religion, i.e., to be wholly Hindu, or wholly Christian, or wholly Mussalman, but I want it to be wholly tolerant with its religions working side by side with one another.

Tolerance does not mean indifference towards one's own faith, but a more intelligent and purer love for it. Tolerance gives us spiritual insight, which is as far from fanaticism as the north pole from the south. True knowledge of religion breaks down the barriers between faith and faith. Cultivation of tolerance for other faiths will impart to us a truer understanding of our own.

Buddhism

Masaharu Anesaki

Masaharu Anesaki was born in Kyoto in 1873, graduated from Tokyo University in 1896, and did further studies in Europe and India before returning to Japan as professor of Buddhism at Tokyo University.

Anesaki often lectured abroad on Japanese culture and was a professor of Japanese studies at Harvard University. In addition to achieving a world reputation as lecturer, he was the author of several books. His "History of Japanese Religions" is regarded as the most comprehensive study of the subject available in English. His other works include "Fundamental Buddhism," "Art, Life and Nature in Japan," "Nichiren, the Buddhist Prophet," "The Religions of Japan," "Buddhist Art," and "A Concordance to the History of Catholic Missions in the 16th and 17th Centuries." The following essay first appeared in the Hibbert Journal in 1905. Anesaki died in 1949.

HOW CHRISTIANITY APPEALS TO A JAPANESE BUDDHIST *

No religion, not even the most catholic or cosmopolitan in its character, can claim an absolute unity and homogeneity. Christ's teaching of the love of our Father in heaven and, as its corollary, of the brotherly love of men can in no way be an exception to this rule. This is too obvious a fact to need a demonstration. It is a well-known fact that even among the Synoptists there are discrepancies as regards their respective views of Christ's person and teaching; still more is this the case with the relations between them and St. John or St. Paul. The Christ of the Roman Catholics is more the world-ruler than the high priest of the Protestants. I never think that Christianity, because of the manifoldness of its historical developments and varieties of personal beliefs, is not a unified religion. The unity of Christianity must be fully recognized, so far as it is founded upon the teaching of Christ and so far as its religion consists in a belief in the person of Christ. Truth is one, but modes of its expression cannot be so. The essence of Christianity is universal, but its adaptation to various hearts and heads needs a certain flexibility. The function of each instrument in an orchestral performance consists in its harmonization with the general concert, and at the same time in the playing of its own peculiar part. The whole concert cannot go on without respect to the characteristics of the different instruments; no instrument can enter into the harmony

* M. Anesaki, "How Christianity Appeals to a Japanese Buddhist," *Hibbert Journal,* vol. IV, no. 1, London, 1905.

of the whole without consonance with the general theme. The question how the grand harmony of various Christian nations is to be accomplished awaits its perfect solution in the future.

But Christianity is not the sole religion in the world. Leaving many undeveloped forms of tribal religions out of account, there is at least one religion which is, or claims to be, as universal in its character as Christianity. A religion which intends, as its ideal, to lead every sentient and non-sentient being into the path of immortality, cannot but be universal. A religious community which is ideally in communion with the Buddhas, the Enlightened in Truth, of the past, present, and future, cannot but be catholic. If Christianity is an absolute religion, not in its actual visible condition, but owing to the universality of its Gospel, Buddhism may claim the same as possessing a similarly universal ideal. "Go ye into all the world, and preach the Gospel to the whole creation"—that was the message of Christ to his disciples after his resurrection. The same mission was given by Gotama, the Buddha, to his sixty disciples, i.e.: "Go forth on your journeys for the weal and the welfare of much people, out of compassion for the world, and for the wealth and the weal and the welfare of angels and mortals. Preach the Truth thoroughly glorious and proclaim a religious life wholly perfect and pure." I am not in a position to convince those who think that Buddhism is a mere diabolic imitation of God's religion of truth of my statement. To the present writer, a student of religions bred in a Buddhist atmosphere, this striking similarity of the two creeds, at least in their formal aspects, is a grave problem to be considered. Is the harmony of these two absolute religions not as much a question of the future as is the harmony of various forms of Christianity? Speaking more concretely, should Buddhism wholly yield its claim and mission to Christianity? Can a Buddhist nation contribute nothing to the civilization of the world and to the progress of humanity without being converted to Christianity? Might she not remain Buddhist and be Christianized in spirit, and, in this way, enter into the world-concert of the future civilization? On the other side, is it impossible that the Christian nations and the Christian civilization, adhering to Christianity, should keep harmony with the Buddhist nations and the Buddhist civilization?

These questions lead us first to the consideration of the fundamental characters of these religions. The difference between these two, which calls our attention, is the intellectual character of Buddhism and the emotional one of Christianity. If we characterize the former as a religion of intellectual resignation, we may call the latter a religion of hope and love and faith. Many critics have found the difference between the two in the monotheism of Christianity and the pantheism or acosmism of Buddhism. Even admitting this kind of characterization, we think it more scientific, in the study of religions, to look first to the main feature of a religion and to its actual influence upon the human mind. The fundamental teaching of Buddhism consists in the conviction of the pain and impermanency of every limited existence, and in the release from it. As a necessary step to this conviction it teaches the constituents of our bodily and mental life, and for the realization of the ideal it practises meditation. The so-called Buddhist metaphysic, which mainly teaches these phenomenal aspects of our life, presupposes a long history of Vedic philosophy, which culminated in the contrast of the true universal self (*ātman*) and the sensuous life (*jīva*). The enlightenment of the pre-Buddhistic philosophy consisted in the abandonment of the empirical self and the realization of the true ego or the absorption into the highest being (*Brahma-nirvāna*). The Buddhistic ideal of Nirvāna, the wisdom of the truth, the meditation leading to it, and the good conduct—all these teachings are founded upon the Brahmanic philosophy. Buddhism teaches the nonentity of the ego, and uses the very term *ātman* for the ego which is to be annihilated. But that means the transcendence of the empirical ego, which is made up of constituents, and after this extinction there remains the universal *Bodhi*, the highest, eternal life in Truth. (This point would require separate elucidation.) In this respect Buddhism is no heterodox branch of the Brahmanic philosophy and religion. Buddhism has grown out of the very philosophical soil of the Brahmanic wisdom. Though the powerful personality of the founder has given the religion a very strong impression of the faith in and the love of the Master, its enlightenment consisted in the intellectual conviction of the truth; and the calm resignation of all worldly interests by the Master has become typical of a Buddhist saint.

On the other side, Christ's religion is a necessary outgrowth of the fervent religion of the Jewish prophets. The idea of an almighty and omniscient Creator, the faith in Jahveh's love for the people of Israel, the expectation of the day of God in a future not very far off—all these intuitive and emotional religious experiences of the prophets have given the religion of Christ heat and vitality. Though not without the melancholy tone of a Jeremiah and of a suffering servant of God, Christ's religion, in its main feature, could not but be religion of hope. Even his suffering shows no trait of weakness, but is predominant in its sublime and tragical character. In his last words, "My God, why hast thou forsaken me?" there sounds in the background an absolute trust in the God who delivered his forefathers, his God ever since he was in his mother's womb, whom he always praised and declared to his brethren. Christ's religion of love and trust is a natural outcome of his fathers' religion, and inherits the very essence of the Jewish monotheism.

Here lies an unmistakable difference between the religions of Buddha and of Christ. The one has grown out of and completed the religion of a serene, intellectual release from the evil of this world, and the other has likewise grown out of and completed the enthusiastic love of the Father in heaven, each respectively in its most universal and complete form. The two religions, viewed in their respective historical sources, show two uncompromising, if not contradictory, aspects of the religious experience of mankind. But are they, each of them, nothing but a succession and continuation of the Brahmanic and the Jewish religions respectively? Buddhism cannot be understood without reference to the idealistic philosophy of the Brahmins, but yet it is not a mere philosophical teaching of nirvāna. In the same way, Christianity is founded upon the Jewish monotheism; but no Christian will think his religion to be merely a religion of Jahveh, the Creator and Ruler of the world, and especially the protector of the sons of Jacob. There is something more in each of them, and there lies the keynote of each religion.

The Brahmins believed in the Highest Being revealed in the mind of a sage (*muni*), but their Highest Deity is a pure Being which is at the same time pure Thinking (*sac-cit*). Though it revealed itself in the mind of every thinking sage, there was lacking the faith in a man in whom the "Being-Thinking" was fully manifested. They aspired after the Logos, but the Logos in flesh was wanting. The weight of their religion fell on, to use Kant's language, the ontological argument; the living moral proof was lacking. What was sought for in the observance of ritual (*rtam*) or in faithfulness to holy tradition (*satyam*) became all embodied in the idea of *dharma*, and the very source of the Dharma was found in the essence of ego, the macrocosmical and microcosmical *ātman*. Buddha appeared indeed as the personification of the *Dharma*, or, to use a more Buddhistic term, of *Bodhi*. He was Bodhisattva as a seeker after truth, and his enlightenment, Bodhi, was expounded in his teaching, Dharma. As an embodiment or incarnation of the Dharma he dared to teach that "he who sees Dharma sees me." What he saw he taught, what he was he revealed. His teaching and his wisdom were nothing but what he himself was in the quintessence of his personality. He is therefore called the Tathāgata, one who has appeared as he was in reality, or, speaking metaphysically, as the personal manifestation of eternal truth. If the doctrine of Buddha's *Dharmātman* or *Dharma-kāya* were not expounded fully in the primitive Buddhist faith, the necessary foundation of the doctrine was implied in the faith in his personality as Buddha or Tathāgata.

When we, conveying this idea, come to Christ, we cannot help noticing the same religious self-consciousness as implied in many sayings of his in the synoptic gospels, and more manifestly expressed in the Johannine representation of Christ, the incarnate Logos. Christ is the Son of God, not merely because he loved God as his Father, but because he was from eternity the very *Word of God*, by which God manifested Himself. He is not one who leads to the way, but himself the Way; not one who preaches truth, but himself the Truth, just as Buddha was the Way (*Magga*) and the Truth (*Bodhi*). Christ strengthened and completed the physico-teleological argument of God's existence in the Jewish religion by the moral evidence of his own personality.

Here we see in both cases personal moral evidence of religion in the persons of the founders. The Buddhist nirvāna is the outcome of a long course of metaphysical thought, and the Christian God is the Creator of the world, the Father and the King. But in each case the centre of gravity in the religious consciousness falls on the personality of the founder, who lived among men and led them to the One who has sent him, or to the ideal which he saw face to face. Faith in a person like this means becoming, through him, one with the Truth he represents and living with him in love. That all may be one, one with the Father, one with the Son, and one with them, is not only the kernel of Christian faith, but the very essence of Buddhist belief. The faith (*saddhā*) in and the love (*pema*) for Buddha, the Lord, lead to nirvāna and "pour forth into nirvāna." Not only the soul of Buddha, but the soul of everyone who has faith in him, who has become one with him in faith and love, pervades the four quarters of the world with thoughts of pity, of sympathy, of deep-felt love, and leaves no being outside. That is the sole way (*ekayāna*) by which every enlightened man, who is free from passion and egotism, goes and comes.

I shall not minimize the differences existing between the two religions, but no one should overlook this cardinal affinity of faith in both. Christianity is certainly the absolute religion, i.e., the religion which requires for its existence no other assistance but its own truth, and the religion which teaches the only way to God by faith in Christ. Does this absoluteness necessarily exclude the truth and absoluteness of another? The existence of two absolute religions is seemingly a contradiction, and it seems that the claims of the one can only be established by the sacrifice of the other. Many a Christian of firm conviction has tried to explain the many apparent similarities of the ideas of other religions with those of Christianity by a theory of diabolic imitations. Here we must ask: Is the Satan who imitates God in His most important characteristics condemnable? Are these "imitations" of Christianity by other religions always insincere and of bad intention, as the disguise of a devil in a monk's garment? I shall not enter into polemic with these ardent believers in Christianity, but, as a student of the world's religions, I wish to find another explanation for these so-called imitations, and especially for what I might call the Christianity in Buddhism.

According to the Christian doctrine of the Trinity, the Father is God, the Son is God, and Holy Spirit also. That God is absolute needs no remark. There are three absolutes in Christianity; but these neither exclude one another, nor melt into one. They are three in person but one in substance. Even among Christians there were and are many sceptics as regards this seeming arithmetical contradiction. This scepticism is merely a product of an over-rationalistic head which has no sympathy with the mystery of faith. Christ is the Son and God is the Father. Still, has not Christ taught that they are one, and that those who love God in the name of Christ are one with them? This oneness of different persons is neither physical nor individual unity, but union in faith and love. One who believes in Christ as the Son of God is in communion with the Father of Christ by virtue of his faith. Christ's Father is our Father, and just as the glory of Christ is the glory of the Father, so is our perfection the perfection of God. I called this a mystery of faith, but in reality it is no mystery. In daily life, the true love of husband and wife or of two friends transcends the difference of personality and makes both lovers feel one in their life. And moreover, this feeling is no mere subjective illusion, but the source of many a human activity. Where there prevails love, harmony, or faith, there is participation, communion, or union; and this union is possible only by virtue of the oneness of essential character or substance. The consonance of two musical notes presupposes the difference of scale, but at the same time the communion of sound-waves. This communion is only possible by virtue of the fundamental affinity of wave-motions. When we admit that there is union in different persons, and that one substance is manifested in different personalities, not merely as a difference of attributes but as a participation of the substance in full, then nothing obstructs our belief in the full divinity of each of the three persons. In this belief we have a right to call ourselves children of God, who can participate and realize the divinity of the Father in full. This is the source of divine authority in Christ's ministry, and the foundation of a Christian's belief in Christ as truly man and truly God.

Viewed in this light, does the absoluteness of the Christian religion necessarily exclude the same claim of another religion, whose fundamental faith is belief in a divine master? Anyone who accepts Christ's personality as the true moral evidence of religious faith must admit, or at least sympathize with, the Buddhist faith in Buddha. One who sees Buddha sees the Dharma, the Logos, eternal Truth, unmade, unchangeable, and the source of immortality. If there were any difference between the Christian concept of God and the Buddhist Dharma, the fundamental and essential identity of the beliefs of both in the incarnate Divinity could not be left out of account. The differences are necessary consequences of the historical circumstances in which the two religions have grown up, and of the different demands of the peoples they intended to lead; but the religious foundation of both is the same. If we call the Buddhist faith in Buddha's person the Christianity in Buddhism, we may, with the same right, see in the Christian doctrine of the Logos the Buddhism in Christianity.

A time may come when all the world will accept the Christian religion, but this will never abolish the difference of tastes or modes of expression. Eastern peoples will hardly lose thoroughly their inheritance of serene meditative faith. Their Christianity will never be the Christianity of a Jew, fervent and sometimes very exclusive. The Greeks demand wisdom and the Jews a sign; the gifts are diverse, but the spirit the same. There are many paths and roads in forests and valleys, but those who have climbed up to the hilltop by any of these routes equally enjoy the same moonlight on the open summit. This is an old Buddhist proverb. Buddhists will never lose this spirit of toleration. There may grow in Japan a form of Christianity without Pope and without Holy Synod, but Buddhism will nevertheless hold its footing therein for ever.

In short, we Buddhists are ready to accept Christianity; nay, more, our faith in Buddha is faith in Christ. *We see Christ because we see Buddha.* The one has come to us in order to release us from the fetters of passion and avarice, and to convince us of an ideal higher than any worldly good. His gospel was that of resignation, attainable by meditation, yet never leaving one to the dreamy quietism of pantheistic or nihilistic philosophy, but purifying human activity by calm enlightenment, and pushing one to the love of all beings by faith in an incarnate Dharma. The other appeared in flesh as Son of Man, to redeem us from sin, to recover us to the love of our Father, from a covetous attachment to our own egotism. His gospel was that of love and hope, but never of fury and vanity. He preached no wisdom, but the wisdom of his believers is holy and leading to the Father, purified by faith and strengthened by hope.

The question of the future depends upon how fully the followers of the two Lords understand each other, and how the two streams of civilization nourished respectively by them in the West and in the East can harmonize with each other and contribute conjointly to the future progress of humanity. The solution of this problem is no matter of merely abstract speculation, but of sympathy and faith. Just as at the fountain-heads of these two streams there appeared the Truth in flesh, the Faith in person, the realization of this harmony in love and faith needs an incarnate person, representative of humanity. The person may be a powerful individual or a nation. If the appearance of Christ or Buddha has not been in vain, if the two streams of civilization have been more than ephemeral, then we can hope not in vain for the *second advent* of Christ or the appearance of the future *Buddha Metteya.*

Turning from this rather speculative side of our view of Christianity and the future of the world's religion, we shall enter into the more practical and historical aspects of the problem. The most visible and tangible product in which a religion manifests its actual influence upon human mind and civilization is art. The one thing which strikes most the mind of an Asiatic in Europe is the grandeur of religious architecture. It has not the impressive but overwhelming grandeur of an Egyptian sepulchre, nor the gigantic but extravagant magnitude of a Mohammedan mosque, but grandeur in proportion, sublimity with harmony. The Gothic tower of a Strasbourg or Rouen Cathedral, pointing imposingly to heaven, rising from among the roofs of human dwellings or along the undulating hillside, appeals to us as something grand and elevating. Standing among the pillars of a cloister like that of the Lateran, or sitting under the vault of a Cappella degli Spagnuoli, no one could restrain himself from uttering a prayer to Him, or singing in praise of Him, who has caused a pious architect to plan this or that impressive building in His service. God does not dwell in a temple built by human hands, yet there is the Divine exhibited to us in these harmonious grandeurs or in these serene beauties. At the same time, while we are impressed and inspired by the sublimity and beauty of the Christian architecture, we cannot but admire the same power manifested before us in the graceful temple of Hōryūji or meditatively serene buildings of Zen-Buddhism.

I shall not enter into description of this Japanese Buddhist architecture, but the similar plan and idea, expressed, though on a smaller scale, in the Buddhist buildings, never fails to excite my wonder. Certainly there is a gap between the tastes of the West and the East, but it is not an unsurmountable one, when we examine into the very root of religious faith which has produced such similar grandeur and harmony.

Passing over to another category of Christian art, we find painting, especially that of the Quattrocento, remarkable in its depth and vitality. In this respect, the works of the Quattrocentisti appeal to our inner heart incomparably more than the later European art, excellent though this be in execution. There is in them not much comparable to the gracefulness of a Raphaelian Madonna, but these earlier artists knew how to paint the deep store of faith or emotion, to attract the beholders and to assimilate their hearts to the inner hearts of the figures depicted. One expects in vain to see the skilful shadings and colourings of modern French painters in a Lippi or a Bellini, but their naive sincerity and sometimes childlike freshness are truly products of piety. I find no necessity of saying more on this subject to the English public, whose taste is now much influenced by Ruskin and who are true lovers of Italian art. What I wish to emphasize is the wonderful similarity existing between the art of the Quattrocento and our old Buddhist painting. My impressions when I first saw Angelico's Madonna in the National Gallery of London, and then in Florence, were simply the feelings I had when I looked at the old paintings of the Takuma school. Not only in intention and depth, but in treatment and colouring, they show a striking similarity. They depicted their piety in figures and colours, and have appealed to the heart of the same emotion. Their paintings were not for the sake of amusement or of dilettantism, but for worship. For them art was not a merry thing, but serious as life. It is a great misfortune for our Japanese painting that it is known in Europe only through the genre of an Utamaro or the caricature of a Hok'sai. But there will come the day when the European public will no more be merely amused with the genre, but will find the existence of deeply religious paintings in Japan, and appreciate the sincerity of its intention. The stream of a similar faith will at last communicate through the inner heart, despite of differences of outward forms and materials.

I write this because I think that art is the universal language of the human heart, and through that channel the heart of religion may be communicated incomparably better than through that of dogmas or of reason. If the kernel of a religion consists in and is founded upon the moral evidence, as brought forth in the personality of its founder, its outward realization is manifested in its religious art. It is much to be regretted that Christianity is now known in the East only by dogmas and creeds, and European art only in its modern secular form. If the Eastern peoples were shown the artistic side of Christianity, and began to talk with pious Christians heart to heart through Christian art, they would be found far more ready to appreciate Christianity than the experiences of missionaries have led them to expect.

As a Christian morality, I find nothing to add to Christ's saying: "*None is good save one, even God.*" Here is the inexhaustible fountain of Christian morality. All moralities flow out of this one and only source. No long sermon, no deliberate ethics can open all the secrets of human conduct without this one key. Anyone, though poor both in knowledge and in property, imbued once with this one thought, is the richest in heaven. Modern ethics endeavours to exclude the idea of God or of the *summum bonum* from its sphere. But the bankruptcy of an ethics without this idea is too clearly shown in utilitarianism to need elucidation. Ethics without the highest good is a mere *Lebensweisheit,* and finally a *Lebensklugheit.* It justifies everything useful to the need of the hour, anything convenient to the *Stärkeren.* Modern European civilization has too many riches and too great possessions to follow Him whom God has destined to die in order to live.

Buddhist ethics is blamed by its Christian critics as lacking the very foundation of morality, God. We do not use the expression God, never Jahveh; but there prevails in Buddhadom an unmistakably idealistic element of morality, i.e., esteem for a good higher than worldly happiness. "*Leaving the good and the evil* (or, merit and sin)" is the motto of Eastern morality, ever since the rhapsodists of the Mahābhārata sang the great epic in praise of virtuous warriors, ready to die for the sake of the *Dharma.* Their moral ideal consisted always in the highest good, transcending any merit or evil of human life. Buddha's teaching of resignation was nothing but the realization of this highest ideal. "This idealism," said a Buddhist father, "is the mother of all the holy men, and love (*karunā*) is her daughter." Though this morality of resignation has been much defiled in the course of its transmission through China, we Japanese Buddhists preserve, at least, an earnest aspiration after this ideal. "No evil," said Shinran (1173-1262), the apostle of Jōdo Buddhism, "is to be feared, except disbelief in Amita's grace; no good is to be esteemed, but faith in our Tathāgata's promise (*pranidhāna*)." A saying of another Buddhist sage, Nichiren (1222-1282), the founder of Hokke Buddhism, which exhorts its followers to sacrifice everything to the *Dharma*, reminds us again of Christ's teaching. And these were no mere teachings, but the morality inculcated by them has tuned the actual life so deeply that self-sacrifice for the sake of one's ideal has become the spirit of our national life. Applied to the morality of the warrior class, it has caused many warriors to die gladly for the sake of their lord or of the nation. Parents as representatives of heaven and earth, as is taught usually, are the most prominent objects of the ideal of self-sacrifice. This spirit of self-sacrifice is the vital force of our morality, and has manifested its power during the present war most remarkably. Is this not a good soil for the plantation of Christian morality?

This remark leads me naturally to a problem, important for us, on the relation of Christianity to our national spirit, which has become a subject of controversy since the introduction of that religion into Japan. As is well known, filial piety is the cardinal virtue of Eastern morality in general, and loyalty to the sovereign was the chief point of Confucian teaching. These two were completely unified in Japan. A Mikado, or Emperor, as the patriarchal head of the people and the benevolent ruler of the country, has been, since the beginning of our history, the object of loyalty and of a kind of filial piety at the same time. This morality has been brought to a clear consciousness by Confucianism, and then universalized by Buddhism. On this ground, the present Emperor, when he issued an edict on the morality of the nation in 1889, expressed his reverence toward the manes of his ancestors, and appealed to his subjects to hold fast to the virtues their ancestors had cherished under his fathers. Here is expressed what critics, both foreign and indigenous, call the ancestor-worship of the Japanese. This view has led, in 1892, to a hot controversy between the conservative thinkers and the converted Christians. The points of the controversy were formulated by its propounder as follows:

1. Christianity pretends to be a universal religion and does not recognize national differences, and this contradicts the fundamental teaching of the edict which is strongly national and patriotic.

2. Christian morality is founded upon a supernatural belief in Divinity, and this is contrary to the practical and naturalistic basis of our morality.

3. The love of Christianity is universal and does not admit special virtues toward ruler and parents, and this is diametrically opposed to the cardinal virtues, filial piety and loyalty, as insisted upon in the edict.

Christianity was accused in this way, and since that time both foreign missionaries and converted Christians have fostered a strong antipathy against these two virtues of filial piety and loyalty. That this representation of Christianity is a very erroneous and partial one, needs no remark; but at the same time I find myself obliged to express my regret as regards the attitude of Christians toward the controversy.

In order to make my position clear, I think it necessary to correct the misconceptions of many about the so-called ancestor-worship of the Japanese. We observe strictly the anniversaries of the deaths of relations, and these rituals are connected with the idea of family unity. Every clan in ancient times had its clan-diety (*Uji-gami*), and this nomination is preserved in the worship of the protectors of villages and communities. One may call this cult ancestor-worship. But these community rituals are not observed in order to invoke the spirits of the dead, but rather to offer our homage toward them and to communicate our faith and merit to them. The expression *tsuizen* means just a communion, i.e., the communion of our spiritual gain to them, who partake in our faith and virtues in the all-embracing spiritual community. This is due to the influence of Buddhism, and not a primitive conception. But that is our actual idea, and it shows how a religion of universal salvation could, adopting the primitive ancestor-worship sanctify, universalize, and spiritualize it. On the other hand, the worship of protecting clan or local deities was never exclusively that of the blood-related. Omitting many historical evidences for the support of this remark, I say simply it was something similar to the hero-worship of the Greeks, or not seldom to the saint-worship of the Catholics. In modern times this kind of cult has gone decidedly into the background, and is not so much in vogue as represented by Lafcadio Hearn. If not quite so ideal as Carlyle's, our hero-worship has been much elevated by Buddhism. Even among Shintoists, the adherents to the primitive religion, the spiritual unity of these worshipped manes of ancestors or of heroes is recognized. Some of them have even tried to establish, out of our traditional Shintoism, a monotheism much akin to that of Zoroastrianism. The imperial edict itself states, at its close, that this morality of piety and loyalty transcends the distance of time and difference of nationalities. This point needs a minuter remark, but it lies now out of my scope. I must now content myself with saying that our primitive faith has been much elevated by Buddhism, and still has enough room to be purified by a more decidedly monotheistic religion such as Christianity.

It is rather singular that Christians have not tried this purification and elevation of the Japanese moral and religious ideas by their love of the Heavenly Father, which is the root of all piety, and absolute obedience toward the Lord of heaven and earth, which is the root of all loyalty. None is good save God; but does the oneness of God exclude all that is good, not beside Him, but within and under Him? The field is ripe, the harvest is truly plenteous. Where are the labourers who know how to burn the tares and to gather the wheat into the barn?

To express my personal conviction in short, it is enough to say: Where there is the faith in Buddha, there may grow the faith in Christ. The two religions may preserve their respective traits, but they must share in the deep-root of religious faith. Japan may remain Buddhist, or be converted to Christianity, but she will in either way keep her own tone of national spirit and civilization, and in this way play a part in the grand concert of humanity.

This will be enough to state the cardinal points of my attitude toward Christianity. But as the editor of the Journal asks me to point out what I think to be the defects of Christian morality, I shall venture to respond to his request. What I wish to point out is certainly not the defects of Christianity itself; but there is one thing which strikes our minds as regards the actual tendency of Christians in Europe. It is the exclusiveness of their attitude toward non-Christian peoples. Apart from the theological or ecclesiastical exclusiveness, there is manifest a moral one, especially in recent years. Not only ignorant monks or farmers, but the educated classes and influential rulers, see in the rise of a Buddhist nation the incarnation of Antichrist or a diabolic power. Everything, however good and beautiful it may be, should be extinguished, if it is not Christian. These words were addressed by an Emperor to his soldiers going to the East, and they were instigated to commit murder for revenge, so that the peoples of the East might remember for a thousand years the terrible vengeance of Christians. These and similar phenomena are by no means products of true Christianity, but only remains of Jewish bigotry. The harmony and concert of the world's religions and nations are made impossible by this un-Christian Christianity. If we should be threatened by a bigotry like this, we are ready to stand against it in the name not only of Buddha but of Christ Himself.

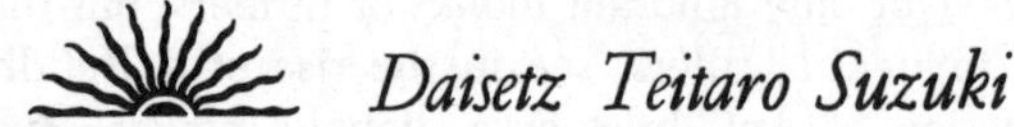

Daisetz Teitaro Suzuki

Daisetz Teitaro Suzuki is well known to Western readers as the author and translator of many books on the subject of Zen Buddhism. Dr. Suzuki was born in the Ishikawa Prefecture in 1870 and graduated from Tokyo University in 1892. From 1897 to 1909 he studied in the United States. He lectured at Tokyo University, Peers School, Columbia University, and Yale University and was for many years professor of Buddhist philosophy at Otani University in Kyoto. He is a member of the Japanese Academy.

Because Dr. Suzuki is well known to Western readers and because he has several attitudes toward Christianity, two selections from his work are presented here. The first selection, "Crucifixion and Enlightenment," appeared in a study of mysticism in Christianity and Buddhism.

*MYSTICISM: CHRISTIAN AND BUDDHIST**

Whenever I see a crucified figure of Christ, I cannot help thinking of the gap that lies deep between Christianity and Buddhism. This gap is symbolic of the psychological division separating the East from the West.

The individual ego asserts itself strongly in the West. In the East, there is no ego. The ego is non-existent and, therefore, there is no ego to be crucified.

We can distinguish two phases of the ego-idea. The first is relative, psychological, or empirical. The second is the transcendental ego.

The empirical ego is limited. It has no existence of its own. Whatever assertion it makes, it has no absolute value; it is dependent on others. This is no more than the relative ego and a psychologically established one. It is a hypothetical one; it is subject to all kinds of conditions. It has, therefore, no freedom.

What is it, then, that makes it feel free as if it were really so independent and authentic? Whence this delusion?

The delusion comes from the transcendental ego being mistakenly viewed as it works through the empirical ego and abides in it. Why does the transcendental ego, thus mistakenly viewed, suffer itself to be taken for the relative ego?

The fact is that the relative ego which corresponds to the *mano-*

* D. T. Suzuki, *Mysticism: Christian and Buddhist,* George Allen & Unwin, Ltd., London, and Harper & Row, Publishers, Incorporated, New York, 1957.

vijñāna of the Yogacara school has two aspects of relationship, outer and inner.

Objectively speaking, the empirical or relative ego is one of many other such egos. It is in the world of plurality; its contact with others is intermittent, mediated, and processional. Inwardly, its contact or relationship with the transcendental ego is constant, immediate, and total. Because of this the inner relationship is not so distinctly cognizable as the outer one—which, however, does not mean that the cognition is altogether obscure and negligible and of no practical worth in our daily life.

On the contrary, the cognition of the transcendental ego at the back of the relative ego sheds light into the source of consciousness. It brings us in direct contact with the unconscious.

It is evident that this inner cognition is not the ordinary kind of knowledge which we generally have about an external thing.

The difference manifests itself in two ways. The object of ordinary knowledge is regarded as posited in space and time and subject to all kinds of scientific measurements. The object of the inner cognition is not an individual object. The transcendental ego cannot be singled out for the relative ego to be inspected by it. It is so constantly and immediately contacted by the relative ego that when it is detached from the relative ego it ceases to be itself. The transcendental ego is the relative ego and the relative ego is the transcendental ego; and yet they are not one but two; they are two and yet not two. They are separable intellectually but not in fact. We cannot make one stand as seer and the other as the seen, for the seer is the seen, and the seen is the seer.

When this unique relationship between the transcendental ego and the relative ego is not adequately comprehended or intuited, there is a delusion. The relative ego imagines itself to be a free agent, complete in itself, and tries to act accordingly.

The relative ego by itself has no existence independent of the transcendental ego. The relative ego is nothing. It is when the relative ego is deluded as to its real nature that it assumes itself and usurps the position of the one behind it.

It is true that the transcendental ego requires the relative ego to give itself a form through which the transcendental ego functions. But the transcendental ego is not to be identified with the relative ego to the extent that the disappearance of the relative ego means also the disappearance of the transcendental ego. The transcendental ego is the creative agent and the relative ego is the created. The relative ego is not something that is prior to the transcendental ego standing in opposition to the latter. The relative ego comes out of the transcendental ego and is wholly and dependently related to the transcendental ego. Without the transcendental ego, the relative ego is zero. The transcendental ego is, after all, the mother of all things.

The Oriental mind refers all things to the transcendental ego, though not always consciously and analytically, and sees them finally reduced to it, whereas the West attaches itself to the relative ego and starts from it.

Instead of relating the relative ego to the transcendental ego and making the latter its starting point, the Western mind tenaciously clings to it. But since the relative ego is by nature defective, it is always found unsatisfactory and frustrating and leading to a series of disasters, and as the Western mind believes in the reality of this troublemaker, it wants to make short work of it. Here we can also see something characteristically Western, for they have crucified it.

In a way the Oriental mind is not inclined toward the corporeality of things. The relative ego is quietly and without much fuss absorbed into the body of the transcendental ego. That is why we see the Buddha lie serenely in Nirvana under the twin Sala trees, mourned not only by his disciples but by all beings, non-human as well as human, non-sentient as well as sentient. As there is from the first no ego-substance, there is no need for crucifixion.

In Christianity crucifixion is needed, corporeality requires a violent death, and as soon as this is done, resurrection must take place in one form or another, for they go together. As Paul says, "If Christ be not risen, then is our preaching vain and your faith is also vain. . . . Ye are yet in sins." (I Corinthians 15:14-17) The crucifixion in fact has a double sense: one individualistic and the other humanistic. In the first sense it symbolizes the destruction of the individual ego, while in the second it stands for the doctrine of vicarious atonement whereby all our sins are atoned for by making

Christ die for them. In both cases the dead must be resurrected. Without the latter, destruction has no meaning whatever. In Adam we die, in Christ we live—this must be understood in the double sense as above.

What is needed in Buddhism is enlightenment, neither crucifixion nor resurrection. A resurrection is dramatic and human enough, but there is still the odor of the body in it. In enlightenment, there are heavenliness and a genuine sense of transcendence. Things of earth go through renovation and a refreshing transformation. A new sun rises above the horizon and the whole universe is revealed.

It is through this experience of enlightenment that every being individually and collectively attains Buddhahood. It is not only a certain historically and definitely ascertainable being who is awakened to a state of enlightenment but the whole cosmos with every particle of dust which goes to the composition of it. I lift my finger and it illuminates the three thousand chiliocosms and an *asamkheyya* of Buddhas and Bodhisattvas greet me, not excluding ordinary human beings.

Crucifixion has no meaning whatsoever unless it is followed by resurrection. But the soil of the earth still clings to it though the resurrected one goes up to heaven. It is different with enlightenment, for it instantly transforms the earth itself into the Pure Land. You do not have to go up to heaven and wait for this transformation to take place here.

Christian symbolism has much to do with the suffering of man. The crucifixion is the climax of all suffering. Buddhists also speak much about suffering and its climax is the Buddha serenely sitting under the Bodhi tree by the river Niranjana. Christ carries his suffering to the end of his earthly life whereas Buddha puts an end to it while living and afterward goes on preaching the gospel of enlightenment until he quietly passes away under the twin Sala trees. The trees are standing upright and the Buddha, in Nirvana, lies horizontally like eternity itself.

Christ hangs helpless, full of sadness on the vertically erected cross. To the Oriental mind, the sight is almost unbearable. Buddhists are accustomed to the sight of Jizo Bosatsu (Kshitigarbha Bodhisattva) by the roadside. The figure is a symbol of tenderness.

He stands upright but what a contrast to the Christian symbol of suffering!

Now let us make a geometric comparison between a statue sitting cross-legged in meditation and a crucified one. First of all, verticality suggests action, motion, and aspiration. Horizontality, as in the case of the lying Buddha, makes us think of peace and satisfaction or contentment. A sitting figure gives us the notion of solidity, firm conviction and immovability. The body sets itself down with the hips and folded legs securely on the ground. The center of gravity is around the loins. This is the securest position a biped can assume while living. This is also the symbol of peace, tranquillity, and self-assurance. A standing position generally suggests a fighting spirit, either defensive or offensive. It also gives one the feeling of personal self-importance born of individuality and power.

When man began to stand on his two legs, this demonstrated that he was now distinct from the rest of the creatures walking on all fours. He is henceforth becoming more independent of the earth because of his freed forepaws and of the consequent growth of his brains. This growth and independence on the part of man are constantly misleading him to think that he now is master of Nature and can put it under his complete control. This, in combination with the Biblical tradition that man dominates all things on earth, has helped the human idea of universal domination to overgrow even beyond its legitimate limitation. The result is that we talk so much about conquering nature, except our own human nature which requires more disciplining and control and perhaps subjugation than anything else.

On the other hand the sitting cross-legged and the posture of meditation make a man feel not detached from the earth and yet not so irrevocably involved in it that he has to go on smelling it and wallowing in it. True, he is supported by the earth but he sits on it as if he were the crowning symbol of transcendence. He is neither attached to the soil nor detached from it.

We talk these days very much about detachment as if attachment is so fatal and hateful a thing that we must somehow try to achieve the opposite, non-attachment. But I do not know why we have to move away from things lovable and really conducive to our social and individual welfare. Kanzan and Jittoku enjoyed their freedom and welfare in their own way. Their life can be considered one of utter detachment as we the outsiders look at it. Śākyamuni spent his seventy-nine years by going from one place to another and teaching his gospel of enlightenment to all sorts of people varied in every way, social, intellectual, and economic, and finally passed away quietly by the river Niranjana. Socrates was born and died in Athens and used his energy and wisdom in exercising his office as the midwife of men's thoughts, bringing down philosophy from heaven to earth and finally calmly taking his cup of hemlock surrounded by his disciples and ending his life of seventy years.

What shall we say about these lives when each of them apparently enjoyed his to the utmost of his heart's content? Is it a life of attachment or of detachment? I would say that, as far as my understanding goes, each had his life of freedom unhampered by any ulterior interest and, therefore, instead of using such terms as attachment or detachment in order to evaluate the life of those mentioned above is it not better to call it a life of absolute freedom?

It is enlightenment that brings peace and freedom among us.

When Buddha attained his supreme enlightenment, he was in his sitting posture; he was neither attached to nor detached from the earth. He was one with it, he grew out of it, and yet he was not crushed by it. As a newborn baby free from all *sankhāras,* he declared, standing, with one hand pointing to the sky and the other to the earth, "Above heaven, below heaven, I alone am the honored one!" Buddhism has three principal figures, symbolizing (1) nativity, (2) enlightenment, and (3) Nirvana, that is standing, sitting, and lying—the three main postures man can assume. From this we see that Buddhism is deeply concerned with human affairs in various forms of peaceful employment and not in any phase of warlike activities.

Christianity, on the other hand, presents a few things which are difficult to comprehend, namely, the symbol of crucifixion. The crucified Christ is a terrible sight and I cannot help associating it with the sadistic impulse of a psychically affected brain.

Christians would say that crucifixion means crucifying the self or the flesh, since without subduing the self we cannot attain moral perfection.

This is where Buddhism differs from Christianity.

Buddhism declares that there is from the very beginning no self to crucify. To think that there is the self is the start of all errors and evils. Ignorance is at the root of all things that go wrong.

As there is no self, no crucifixion is needed, no sadism is to be practiced, no shocking sight is to be displayed by the roadside.

According to Buddhism, the world is the network of karmic interrelationships and there is no agent behind the net who holds it for his willful management. To have an insight into the truth of the actuality of things, the first requisite is to dispel the cloud of ignorance. To do this, one must discipline oneself in seeing clearly and penetratingly into the suchness of things.

Christianity tends to emphasize the corporeality of our existence. Hence its crucifixion, and hence also the symbolism of eating the flesh and drinking the blood. To non-Christians, the very thought of drinking the blood is distasteful.

Christians would say: This is the way to realize the idea of oneness with Christ. But non-Christians would answer: Could not the idea of oneness be realized in some other way, that is, more peacefully, more rationally, more humanly, more humanely, less militantly, and less violently?

When we look at the Nirvana picture, we have an entirely different impression. What a contrast between the crucifixion-image of Christ and the picture of Buddha lying on a bed surrounded by his disciples and other beings non-human as well as human! Is it not interesting and inspiring to see all kinds of animals coming together to mourn the death of Buddha?

That Christ died vertically on the cross whereas Buddha passed away horizontally—does this not symbolize the fundamental difference in more than one sense between Buddhism and Christianity?

Verticality means action, combativeness, exclusiveness, while horizontality means peace, tolerance, and broad-mindedness. Being active, Christianity has something in it which stirs, agitates, and disturbs. Being combative and exclusive, Christianity tends to wield an autocratic and sometimes domineering power over others, in spite of its claim to democracy and universal brotherhood.

In these respects, Buddhism proves to be just the opposite of Christianity. The horizontality of the Nirvana-Buddha may sometimes suggest indolence, indifference, and inactivity though Buddhism is really the religion of strenuousness and infinite patience. But there is no doubt that Buddhism is a religion of peace, serenity, equanimity, and equilibrium. It refuses to be combative and exclusive. On the contrary, it espouses broad-mindedness, universal tolerance, and aloofness from worldly discriminations.

To stand up means that one is ready for action, for fighting and overpowering. It also implies that someone is standing opposed to you, who may be ready to strike you down if you do not strike him down first. This is "the self" which Christianity wants to crucify. As this enemy always threatens you, you have to be combative. But when you clearly perceive that this deadly enemy who keeps you on the alert is non-existent, when you understand that it is no more than a nightmare, a mere delusion to posit a self as something trying to overpower you, you then will be for the first time at peace with yourself and also with the world at large, you then can afford to lie down and identify yourself with all things.

After all is said there is one thing we all must remember so as to bring antagonistic thoughts together and see how they can be reconciled. I suggest this: When horizontality remains horizontal all the time, the result is death. When verticality keeps up its rigidity, it collapses. In truth, the horizontal is horizontal only when it is conceived as implying the tendency to rise, as a phase of becoming something else, as a line to move to tridimensionality. So with verticality. As long as it stays unmoved vertically, it ceases to be itself. It must become flexible, acquire resiliency, it must balance itself with movability.

(The cross [Greek] and the swastika are closely related, probably derived from the same source. The swastika however is dynamic whereas the cross symbolizes static symmetry. The Latin cross is most likely the development of a sign of another nature.)

In the following essay, Suzuki–engaging in dialogue with the Trappist poet and priest, Thomas Merton–speaks more often of Zen Buddhism than of Christianity. However, the reader should note that Suzuki's remarks are made in juxtaposition to the Christian point of view expressed by Merton.
The meeting ground for this dialogue was a new translation of selections from the "Verba Seniorum"; it was felt by the publishers, New Directions, that the "Verba," in their austere simplicity, bore a remarkable resemblance to some of the stories told by the Zen Masters.

KNOWLEDGE AND INNOCENCE *

When I speak about Zen to the Western audience, mostly brought up in Christian tradition, the first question generally asked is: "What is the Zen concept of morality? If Zen claims to be above all moral values, what does it teach us ordinary mortals?"

If I understand Christianity correctly, it derives the moral authority from God who is the giver of the Decalogue, and we are told that if we violate it in any way we shall be punished and thrown into everlasting fire. It is for this reason that atheists are regarded as dangerous people, for they have no God and are no respecters of moral codes. The Zen-man, too, having no God that corresponds to the analogical Christian God, but who talks of going beyond the dualism of good and evil, of right and wrong, of life and death, of truth and falsehood, will most likely be a subject of suspicion. The idea of social values deeply ingrained in Western minds is intimately connected with religion so that they are led to think religion and ethics are one and the same, and that religion can ill afford to relegate ethics to a position of secondary importance. But, Zen seems to do this, hence the following question: [1] "Dr. Suzuki writes: 'All the moral values and social practice

* D. T. Suzuki, "Knowledge and Innocence," *New Directions 17*, 1961.

[1] This question was submitted to me by one of the members taking part in the Third East-West Philosophers' Conference at the University of Hawaii, June-July, 1959. It was based on the paper I contributed to this conference. My answer which follows here requires further elaboration for which I have no time just now. It involves my view on the Judaeo-Christian creation account.

come out of this life of Suchness which is Emptiness.' If this is so, then 'good' and 'evil' are secondary differentiations. What differentiates them and how do I know what is 'good' other than 'evil'? In other words, can I—and if so, how can I—derive an ethics from the ontology of Zen Buddhism?"

We are all social beings and ethics is our concern with social life. The Zen-man too cannot live outside society. He cannot ignore the ethical values. Only, he wants to have the heart thoroughly cleansed of all impurities issuing from "Knowledge"[2] which we acquired by eating the fruit of the forbidden tree. When we return to the state of "Innocence"[2] anything we do is good. St. Augustine says: "Love God and do as you will." The Buddhist idea of *anābhoga-caryā*[3] corresponds to Innocence. When Knowledge is awakened in the Garden of Eden where Innocence prevails, the differentiation of good and evil takes place. In the same way, out of the Emptiness of the Mind a thought mysteriously rises and we have the world of multiplicities.[4]

The Judaeo-Christian idea of Innocence is the moral interpretation of the Buddhist doctrine of Emptiness which is metaphysical, whereas the Judaeo-Christian idea of Knowledge epistemologically corresponds to the Buddhist notion of Ignorance though superficially Ignorance is the opposite of Knowledge. Buddhist philosophy considers discrimination of any kind—moral or metaphysical—the product of Ignorance which obscures the original light of Suchness which is Emptiness. But this does not mean that the whole world is to be done away with because of its being the outcome of Ignorance. It is the same with Knowledge, for Knowledge is the outcome of our having lost Innocence by eating the forbidden fruit. But no Christians or Jews, as far as I am aware,

[2] Throughout this paper, "Innocence" is to be taken as the state of mind in which inhabitants of the Garden of Eden used to live around the tree of life, with eyes not opened, all naked, not ashamed, with no knowledge of good and evil; whereas "Knowledge" refers to everything opposite of "Innocence," especially a pair of discriminating eyes widely opened to good and evil.

[3] See D. T. Suzuki, trans., *Lankāvatāra Sūtra,* Routledge & Kegan Paul., Ltd., London, 1957, pp. 32, 43, 89, etc., where the term is translated "effortless" or "no striving" act.

[4] D. T. Suzuki, trans., *Asvaghosa's Awakening of Faith,* Open Court Publishing Company, Chicago, 1900, pp. 78-79.

have ever attempted to get rid of Knowledge in order to regain Paradise whereby they might enjoy the bliss of Innocence to its full extent as they originally did.

What we are to realize, then, is the meaning of "Knowledge" and "Innocence," that is to say, to have a thoroughly penetrating insight into the relationship between the two opposing concepts—Innocence and Original Light on the one side, and Knowledge and Ignorance on the other. In one sense they seem to be irreducibly contradictory, but in another sense they are complementary. As far as our human way of thinking is concerned, we cannot have them both at the same time, but our actual life consists in the one supporting the other, or better, that they are inseparably co-operating.

The so-called opposition between Innocence and Knowledge or between Ignorance and the Original Light is not the kind of opposition we see between black and white, good and evil, right and wrong, to be and not to be, or to have and not to have. The opposition is, as it were, between container and the contained, between the background and the stage, between the field and the players moving on it. The good and the evil play their opposing parts on the field which remains neutral and indifferent and "open" or "empty." It is like rain that falls on the just and on the unjust; it is like the sun rising on the good and on the evil, on your foes and on your friends. In a way, the sun is innocent and perfect as is the rain. But man who has lost Innocence and acquired Knowledge differentiates just from unjust, good from evil, right from wrong, foes from friends. He is, therefore, no longer innocent and perfect, but highly "morally" conscious. To be "moral" apparently means the loss of Innocence, and the acquirement of Knowledge, religiously speaking, is not always conducive to our inner happiness or divine blessings. The outcome of "moral" responsibility may sometimes lead to the violation of civil laws. The outcome of the "great hermit's" inner goodness in releasing the robbers from jail (cf. *Wisdom of the Desert #37*) [5] may be far from being desirable.

[5] "There was once a great hermit in the mountains and he was attacked by robbers. But his cries aroused the other hermits in the neighborhood, and they ran together and captured the robbers. These they sent under guard to the town and the judge put them in jail. But then the brothers were very ashamed and sad because, on their account, the robbers had been turned over to the

Innocence and Knowledge must be kept well balanced. To do this Knowledge must be disciplined and at the same time the value of Innocence must be appraised in its proper relation to Knowledge.

In the *Dhammapada* (verse 183) we have:

Not to do anything that is evil,
To do all that is good,
To thoroughly purify the heart:
This is the teaching of Buddhas.

The first two lines refer to Knowledge whereas the third is the state of Innocence. "To purify" means "to purge," "to empty" all that pollutes the mind. The pollution comes from the egocentric consciousness which is Ignorance or Knowledge which distinguishes good from evil, ego from non-ego. Metaphysically speaking, it is the mind that realizes the truth of Emptiness, and when this is done it knows that there is no self, no ego, no *ātman* that will pollute the mind, which is a state of zero. It is out of this zero that all good is performed and all evil is avoided. The zero I speak of is not a mathematical symbol. It is the infinite—a storehouse or womb (*garbha*) of all possible good or values.

zero = infinity, and infinity = zero

The double equation is to be understood not only statically but dynamically. It takes place between being and becoming. For they are not contradicting ideas. Emptiness is not sheer emptiness or passivity or Innocence. It is and at the same time it is not. It is Being, it is Becoming. It is Knowledge and Innocence. The Knowledge to do good and not to do evil is not enough; it must come out of Innocence, where Innocence is Knowledge and Knowledge is Innocence.

---

judge. They went to Abbot Poemen and told him all about it. And the elder wrote to the hermit saying: Remember who carried out the first betrayal, and you will learn the reason for the second. Unless you had first been betrayed by your own inward thoughts, you would never have ended by turning those men over to the judge. The hermit, touched by these words, got up at once and went into the city and broke open the jail, letting out the robbers and freeing them from torture." *The Wisdom of the Desert,* XXXVII.

The "great hermit" is guilty of not realizing Emptiness, that is, Innocence, and Abbot Poemen commits an error in applying Innocence minus Knowledge to the affairs of the world. The robbers are to be consigned to prison, for the community will suffer; as long as they are outlaws they must be deprived of their liberty—this is the way of the world in which we carry on our business of earning bread by hard, honest labor. Our business is possible only by living in the world of Knowledge because where Innocence prevails there is no need of our laboring: "All that is needed for our existence is given freely by God." As long as we live a communal life, all kinds of law are to be observed. We are sinners, that is, we are knowers not only individually but collectively, communally, socially. The robbers are to be confined in prison. As spiritual beings we are to strive after Innocence, Emptiness, enlightenment and a prayerful life. "The great hermit" must lead a life of penance and prayer but not interfere with the laws of the land that regulate our secular life. Where secular life goes on, Knowledge predominates, and hard and honest labor is an absolute necessity, and, further, each individual is entitled to the fruit of his work. "The great hermit" had no right to release the robbers thereby threatening the peace of law-abiding fellow beings. When Knowledge is not properly exercised strange, irrational phenomena will take place. The hermit is no doubt a good social member and he means no harm to any of his fellow beings; the robbers are those bent on disturbing the peace of the community to which they belong. They must be kept away from the community. The hermit deserves to be imprisoned for having violated the law by freeing the antisocial members. The good man is punished while the bad men roam about free and unhampered annoying peace-loving citizens. This, I am sure, is far from the hermit's aspirations.

The metaphysical concept of Emptiness is convertible in economic terms into poverty, being poor, having nothing: "Blessed are those who are poor in spirit." Eckhart defines: "He is a poor man who wants nothing, knows nothing, and has nothing." (Blakney, p. 227) This is possible when a man is empty of "self and all things," when the mind is thoroughly purified of Knowledge or Ignorance, which we have after the loss of Innocence. In other words, to gain

Innocence again is to be poor. What strikes one as somewhat strange is Eckhart representing a poor man as knowing nothing. This is a very significant statement. The beginning of Knowledge is when the mind is filled with all kinds of defiled thought among which the worst is "self." For all evils and defilements start from our attachment to it. As Buddhists would say, the realization of Emptiness is no more, no less than seeing into the non-existence of a thingish ego-substance. This is the greatest stumbling block in our spiritual discipline, which, in actuality, consists not in getting rid of the self but in realizing the fact that there is no such existence from the first. The realization means being "poor" in spirit. "Being poor" does not mean "becoming poor"; "being poor" means to be from the very beginning not in possession of anything and not giving away what one has. Nothing to gain, nothing to lose; nothing to give, nothing to take; to be just so, and yet to be rich in inexhaustible possibilities—this is to be "poor" in its most proper and characteristic sense of the word, this is what all religious experiences tell us. To be absolutely nothing is to be everything. When one is in possession of something, that something will keep out all other somethings from coming in.

In this respect, Eckhart had a wonderful insight into the nature of what he calls *die eigentlichste Armut.* (Quint, p. 309) We are generally apt to imagine that when the mind or heart is emptied of "self and all things" a room is left ready for God to enter and occupy it. This is a great error. The very thought, even the slightest, of making room for something is a hindrance as monstrous as the mountain. A monk came to Ummon, the great Zen master (who died in 949), and said: "When a man has not one thought occupying his consciousness, what fault has he?" Ummon roared: "Mount Sumeru!" Another Zen master, Kyōgen Chikan,[6] has his song of poverty:

Last year's poverty was not yet perfect;
This year's poverty is absolute.
In last year's poverty there was room for the head of a gimlet;
This year's poverty has let the gimlet itself disappear.

[6] Disciple of Isan Reiyū, 770-853.

Eckhart's statement corresponding to Kyōgen's runs in this wise where he is typically Christian:

> If it is the case that a man is emptied of things, creatures, himself and God, and if still God could find a place in him to act, then we say: as long as that (place) exists, this man is not poor with the most intimate poverty (*eigentlichste Armut*). For God does not intend that man shall have a place reserved for him to work in, since the true poverty of spirit requires that man shall be emptied of God and all his works, so that if God wants to act in the soul, he himself must be the place in which he acts—and that he would like to do. For if God once found a person as poor as this, he would take the responsibility of his own action and would himself be the scene of action, for God is one who acts within himself. It is here, in this poverty, that man regains the eternal being that once he was, now is, and evermore shall be. (Blakney, pp. 230-231)

As I interpret Eckhart, God is at once the place where He works and the work itself. The place is zero or "Emptiness as Being," whereas the work which is carried on in the zero-place is infinity or "Emptiness as Becoming." When the double equation, zero = infinity and infinity = zero, is realized, we have the *eigentlichste Armut,* or the essence of poverty. Being is becoming and becoming is being. When the one is separated from the other, we have a poverty crooked and limping. Perfect poverty is recovered only when perfect emptiness is perfect fullness.

When a monk [7] has anything to loan and when he feels anxious to have it returned, he is not yet poor, he is not yet perfectly empty. Some years ago when I was reading stories of pious Buddhists I remember having come across one of a farmer. One evening he heard some noise in the garden. He noticed a young man of

[7] "A certain brother asked of an elder, saying: If a brother owes me a little money, do you think I should ask him to pay me back? The elder said to him: Ask him for it once only, and with humility. The brother said: Suppose I ask him once and he doesn't give me anything, what should I do? Then the elder said: Don't ask him any more. The brother said again: But what can I do, I cannot get rid of my anxieties about it, unless I go and ask him? The elder said to him: Forget your anxieties. The important thing is not to sadden your brother, for you are a monk." *The Wisdom of the Desert,* XCVIII.

the village atop a tree stealing his fruit. Quietly, he went to the shed where he kept his ladder and took it under the tree so that the intruder might safely make his descent. He went back to his bed unnoticed. The farmer's heart emptied of self and possession could not think of anything else but the danger that might befall the young village delinquent.

There is a set of what may be called fundamental moral virtues of perfection in Mahāyāna Buddhism known as the Six Pāramitā. Followers of the Mahāyāna are expected to exert themselves to practice these virtues in their daily life. They are (1) *dāna,* "giving"; (2) *sīla,* "observing the precepts"; (3) *vīrya,* "spirit of manhood"; (4) *ksānti,* "humility" or "patience"; (5) *dhyāna,* "meditation"; and (6) *prajñā,* "transcendental wisdom," which is an intuition of the highest order.

I am not going to explain each item of the six virtues here. All that I can try is to call the attention of our readers to the order in which they are set. First comes *dāna,* to give, and the last is *prajñā,* which is a kind of spiritual insight into the truth of Emptiness. The Buddhist life starts with "giving" and ends in prajñā. But, in reality, the ending is the beginning and the beginning is the ending; the Pāramitā moves in a circle with no beginning and no ending. The giving is possible only when there is Emptiness and Emptiness is attainable only when the giving is unconditionally carried out—which is *die eigentlichste Armut* of Eckhart.

As prajñā has been frequently the subject of discussion, I shall limit myself to the exposition of dāna, giving. It does not just mean giving in charity or otherwise something material in one's possession as is usually understood when we talk of "giving." It means anything going out of oneself, disseminating knowledge, helping people in difficulties of all kinds, creating arts, promoting industry or social welfare, sacrificing one's life for a worthy cause and so on. But this, however noble, Buddhist philosophers would say, is not enough as long as a man harbors the idea of giving in one sense or another. The genuine giving consists in not cherishing any thought of anything going out of one's hands and being received by anybody else; that is to say, in the giving there must not be any thought of a giver or a receiver and of an object going through this transaction. When the giving goes on thus in Emptiness, it is the deed of dāna, the first Pāramitā, directly flowing out of prajñā, the final Pāramitā. According to Eckhart's definition, as was quoted above, it is poverty in its genuine sense. In another place he is more concrete by referring to examples:

> St. Peter said, "We have left all things." St. James said, "We have given up all things." St. John said, "We have nothing left." Whereupon Brother Eckhart asks, When do we leave all things? When we leave everything conceivable, everything expressible, everything audible, everything visible, then and then only we give up all things. When in this sense we give up all, we grow aflood with light, passing bright with God. (Evans, p. 423)

Kyōgen the Zen master says: "This year's poverty has let the gimlet itself disappear." This is symbolical. In point of fact it means that one is dead to oneself, corresponding to:

Visankhāragatam cittam,[8]
Gone to dissolution is the mind,
Tankhānam khayam ajjhagā.[9]
The cravings have come to an end.

This is part of the verse ascribed to Buddha when he attained the supreme enlightenment, and it is known as the "Hymn of Victory." The gimlet is "dissolved," the body is "dissolved," the mind is "dissolved," all is "dissolved"—is this not Emptiness? In other words, it is the perfect state of poverty. Eckhart quotes St. Gregory: "No one gets so much of God as the man who is thoroughly dead." (Evans, p. 206) I do not know exactly in what sense St. Gregory uses the word "dead." But the word is most significant if it is understood in reference to Bunan Zenji's [10] poem:

[8] Buddhist texts are quoted by D. T. Suzuki and Fumio Masutani without complete citations. It is impossible to give accurate cross references, since undoubtedly some of the translations are those of the author. The reader is referred to an accessible English edition of the text in question. Editor.

[9] *Dhammapada,* verse 154, Max Muller, trans., *Sacred Books of the East,* University Press, 1881, Clarendon, Oxford, vol. X.

[10] Lived 1603-1676.

While alive, be dead,
Thoroughly dead—
All is good then,
Whatever you may do.

Emptiness, poverty, death or dissolution—they are all realized when one goes through the experience of "breaking-through" (*Durchbrechen,* Evans, p. 221), which is nothing else but "enlightenment" (*sambodhi*). Let me quote a little more from Eckhart:

> In my breaking-through . . . I transcend all creatures and am neither God nor creature: I am that I was and I shall remain now and forever. Then I receive an impulse (*Aufschwung*) which carries me above all angels. In this impulse I conceive such passing riches that I am not content with God as being God, as being all his godly works, for in this breaking-through I find that God and I are both the same. . . . (Evans, p. 221)

I do not know how my Christian readers would take these statements, but from the Buddhist point of view one reservation is needed, which is: However transcendental and above all forms of conditionality this experience itself of "breaking-through" may be, we are liable to formulate a distorted interpretation of the experience. The Zen master therefore will tell us to transcend or "to cast away" the experience itself. To be absolutely naked, to go even beyond the receiving of "an impulse" of whatever nature, to be perfectly free from every possible remnant of the trappings we have put on ourselves ever since the acquisition of Knowledge —this is the goal of the Zen training. Then and only then do we find ourselves again to be the ordinary Toms, Dicks and Harrys as we had been all along. It was Jōshū, one of the greatest masters of the T'ang, who confessed something like this: "I get up early in the morning and look at myself—how poorly dressed I am! My upper robe is nearly reduced to tatters, my surplice somewhat holding its shape. My head is covered with dirt and ashes. When I first started the study of Zen, I dreamed of becoming a fine imposing clergyman. But I never imagined that I should be living in this tottering shanty and eating scanty meals. After all, I am a poor beggar-monk."

A monk came to this man and asked: "When a man comes to you free of all possible possession, how would this do?" Jōshū answered: "Throw it away!"

Still another came and asked: "Who is Buddha?" Jōshū retorted instantly: "Who are you?"

An old woman visited Jōshū saying: "I am a woman who according to Buddhism lives under five obstructions; [11] how can I surpass them? Jōshū advised her: "Pray that all beings may be born in Paradise, but as to myself, let me forever remain in this ocean of tribulations."

We may enumerate a number of virtues to be pursued by monks, Buddhist or Christian, such as poverty, tribulation, discretion, obedience, humility, not-judging-others, meditation, silence, simplicity and some other qualities, but the most fundamental one is in my opinion poverty. Poverty corresponds ontologically to Emptiness and psychologically to selflessness or Innocence. The life we used to enjoy in the Garden of Eden symbolizes Innocence. How to regain (or perhaps better how to recognize that we already possess) this primitive-mindedness in the midst of industrialization and the universal propagandism of "an easy life" is the grave question given to us modern men for successful solution. How to actualize the transcendental wisdom of prajñā in a world where the growth of Knowledge is everywhere encouraged in a thousand and one ways? A solution is imperatively demanded of us in a most poignant manner. The day of the Desert Fathers is forever gone and we are waiting for a new sun to rise above the horizon of egotism and sordidness in every sense.

[11] A woman is said not to be qualified to be (1) Mahābrahman, "supreme spirit," (2) Sakrendra, "king of the heavens," (3) Māra, "evil one," (4) Cakravartin, "great lord" and (5) Buddha.

Fumio Masutani

Fumio Masutani, who was born February 16, 1902, is a disciple of the Jodo Shaw sect of Buddhism. He is lecturer at the University of Tokyo, Taisho University, and Rikkyo University and a professor of foreign languages at Tokyo University.

He is author of over ten books in Japanese dealing with various phases of Buddhism in general and Jodo Shaw in particular. He recently participated in a symposium sponsored by the International Institute for the Study of Religions held in Tokyo. The results of this discussion were published in a book entitled "Living Buddhism in Japan." The following essay first appeared in Dr. Masutani's first book to have been written in English.

A COMPARATIVE STUDY OF BUDDHISM AND CHRISTIANITY *

I

The religion of Buddha is based on the confidence in the reasoning man (*homo sapiens*) while that of Jesus is definitely antipodal to the former.

In the philosophical study of man, man is often defined as an intermediate being. Indeed, we have a tendency for good, but at the same time we have a tendency for evil. This fact cannot be denied. Speaking in Christian terms, we live "twixt heaven and earth." We are intermediate beings, also as to reason. We have a desire to go our way following the guidance of reason. But at the same time we have an inclination to live an irregular and degenerate life against reason. Who can deny this? Thus, we are intermediate beings to the last, wanderers between good and evil, fighters against both lust and reason. Pascal said in his *Pensées:*

> If he had only reason without passion. . . . If he had only passion without reason. . . . But having both, he cannot be without strife, being unable to be at peace with the one without being at war with the other. (*Pensées,* 412)

Thus man is always divided against himself. As long as introspection goes on in our minds, we have to admit that this is our

* F. Masutani, *A Comparative Study of Buddhism and Christianity,* The Young East Association, Tokyo, 1957, pp. 17-20, 26-32, 163-174.

true state. As a result of such introspection, people are presently divided into two camps.

The so-called theories of man's "inherent good" and "inherent evil," which have been pitted against each other in the history of Oriental thought, can be found also in the history of Occidental thought. There the antagonism of these two most fundamental ideas has presented itself in the form of strife or interchange between Hellenism and Hebraism. Hellenism, the trend of rationalism originating in Greece, takes the stand on the "inherent good" theory and, convinced of the superiority of human reason, strides proudly heavenward; while Hebraism, originating among the Semites, takes the stand on the theory of "inherent evil," and leads a life of the "vale of tears," lamenting man's sin. Jesus' religion was the largest and the most beautiful flower that bloomed in the field of Hebraism. Here we will discover that reason, which is supposed to be something man should be proud of, is utterly given up. However proud we may be of our reason and wisdom, they are after all limited. What is unlimited and absolute is beyond the reach of our human reason. If so, what could we be really proud of? What is it that we could really be praised for? Reason has thus become a thing we cannot be proud of any more. Humility in respect of one's own reason and wisdom becomes a virtue to be praised, instead. And man, who has abandoned the idea of superiority of reason, realizes in essence his limitation before the Absolute. The limitation is to be grasped through man's recognition of himself as a mortal being, burdened with sin. Of these two, death and sin, sin is emphasized more than death. To make sin the basic cause of death is a remarkable characteristic of this interpretation of man.[1]

The ground on which the religion of Jesus Christ stood was clearly the one that upheld this interpretation. It stood on the conviction of man's frailty and transiency, especially on the conviction of man's sinfulness.

"Those who are well have no need of a physician, but those who are sick. . . . For I came not to call the righteous, but sinners," said Jesus. (Matthew 9:12-13) Riveting his eyes only upon the least, the foolish, the weak, and the sinful, he came to them for

[1] Cf. Romans 6:23: "For the wages of sin is death."

help, became their friend, and preached them God's love and His reign.

> Come to me, all who labor and are heavy-laden, and I will give you rest. (Matthew 11:28)

This plainly expresses the fundamental character of Jesus' religion.

Paul, who had developed world evangelism for the Christian church after the death of Jesus, contributed many well-defined interpretations to Christianity. In interpreting Jesus' life and his death on the cross, he explained that Jesus' whole life was a revelation of God's desire for man's salvation, and that his innocent blood on the cross was shed to atone for man's sin. The creation, Adam's degeneration, and the birth of sin mythically narrated in the Old Testament had prepared such an interpretation for Paul. Paul started from here. He said, "Therefore as sin came into the world through one man and death through sin, and so death spread to all men because all men sinned." (Romans 5:12) He also said, "Death reigned from Adam to Moses, even over those whose sins were not like the transgression of Adam, who was a type of the one who was to come." (Romans 5:14) Every one of us is also burdened with sin—the sin originating in Adam's disobedience to God's commandments. It follows that, because of this, man, although he is eager to do good, cannot do good, while he is apt to do evil which he is not desirous of doing.

Augustine said, "It was possible for man not to sin (*posse non peccare*), but after Adam, it is impossible for man not to sin (*non posse non peccare*)." If this is so, it is hardly possible for such a miserable man to think that he can save himself by his own merits. There is only one way left. It is to receive God's grace through Jesus' redemption, believing in him. There is no alternative. It was such consciousness of original sin and the grace of God that constituted the framework of Jesus' religion.

This is quite a contrast to Buddha's teaching characterized by reason. It is no longer the self that one can depend on. It is not reason but the consciousness of man's powerlessness and sinfulness that leads man to God's love. Accordingly, this way is tightly closed to those who boast of their own reason, and only opened to those who believe in Jesus. This is not a belief to be had after understanding and being convinced of what is preached. The desire for reasoning is rejected here completely: "The son of God was crucified. Because this is a shameful thing, I am not ashamed of it. The son of God died. Because this is a ridiculous thing, I should believe it to the utmost. He was buried and was resurrected. Because this is impossible, it is very certain."[2]

Insufficiency of rational understanding does not mean insufficiency of belief. On the contrary, the believers thought that the less they were concerned over reason the firmer their belief became. Father Tertullianus said, "I believe it because it is absurd (*Credo quia absurdum est*)."

This way is entirely different from the way of Buddha. Buddha taught that we should depend on ourselves and the *dharma* as refuge, and on nothing else. In Christianity, the spirit of self-reliance and the desire for reasoning are to be abandoned; the flower of faith is to bloom only through belief in Jesus. The two ways are quite separate ones. Consequently, their interpretations of man are also diametrically opposed to each other. One upholds reason and urges us to develop it, the other denounces human reasoning and exhorts us to be saved by God in humble consciousness of our sin. They both start as wanderers between darkness and light, and resolutely reject darkness with the hope of becoming the child of light, and yet they march along two paths which are entirely different from each other.

In contrast to Buddhism, we can find nothing theoretical in what Jesus preached. He made his appearance in public all of a sudden around the age of thirty, and made his exit in like manner. During the time he only preached the glad tidings of the Lord. "Repent, for the kingdom of heaven is at hand." This was what John the Baptist had once cried by the Jordan. (Matthew 3:2) Jesus tried to spread this very saying among people and convince them of it through parables and miracles.

The kingdom of God will come—this idea was not original either.

[2] The saying of Tertullianus (about 160-222).

It was a belief which had been cherished of old among his fellow men, and which he had also entertained, being born and brought up in this tradition. We can say the same thing in respect of other traditions such as the Lord's Day, the Last Judgement and the End of the World. He as well as John the Baptist felt that the Last Judgement, the End of the World, and the arrival of the kingdom of God were all near at hand. He believed that "the ax is laid to the root of the trees." (Matthew 3:10) And like John he cried that the kingdom God was near at hand, and urged the people to repent without delay in order to prepare for the day. Such a teaching as this must be said to be far from being theoretical.

As is well known, the writers of the Gospel, describing Jesus' manner of preaching, said, "For he taught them as one who had authority, and not as the scribes." (Matthew 7:29) The Gospel, according to one of the writers, states that people were amazed at his teaching, saying to one another, "What is this?" (Mark 1:27) or "What a word is this?" (Luke 4:36) These passages enable us to see the character of his sermons.

It was not that Jesus preached what was entirely new or what had never been known to them at all that made people listen to his sermons and open their eyes in wonder. Their amazement was due to the way he preached. They were amazed at and attracted by his fresh and unique manner of expression totally different from what they had been used to. The writers of the Gospel were right in saying, "not as their scribes." Here the word "scribe" means "a scholar of the sacred law." Being expert annotators, these scribes would often come to the synagogues to read aloud and comment on the Bible, apparently in a very formal and dull way, and very particular about trifles. There was nothing in their talks that would make the law vibrant with life. Jesus often preached on the Sabbath in the synagogue of Capernaum in Galilee. To the ears of those who had been so used to the complicated and dry sermons of the scribes, his sermons sounded extremely fresh and appealing. They were such vital words that they inspired all who heard him. They may be called "the words of life" or "live words," if we call Buddha's "the words of wisdom" or "wise words."

However, Jesus' sermon described in the passage "He taught them as one having authority," was somewhat different from the sermons of religious fanatics and roaring prophets. True, Jesus often flung violent words at people. He said, "If your right eye causes you to sin, pluck it out and throw it away." (Matthew 5:29) He also said, "If your right hand causes you to sin, cut it off and throw it away." (Matthew 5:36) On another occasion he urged them to make a resolute choice, saying, "No one can serve two masters." (Matthew 6:24) But he did not tell it like fanatical prophets. He always remained free and cheerful in mind. While inducing them to make an uncompromising decision, he talked of the sun and the genial rain. While shaking their souls with words of ardor, he cast his eyes full of love on flowers, children, lilies of the field and birds of the air. (Matthew 6:26-30) Even amid acute tensions, he let his mind affectionately linger on all creation, and his words were decorated with beautiful allegories. A sermon of this kind was naturally very far from being theoretical. It did not show a slightest sign of a man of reason trying to prove or teach something to another man of reason.

The tree is known by its fruit. By observing the disciples of both Buddha and Jesus, we can also tell to what kind of people their religions belonged, respectively.

Sariputta was a typical disciple of Buddha. According to an old sutra, Buddha once praised him, saying, "Sariputta is the one who justly drives the wheel of the *dharma* as Buddha has driven. If anyone talks of 'one being a Buddha's son, born from his mouth, born from the *dharma*, heir to the *dharma*,' Sariputta is the very first to win the title." [3] Together with Moggalana, Sariputta was once a disciple of a heathen ascetic. Both Moggalana and Sariputta encouraged each other in seeking the final solution, and promised to share the result mutually in case either of them found it. One day in the city of Rajagaha, Sariputta was deeply impressed with the sight of a *bhikkhu* begging food. Sariputta thought that the *bhikkhu* must be one of those who had attained wisdom, if there were any such men in the world. In his gait, in his eyes, and in his quiet yet dignified manner, he had no fault to be found. Who was the teacher of this man? What sort of teaching did he

[3] *Majjhima-nikaya,* V. Trenckner, ed., Humphrey Milford, London, 1888, 111 *Anupada-sutta.*

profess? Sariputta waited till he finished begging, approached, and asked questions. The *bhikkhu* answered, "I am a follower of Buddha." When Sariputta asked for information about his teachings, he apologized for being a novice and unable to tell much. What he only said is recorded in a sutra as follows:

> *Of all things which proceed from a cause,*
> *The* Tathagata *has explained the cause,*
> *And also has explained their ceasing.*
> *This the great Adept has proclaimed.*[4]

This quatrain reveals something of the law of causality, and Sariputta could understand what the *bhikkhu's* teacher had taught, as soon as he heard it. The sutra describes that "he gained penetrating eyes for truth (*dharma*) at once." He told it to Moggalana, and both became followers of Buddha.

The circumstances leading to Sariputta's conversion show clearly what high culture and intelligence he had had already. Had he not been a man of excellent intelligence, it would have been entirely impossible for him to grasp what the quatrain meant. Besides, he and Moggalana belonged to the Brahman caste. They were thus distinguished both in birth and culture, and were typical of Buddha's disciples.

Both Buddha and Jesus said, "He who has ears to hear, let him hear." (Matthew 11:15) Jesus also said, "You shall indeed hear but never understand, and you shall indeed see but never perceive." (Matthew 13:14) The Buddhist term *ki* (degree of man's fitness for receiving the truth) also expresses what is meant here. Now, what sort of men have the "ears to hear" or a good *ki*?

Buddha's way is, in short, the way "to perceive with wisdom." "Fools filled with illusions and tied with passions" were far from his religion. It is difficult to approach this religion without intelligence, and to enter it without a contemplative spirit.

> *O bhikkhus!* I preach how to extinguish the worldly passions of what we know and see. I don't tell you of what I do not know or see. Now *bhikkhus*! What is right knowledge and right observation that will

[4] *Vinaya-pitaka,* Hermann Olderberg, ed., Williams & Norgate, London, 1880, *Mahavagga,* 1, 23, 5.

> enable us to extinguish the passions? It is those who have recognized the suffering of life that have really extinguished the passions.[5]

Thus preached Buddha, and the teaching contained the Four Noble Truths. It begins with the recognition of the bitterness of life, and then proceeds to the perception of its cause, the comprehension of the principle for overcoming it, and the actual means for overcoming it. However, those who neither know nor see have no means of overcoming the bitterness of life through this way. One must first of all know, if he wishes to follow the way. He must grasp the actuality of life through proper contemplation. He must then penetrate into the path to be followed, with a resolute will. Only those who were able to do these things were qualified to follow Buddha. Intelligence was the sole prophet, proper understanding the sole prayer, and the righteous *dharma* the sole guide for them. What kind of people was it that could follow such a teaching?

Buddha's order stressed the equality of all men. None was denied entrance into his order because of his caste or poverty. He did not like the caste system Brahmanism had set up. He said man could become a sage not by birth but by his own accomplishment. The gate of his religion was thus wide open to all. Yet those who could actually go through it were inevitably limited to the few with "the eye to perceive and the ear to hear." Those who were weak in their power of observation, reflection, contemplation and practice could not enter it. Evidently the religion belonged to "the wise, and not to the fool." Therefore those who actually constituted the realm of early Buddhism were chiefly young, intelligent men of noble birth. This shows that his religion was solely for the reasoning men.

Jesus' disciples constituting the early Christian order were in marked contrast to their counterparts in the early Buddhist order.

Among Jesus' disciples, one comparable with Sariputta in position was Simon nicknamed *Kepba* (meaning stone, which was *Petros* in Greek). Jesus told Simon, "And I tell you, you are Peter, and on this rock I will build my church, and the powers of death

[5] *Itivuttaka*, E. Windisch, ed., Pali Text Society, London, 1889, 102.

shall not prevail against it. I will give you the keys of the kingdom of heaven, and whatever you bind on earth shall be bound in heaven, and whatever you loose on earth shall be loosed in heaven." (Matthew 16:18-19) This man, the greatest of all of Jesus' disciples, had been a fisherman by the Sea of Galilee. Soon after Jesus started preaching the gospel, Simon was casting a net into the sea and heard Jesus calling to him, "Follow me, and I will make you fishers of men." He abandoned his net, and followed Jesus at once. (Matthew 4:18-19) Since, in Capernaum where he had been living, people had the habit to work, his being a fisherman did not necessarily mean that he was of humble birth. The utmost humbleness of the disciples emphasized by the preachers at church in order to enhance the wonderfulness of the origin of Christianity does not represent their true nature. Simon called Peter, seems to have been quite a prominent figure among his colleagues. However, it is clear that Jesus' disciples decidedly did not belong to the so-called noble class. And, to what we call intelligence or culture in the Greek sense, they were all perfect strangers. Here we cannot but find in Simon Peter a man entirely different from Sariputta, the first man of his day in intelligence, in birth, and in the practice of austerities.

And Peter was virtually a representative type of those who followed Jesus. They were all strangers to intelligence and refinement, and lived in a world quite different from that of the upper class. They formed a becoming audience for the parables of fishing, sowing, reaping, the fig tree, and so forth. Among them, Matthew and a few others occupied a social position slightly different from the rest. Matthew was a tax collector, and probably accustomed to writing. This is one of the reasons why Matthew is thought to have written a document that became the basis of the Gospel. But he was a petty official remote from the high tax surveyor called "publicani" in Rome. Tax collectors were never respected by others. They were despised just like murderers or highwaymen because of the nature of their occupation. Even the other writers of the Gospel placed them in the same category with sinners by saying, "Many tax collectors and sinners came. . . ."

We find these aspects also in the Epistles of Paul. He wrote, "For consider your call, brethren; not many of you were wise according to worldly standards, not many were powerful, not many were of noble birth." (Corinthians 1:26) In the next verse it is also written, "But God chose what is foolish in the world to shame the wise, God chose what is weak in the world to shame the strong." Such were the people that gathered around Jesus who preached the gospel and repentance. They were all naive, fragile in mind, with no intelligence. Not a bit of the elements of Greek culture could be found in them. However, they were full of warm feelings and good faith. Jesus' sermon on the kingdom of God could sink into the hearts of these people, uncultured but naive and honest, like the rain on a field of parched soil. Here we can see clearly the nature of Jesus' religion.

On one occasion someone brought a little child to Jesus that he should touch him. His disciples tried to interrupt it, but Jesus reprimanded them, saying, "Let the children come to me, do not hinder them; for to such belongs the kingdom of God. Truly, I say to you, whoever does not receive the kingdom of God like a child shall not enter it." (Mark 10:14-15) And he took the child in his arms, put his hands upon him, and blessed him. Here again we can clearly see Jesus' view of man.

II

What is the first commandment of religious practice in Buddhism? We may say that it is mercy (*maitra*). What is the core of religious practice in Christianity? It is no doubt love (*agape*). Though the two are different in expression from each other, they will fall under the same category of virtue: "love." Then, in what sense are these different from the "love" as a social virtue? And what differences are there between Buddhistic mercy and Christian love? By analyzing these differences, we may come to understand more concretely the features of religious practice.

A passage from the First Epistle of Paul to the Corinthians is, I suppose, one of the most impressive teachings for Christians about the duty of love, which always lies in the deep of their hearts and comes out at times to encourage them to do the duty.

> If I speak in the tongues of men and of angels, but have not love, I am a noisy gong or a clanging cymbal. And if I have prophetic

> powers, and understand all mysteries and all knowledge, and if I have all faith, so as to remove mountains, but have not love, I am nothing. If I give away all I have, and if I deliver my body to be burned, but have not love, I gain nothing. Love is patient and kind; love is not jealous or boastful; it is not arrogant or rude. Love does not insist on its own way; it is not irritable or resentful; it does not rejoice at wrong, but rejoices in the right. Love bears all things, believes all things, hopes all things, endures all things. Love never ends; as for prophecy, it will pass away; as for tongues, they will cease; as for knowledge, it will pass away. . . . So faith, hope, love abide, these three; but the greatest of these is love. (I Corinthians 13:1-13)

Many Christians get these words by heart exactly to the letter, and draw up from them encouragement as well as strength to support their religious practice. For they are taught to believe that in these words lie the summary of all good things and the foundation of all righteous practices, and even that they need not bear any other responsibility than that of love. Paul preaches this in the epistle to the Romans as follows:

> Owe no one anything, except to love one another; for he who loves his neighbor has fulfilled the law. The commandments, "You shall not commit adultery, You shall not kill, You shall not steal, You shall not covet," and any other commandment, are summed up in this sentence, "You shall love your neighbor as yourself." Love does not wrong to a neighbor; therefore love is the fulfilling of the law. (Romans 13:8-10)

Love is the fulfilling of the law, and the realization of all religious practices. Therefore they need neither think of anything but the practice of love, nor bear any duty but that of love. Paul often emphasized this idea, which, of course, he had himself learned from Jesus. It was after Jesus' entry into Jerusalem that a scribe, who had been listening to Jesus' skillful discussion, went a few steps forward and asked him, "Which commandment is the first of all?" Then Jesus answered, "The first is, 'Hear, O Israel: The Lord our God, the Lord is one; and you shall love the Lord your God with all your heart, and with all your soul, and with all your mind, and with all your strength.' The second is this 'You shall love your neighbor as yourself.' There is no other commandment greater than these." (Mark 12:28-31) Jesus said these words, quoting from the Old Testament. The first commandment is found in Deuteronomy 6:4:

> Hear, O Israel: The Lord our God is one Lord; and you shall love the Lord your God with all your heart, and with all your soul, and with all your might.

And the second commandment is found in Leviticus 19:18:

> You shall love your neighbor as yourself.

Perhaps Jesus answered with a legal term because he was asked by a lawyer.

Hearing Jesus' answer, the scribe affirmed Jesus' words, saying:

> You are right, Teacher; you have truly said that he is one, and there is no other but he; and to love him with all the heart, and with all the understanding, and with all the strength, and to love his neighbor as oneself, is much more than all whole burnt offerings and sacrifices. (Mark 12:32-33)

And no man after that dared ask Jesus any question, the Gospel describes.

The old religion of Israel, which was written in the Old Testament, possessed many formalities as its religious practices. There were burnt offerings, sacrifices, and circumcisions, and the commandments of the law were becoming more and more complicated year after year. Jesus, under these circumstances, preached only one commandment, love. To love God and to love man—in these two he condensed all the commandments. Thus he once said, "On these two commandments depend all the law and the prophets." (Matthew 22:40) Paul expressed this idea by saying that love is the fulfilment of the law and that people should owe no man anything but to love one another. Herein lies a characteristic feature of Christianity, which is said to be the "religion of love."

It may be said that Christianity is the "religion of love," while Buddhism is the "religion of mercy." As was often mentioned before, what Buddha preached was the way of self-control. He taught by his words and deeds that we should control ourselves, aiming at the establishment of the highest personality.

> Self is the lord of self, who else could be the lord? With self well subdued, a man finds a lord such as few can find.[6]

This passage from the *Dhammapada* most aptly expresses the characteristics of Buddha's teachings. Therefore, those who want to follow his way must proceed first of all toward themselves; they must observe themselves, and reform and establish themselves. Another passage of the *Dhammapada* says:

> Well-makers lead the water; fletchers bend the arrow; carpenters being a log of wood; good people fashion themselves.[7]

However, when we turn our eyes that are thus concentrated upon ourselves, and look at people, we see that they are just as we are. Is it all right to give only a cold look upon them? Of course, not. Buddha taught, "Learn to be merciful to the whole world." There is a sutra named *Sutra of Mercy* in the *Sutta-nipata*, in which Buddha preaches as follows:

> Whatever is to be done by one who is skilful in seeking what is good, having attained that tranquil state of *nibbana:*—Let him be able and upright and conscientious and of soft speech, gentle, not proud.
>
> And contented and easily supported and having few cares, unburdened and with his senses calmed and wise, not arrogant, without showing greediness when going his round in families.
>
> And let him not do anything mean for which others who are wise might reprove him; may all beings be happy and secure, may they be happy-minded.
>
> Whatever living beings there are, either feeble or strong, all either long or great, middle-sized, short, small or large,
>
> Either seen or which are not seen, and which live far or near,

[6] *Dhammapada,* 160, Max Muller, trans., *Sacred Books of the East,* Clarendon, Oxford University Press, 1881, vol. X.

[7] *Ibid.,* 145.

> either born or seeking birth, may all creatures be happy-minded.
>
> Let no one deceive another, let him not despise another in any place, let him not out of anger or resentment with harm to another.
>
> As a mother at the risk of her life watches over her own child, her only child, so also let every one cultivate a boundless friendly mind towards all beings.
>
> And let him cultivate goodwill towards all the world, a boundless friendly mind, above and below and across, unobstructed, without hatred, without enmity.
>
> Standing, walking or sitting or lying, as long as he be awake, let him devote himself to this mind; this way of living they say is the best in this world.[8]

We should not remain for a long time in the dark, blinded with worldly passions and desires in the environment of the common run of men. We should resolutely come out of the dark, and return to ourselves, to establish a new and sublime personality. This was the way that Buddha brought into the world. However, even when we have begun to follow his way, we are still a resident of this world; and even when we walk along the road of the outside world, we still remain with people in this world. Then, what should be our religious practice toward our fellow creatures? Needless to say, the principle of our practice is mercy. Buddha taught people to wish, "May all living creatures be blessed, and live in ease and comfort." He also taught, "Not doing whatever things which may be criticized by others, only learn to have this mercy."

Christians often say, "God is love," while Buddhists say, "The mind of Buddha is great mercy." By these sayings we can estimate what value is set upon these items in the two religions.

In Buddhism, the world *kama* (love) is often spoken of with some unfavorable feeling. As it is thought to be the origin of desire, it is sometimes referred to as a synonym of sexual love. Or again, as it is thought to be the consuming strength similar to that of a thirsty man, it is often called *trishna* or "craving thirst." It is also recalled that a certain sutra warns us of its limitless craving:

[8] *Sutta-nipata,* Lord Chalmers, trans., Harvard University Press, Cambridge, Mass., 1932, *Metta-sutta* 143-151.

"As the sea drinks up infinitely the water of rivers, craving thirst cannot be satisfied for ever." [9]

Careful readers, however, will see that it is the original vital force of life which exists before good and evil. Physicists say that all things have attraction. Then, is it not true that this world is "the world for us" because we have such attraction? Like Kant, Buddha thought that by the mutual relations between the subjectivity of cognition and the objectivity of the object, all cognition would be formed. No other world would exist but that made by such relations. On one occasion, he talked on this:

> Disciples, I am going to explain what is "everything." Listen to me carefully. What do we call "everything"? Eyes and colour, ears and voice, the nose and smell, the tongue and taste, the body and feeling, the mind and the law; disciples, these are "everything." [10]

He further added that "everything" besides the above-mentioned "everything" was only a word and did not exist in their world. Then, what is it that combines and connects eyes and colour, ears and voice, the nose and smell, the tongue and taste, the body and feeling, and the mind and the law, or in short, the subjectivity of cognition and the objectivity of the object? It is *kama* or love. It is the power to combine and the energy to attract one another.

Now we cannot but recall the Fourfold Noble Truths preached in his first sermon. Then he taught, as the First Truth of suffering (*dukkha*), that we should observe the actual conditions of life. And as the Second Truth, he taught that we should see the reason or cause of the actual state of life. This is called the truth of the cause of suffering (*dukkha-samudaya*). It explains why this life of suffering has come about. He taught the reason, saying: The cause of suffering lies in the craving thirst that, coupled with pleasure and lust, craves for satisfaction everywhere: namely, the craving for passion (*kama-tanha*), the craving for existence (*bhava-tanha*), and the craving for vanity (*vibhava-tanha*).

[9] *Do-sen: Gyoji-sho* (a commentary of Vinaya), 1, 2, Taishō, vol. 40, p. 127. English edition not available. Editor.

[10] *Samyutta-nikaya,* L. Feer, ed., Pali Text Society, London, 1898, 35, 23.

The former half of this passage reminds us of "the blind will for life" (*blinder Wille zum Leben*) of Schopenhauer. Nobody knows why we crave and desire. But there is a power that seems to push us up, if we may say so, in the fundamental darkness. It is "the blind will for life," and in Buddhism "love" is originally thought to be such a will. It becomes the power which connects our subjectivity to the object, and as a result, our world is formed. Buddha classifies such "love" into three categories, namely, sexual love, love for life, and love for vanity. This reminds us of Hobbes' "three natural desires," the two of which are the desires for existence, the first being sexual love, the second the desire to eat, and the third, which is peculiar to human beings, being vanity. These three kinds of desire exactly correspond to the three kinds of love mentioned by Buddha. If these kinds of desire or love enable our world to be formed, then, they must be originally the source of life that exists before good and evil; and to use a Buddhistic term, they must be "things neither good nor wrong." But when they are brought into the world of value, we cannot say that they are good without modification. Man has made good fields through cultivation out of natural wildernesses. This is also the principle of culture, and even linguistically speaking, the words culture and cultivation have the same root. When a Brahman said to Buddha, "You have to cultivate the ground and obtain food by yourself," Buddha answered, "I cultivate, too." [11] In the spiritual world, if we can turn the natural and vulgar into something good, by developing them, this must be culture and cultivation.

Love is the power that attracts mutually, and is the basic power that forms our whole world through its mutual attraction and combination. Without this, men and women would not be united, parents and children would not love each other, neighbours would not be on friendly terms, and our world would not be formed. Its natural state, however, is not always good. Even animals lead a cooperative life between males and females. The love of parent and child can be seen even among birds. Attraction between close objects exists even in the physical world. Until today, mankind has been criticizing, denying, controlling, and elevating such a natural state of love. And it is Buddhism and Christianity that

[11] *Ibid.*, 6, 11.

have taught to enhance this love and to permeate it universally among all humanity.

But as for the process that led to such an idea of love of all humanity, the two religions took quite different roads.

The practice of love in Christianity is, in short, to imitate God's love. Christian love is called *agape* as against human love, which is called *eros,* because it is thought that however highly human and animal love may be enhanced and purified, it can never be equal to God's love. *Agape* and *eros* are different kinds of love.

As mentioned before, a passage of the Sermon on the Mount teaches:

> You have heard that it was said, "You shall love your neighbor and hate your enemy." But I say to you, Love your enemies and pray for those who persecute you, so that you may be sons of your Father who is in heaven. (Matthew 5:43-45)

This passage leaves nothing unsaid as to the basic principle of Christian love. The natural state of man's love is to love those that are close to himself, namely, to love his wife, to love his children, to love his parents, to love his brothers, to love his friends, and to love his relatives. The closer the object of love is, the stronger is his love toward it; and the farther the object of love is, the weaker is his love toward it. It has generally been encouraged to hate an enemy extremely and to fight a foe bravely. Jesus, however, said, "Love your enemies and pray for those who persecute you." He also said, "If any one strikes you on the right cheek, turn to him the other also." (Matthew 5:39) This is quite different from the natural state of human love and hatred. Then why did Jesus teach these things? How can man be able to do these things? The answer was, "That you may be sons of your Father who is in heaven."

Jesus continued:

> For he makes his sun rise on the evil and on the good, and sends rain on the just and on the unjust. For if you love those who love you, what reward have you? Do not even the tax collectors do the same? . . . You, therefore, must be perfect, as your heavenly Father is perfect. (Matthew 5:45-48)

Only by wishing to be perfect, man can become the child of the Father who is in heaven. Only by wishing to be perfect, man can enter the love of God at a bound from the natural state of human love.

Paul once sent a letter to the Corinthians, saying, "Be imitators of me, as I am of Christ." (I Corinthians 11:1) This shows that imitation is the principle of Christian practice. To imitate Paul is to imitate Jesus; to imitate Jesus is to imitate the Father in heaven; and to imitate the Father in heaven is to wish to be as perfect as God. Here is the principle of the practice of Jesus' followers. It is not to be planned by our absurd knowledge; it is not to be calculated by our selfish and erroneous thinking; but it is to imitate Jesus and the Father in heaven, casting aside all things.

This imitation must therefore be realized in deeds as its practice. Jesus once warned his disciples, saying:

> Not every one who says to me, "Lord, Lord," shall enter the kingdom of heaven, but he who does the will of my Father who is in heaven. (Matthew 7:21)

He also said more concretely:

> So if you are offering your gift at the altar, and there remember that your brother has something against you, leave your gift there before the altar and go; first be reconciled to your brother, and then come and offer your gift. (Matthew 5:23-24)

This shows well that Jesus' teachings are behavioristic. And Christian love as the imitation of the Father in heaven must also be embodied in our deeds. It is thought that we are imitating God and loving God, and imitating Jesus and loving Jesus if we actually extend our hand of love to neighbours, to the poor, and to "the least." Jesus said,

> Truly, I say to you, as you did it not to one of the least of these, you did it not to me. (Matthew 25:45)

Thus the love of God and the love of man are combined into one through practice.

It may be said that the basic principle of universal love in Buddhism is mercy, which extends over all living creatures through the feeling of the same sorrow. Because of this, it is not "love" which is the natural power of combination, but it is more appropriate to be called "mercy."

Buddha was once visited in Jeta Grove by a Brahman named Sangarava. He asked Buddha a question:

> It seems to me that the way of *samana* (wanderer) is to seek only one's happiness, because it aims at obtaining one's tranquillity and deliverance from worldly bonds. Are not the teachings for one's happiness inferior to those for many people? [12]

The question is reasonable, for Buddha's teachings seem, at a first glance, to aim only at one's happiness. Even those who called themselves Mahayanists in later days were not free from such a misunderstanding. Buddha gave a negative answer to the question, explaining the reason roughly as follows:

> I went forth into the homeless life in search of the solution of my sufferings, and found the truths through which I could obtain the solution. Therefore I teach people to come to the solution of their sufferings also through the truths; and if many people could also reach the solution of their sufferings through the truths they should never be called the truths for only one's happiness.[13]

Needless to repeat, Buddha began to search for the truths by thoroughly examining his own sufferings. At first sight, his life before he went into the homeless life had seemed very happy; however, he found that he also bore heavily such human sufferings as birth, decay, disease, and death, and so he entered the homeless life in search of a solution. Now when he lifted his eyes turned so far toward himself, he saw that people, just as he had been before, were thoughtlessly spending every day, without knowing the heavy human sufferings they bore. So he taught them:

[12] *Anguttara-nikaya,* R. Morris and E. Hardy, eds., Pali Text Society, London, 1900, 3, 60.

[13] *Ibid.*

> You must open your eyes and set them upon yourselves. And if you can be convinced of my teachings, you must obtain the solution through them.

This was the spirit of Buddha's forty-five-years gospel-preaching since he attained enlightenment.

We now recall that in his teachings, he said:

> Go now for the benefit of the many, for the welfare of mankind, out of compassion for the world.[14]

At first glance this sems to concentrate on the individual. The teachings, however, unite everybody at the depth of one's self. And only at the depth of one's self, one can really realize that others also bear the same heavy burden of human sufferings. This is what we call in Buddhism the feeling of compassion for the same suffering and same sorrow. Only he who sheds tears over himself can shed tears over others. Out of compassion flows forth the spirit of mercy.

> *Man's thought can go anywhere.*
> *Wherever one may go, however,*
> *One may find nothing dearer than oneself.*
> *The same is with others.*
> *Therefore, one who loves oneself,*
> *Should not hurt others.*[15]

Here is the basic form of compassion for others. When one softly applies his personal observation to others, there will be the feeling of mercy. A certain sutra explains, "Compassion is mercy, while grief is sorrow." [16] Only when there is the feeling of deep grief, there will be the feeling of comprehensive compassion. Mercy is a universal love thus formed in human beings, and it can go far beyond the pale of natural human love only when it is based on the complete realization of human suffering.

[14] *Vinaya-pitaka,* 11, 1.

[15] *Samyutta-nikaya,* 3, 8.

[16] *Daijo-Gisho* (the syllabi of Mahayana Buddhism), vol. 7, Taishō, vol. 44, p. 686.

Judaism

Leo Baeck

Leo Baeck's publications number over four hundred in all. The author of this voluminous production was born in 1873 in Lissa, Posen. In 1897 he received a rabbinical diploma. Among his many works are "Essence of Judaism," "Interrelations of Judaism, Science, Philosophy and Ethics," and "Judaism, the Jew and the State of Israel." By the time of World War II, Leo Baeck had become the acknowledged leader of German Jewry.

In 1955, one year before his death, he was instrumental in founding the scholarly research institute which bears his name: The Leo Baeck Institute in New York, Jerusalem, and London. The primary purpose of this institute is to retrace, collect, and thereby preserve the history of German-speaking Jewry.

JUDAISM AND CHRISTIANITY *

If we classify types of piety in accordance with the manner in which they have historically become types of religion, then we encounter two forms above all: classical and romantic religiousness, classical and romantic religion. The distinction and opposition between these two types is exemplified especially by two phenomena of world history. One of these, to be sure, is connected with the other by its origin and hence remains determined by it within certain limits; and yet the significant dividing line separates them clearly. These two religions are Judaism and Christianity. In essential respects they confront each other as the classical religion and the romantic religion.

What is the meaning of romantic? Friedrich Schlegel has characterized the romantic book in these words: "It is one which treats sentimental material in a phantastic form." In almost exactly the same words one might also characterize romantic religion. Tense feelings supply its content, and it seeks its goals in the now mythical, now mystical visions of the imagination. Its world is the realm in which all rules are suspended; it is the world of the irregular, the extraordinary and the miraculous, that world which lies beyond all reality, the remote which transcends all things.

We can observe this disposition of the soul in relative historical proximity when we consider the German romantic of the last century. For him, everything dissolves into feeling; everything

* Leo Baeck, *Judaism and Christianity*, Walter Kaufmann, trans., The Jewish Publication Society of America, Phialdelphia, 1958.

becomes mere mood; everything becomes subjective; "thinking is only a dream of feeling." Feeling is considered valid as such; it represents the value of life which the enthusiastic disposition wants to affirm. The romantic becomes enraptured and ecstatic for the sake of ecstasy and rapture; this state becomes for him an end in itself and has its meaning within itself. His whole existence is transformed into longing—not into the longing for God, in which man, raising himself above the earth, overcomes his earthly solitude; nor into the powerful longing of the will which thirsts for deeds; but into that sweet wavelike longing which pours itself out into feelings and becomes intoxicated with itself. Suffering and grief, too, become a good to him, if only the soul is submerged in them. He revels in his agonies as much as in his raptures.

Thus something agitated and excited, something overheated or intoxicated easily enters the feelings—and not only the feelings, but the language, too. Every expression seeks to excel in this direction; voluptuousness becomes a much sought-after word. The feelings talk in terms of superlatives; everything has to be made ecstatic. Fervently, the romantic enjoys the highest delight and the deepest pain almost day after day; he enjoys the most enchanting and the most sublime; he enjoys his wounds and the streaming blood of his heart. Everything becomes for him an occasion of enraptured shuddering, even his faith, even his devotion. Thus Novalis praises his Christianity for being "truly the religion of voluptuousness."

These souls can always be so full of feeling because their abundant suffering is, for the most part, only reverie and dream; almost all of it is merely sentimental suffering. They like so much to dream; the dim distances, twilight and moonlit night, the quiet, flickering hours in which the magic flower lowers its blossoming head, represent the time for which they are wearily waiting. They love the soft, the sweet illusion, the beautiful semblance; and whereas Lessing had said to God, "Give me the wrestling for the truth," the romantics implore, "Accord me lovely illusions." They want to dream, not see; they shun the distinctness of what is clearly beheld in the light, to the very point of antipathy against fact. Disgruntled they confront reality; and in its stead they seek the less clear attraction of fluctuating feelings to the point of outright delight in confusion. What is within and without becomes for them a semblance and a glimmer, resounding and ringing, a mere mythical game; and the world becomes a sadly beautiful novel, an experience to be felt. As Hegel once put it: "The sense for content and substance contracts into a formless weaving of the spirit within itself."

The desire to yield to illusion, justifiable in art, here characterizes the entire relation to the world. In the deliberately sought-out twilight of longing and dream, the border lines of poetry and life are effaced. Reality becomes mere mood; and moods, eventually, the only reality. Everything, thinking and poetry, knowledge and illusion, all here and all above, flows together into a foaming poem, into a sacred music, into a great transfiguration, an apotheosis. In the end, the floods should close over the soul, while all and nothing become one, as the grandson of the romantics celebrates it:

> *"In the sea-like rapture's billowy swell,*
> *In the roaring waves of a drowsy smell,*
> *In the world-breath's flowing all—*
> *To drown—*
> *To sink down—*
> *Unconsciousness—*
> *Highest bliss."*

In this ecstatic abandonment, which wants so much to be seized and embraced and would like to pass away in the roaring ocean of the world, the distinctive character of romantic religion stands revealed—the feminine trait that marks it. There is something passive about its piety; it feels so touchingly helpless and weary; it wants to be seized and inspired from above, embraced by a flood of grace which should descend upon it to consecrate it and possess it—a will-less instrument of the wondrous ways of God. When Schleiermacher, defined religion as "the feeling of absolute dependence," he condensed this attitude into a formula.

Romanticism therefore lacks any strong ethical impulse, any will to conquer life ethically. It has an antipathy against any practical idea which might dominate life, demanding free, creative obedience for its commandments and showing a clearly determined way to the goals of action. Romanticism would like to "recover from purpose." All law, all that legislates, all morality with its commandments is repugnant to it; it would rather stay outside the sphere of good and evil; the highest ideal may be anything at all, except the distinct demands of ethical action. From all that urges and admonishes, the romantic turns away. He wants to dream, enjoy, immerse himself, instead of clearing his way by striving and wrestling. That which has been and rises out of what is past occupies him far more than what is to become and also more than what wants to become; for the word of the future would always command. Experiences with their many echoes and their billows stand higher in his estimation than life with its tasks; for tasks always establish a bond with harsh reality. And from this he is in flight. He does not want to struggle against fate, but rather to receive it with an ardent and devout soul; he does not want to wrestle for his blessing, but to experience it, abandoning himself, devoid of will, to what spells salvation and bliss. He wants no way of his own choosing. For the romantic the living deed is supplanted by the grace whose vessel he would be; the law of existence, by mere faith; reality, by the miracle of salvation. He wants to exist, without having an existence of his own; he wants less to live than to experience—or, to use the German, he prefers *erleben* to *leben*.

Therefore the romantic "personality" is also something totally different from, say, the Kantian personality who confronts us as the bearer of the moral law and who finds himself, and thus his freedom, in being faithful to the commandment. The romantic, too, loves his own being; but he seeks this individuality in the fluid world of his feelings which, capable of the quasi miraculous, can enter into everything and mean everything. Only out of this emotional experience, which becomes for him the measure of all things, does he derive what is good and evil for him. It is not through ethical action and not through clear knowledge that he expects to find the way to himself. He believes that he can become certain of himself only in self-contained feeling, in emotional self-contemplation which does not give expression to the emotions but dwells on them and all-too-easily becomes sheer virtuosity of feeling, admiring itself in the mirror of introspection and preening its own beautiful soul. There is, therefore, no more unromantic remark than Goethe's when he says that man comes to know himself by doing his duty and living up to the demands of the day. The romantics say instead: experience yourself and revel in yourself.

It is for these reasons that romanticism is usually oriented backwards, that it has its ideal in bygone ages, in the paradise of the past. It does not want to create but to find again and restore. After all, whoever prefers to feel and dream soon sees himself surrounded by ancient images; and only those who direct their will toward fixed tasks know themselves to be standing in a living relationship to the future. Therefore it is also given to romanticism to hearken to the voices from former times. Romanticism is especially qualified for this because, with its abundance of emotion, it is capable of reflecting all the recesses and mysteries of the human soul and to feel its way into different individualities. It has discovered the poetry of transitions, also the poetry of the divisions and clefts of the soul; it has known how to comprehend the radiation that emanates from the individual phenomenon and has cultivated the devotion to what is minute. Man with his contradictions is its subject. Hence romanticism has produced the artists of biography and cultivated the kind of history which demands empathy. But only this kind; it has not shown much vision regarding over-all connections or the ideas of the centuries. Romanticism remains lyrical even when it contemplates the seriousness of great events, and history becomes for it a game in which one becomes absorbed. One will here look in vain for the great message of the past. The strength and weakness of emotion determines the power and the impotence of romanticism.

It is the same everywhere. It is always feeling that is supposed to mean everything. Hence the capacity for feeling defines the dimensions and the limits of romanticism. We see this at close range in its representatives of the last century with their merits and their weaknesses. In opposition to the exclusive rule of the sober understanding, romanticism had legitimately demanded another right and another value. But romanticism itself soon fell victim to the same fundamental mistake which it had arisen to combat; for almost immediately it, too, claimed exclusive validity. It elevated pure feeling above everything else, above all conceptual and all obligatory truth—and eventually not only above everything else but in place of everything else. It strove to drown in beautiful illusion more and more of reality with its commandment, and to let the profound seriousness of the tasks of our life fade into a mere musical mood, to let them evaporate into the floating spheres of existence.

It gave its name to a whole generation in the last century; and yet romanticism is not applicable merely to a particular epoch, to a mere period of history. Romanticism means much more: it designates one of the characteristic forms which have emerged again and again in the development of mankind—a certain type in which, from time immemorial, religious life in particular has manifested itself. To be sure, historical types, just like human types, never appear quite pure. Whatever exists is a mixture; nowhere does life know sharp boundaries and distinctions; it is never an equation without any remainder. There are certain romantic elements in every religion, no less than in every human soul. Every religion has its dream of faith in which appearance and reality seek to mingle; each has its own twilight valley; each knows of world-weariness and contempt for the factual. But in one religion this is merely a quiet path alongside the road, a sound which accompanies, a tone which also vibrates. In another religion it fixes the direction; it is the dominant basic chord which determines the religious melody and gives it its character. Thus, depending on whether this or a wholly different motif is the decisive one, the romantic religion distinguishes itself quite clearly from the classical. And in this sense it may be said: Judaism is the classical religion and Christianity, compared with it, the romantic religion.

Christianity accepted the inheritance of ancient—Greek and oriental—romanticism. At an early date, the traditional national religion in the Hellenic lands had been joined by a victorious intruder, probably from the north: another religion—darker, phantastic and sentimental—the Dionysian or Orphic cult of which much might be said, but certainly not: "What distinguished the Greeks? Reason and measure and clarity." It had all the traits of romanticism: the exuberance of emotion, the enthusiastic flight from reality, the longing for an experience. Holy consecrations and atonements were taught and ecstatically tasted with reeling senses. They aimed to relate man to the beyond; they aimed to make him one with the god and thus grant him redemption from primordial sin and original guilt. For this, it was said, could not be attained by mortal man with his own power, but must be a gift of grace which had to descend from hidden regions and to which a mediator and savior, a god, who once had walked on earth had shown the way. Marvelous traditions told of this and handed on the stories of the redeeming events and their mysteries, that they might be renewed again and again in the believers. Mystical music dramas, showy, phantastic presentations, seemingly removed into mysterious distances by the twilight, granted the weary, drowsy soul the beautiful dream, and the sentimental longing its fulfillment: the faith that it belonged to the elect.

In the official religion, this wish of the individual to be chosen and to stand before the god, this individual desire to be important and attain eternal life and bliss, had not found satisfaction. Now all this was offered to him by this enthusiastic religion of moods. And thus it was that this religion found its way more and more into the souls; it became the new religion which gradually decomposed the old naïve faith and the classical spirit of the Greeks, and eventually destroyed it.

Moreover, it had received further strength from all sides, wherever religious romanticism had a home: from the oriental and Egyptian mysteries, from the cults of Mithras and Adonis, of Attis and Serapis. In essentials they were all alike: they shared the sentimental attitude which seeks escape from life into living experience and turns the attention towards a phantastic and marvelous beyond. What they proclaimed, too, was at bottom always the same. It was the faith in a heavenly being that had become man, died, and been resurrected, and whose divine life a mortal could share through mysterious rites; the faith in a force of grace, entering the believer from above through a sacrament, to redeem him from the bonds of earthly guilt and earthly death and to awaken him to a new life which would mean eternal existence and blessedness. The roving yearning of a weary age was only too ready to become absorbed in these conceptions of resurrection and apotheosis, of instruments of grace and consecrations; and it even sought them out everywhere. From all lands the mysteries could flow together in mighty waves.

The tide moved along a free and wide course. The region from the Euphrates to the Atlantic Ocean had under Roman rule become the place of a matchless mixture of peoples fused into a cultural unity. Just like the ancient states, the old pagan religions, too, had more and more lost their boundaries and their former definiteness. A cosmopolitan yearning and hope gripped and united all of them. The way was prepared for a new faith without limits or boundaries. In the world-wide empire it could become the world religion and the world philosophy. Whatever it was that a human being might seek, it promised everything to everybody—mystery and knowledge, ecstasy and vision, living experience and eternity. It was everything and took the place of everything and therefore finally overcame everything. The great romantic tide thus swept over the Roman empire, and the ancient world drowned in it. Even as the old naïve poetry of the gods perished in the sentimental myth of the redeeming savior, so what was classical vanished, along with its sure sense of law and determination, and gave way to the mere feeling of a faith which was sufficient unto itself.

What is called the victory of Christianity was in reality this victory of romanticism. Before Christianity took its course, that through which it eventually became Christianity—or, to put it differently, whatever in it is non-Jewish—had already become powerful enough to be reckoned as a world faith, as a new piety which united the nations. The man with whose name this victory is connected, Paul, was, like all romantics, not so much a creator of ideas as a connector of ideas; the genius of seeing and establishing such connections was characteristic of him. He must be credited with one achievement—and this single achievement was of world-historical significance and truly something great—that he carried living Jewish ideas into the mysteries which even then commanded the allegiance of a whole world. He knew how to fuse the magic of the universal mysteries with the tradition of revelation of the secrecy-wrapt Jewish wisdom. Thus he gave the ancient romanticism a new and superior power—a power taken from Judaism. It was this blend, compounded by him, that the world of the dying Roman empire—Orient and Occident, which had become one world—accepted.

In Paul's own soul, this union in which romantic and Jewish elements were to be combined, had prevailed after a period of transition. Subjectively, this union represented the story of his struggles which became the story of his life. The images of his homeland, Asia Minor, had early revealed to him the one element, romanticism; the parental home and the years of his studies had presented him with the other, the Jewish one. Then, in the land of his people, he had found those who longingly awaited the helper and liberator of whom the prophets had spoken—some hoping that he might come, others waiting that he might return. Eventually he discovered himself among those who were thus waiting—those whose eyes were fixed on the image of their messiah, their Christ, who had died young and would return when his day came—an image similar in many of its features to that offered by his pagan homeland in its mysteries. The pagans in those days were aware of Judaism; and Jews, too, paid attention to the thinking and seeking of paganism. Thus the promises and wisdom from here and there, from paganism and from Judaism, entered into his unrest and doubts which pulled him hither and thither, looking and listening far and wide, in his craving for the certainty of truth. He did not want merely to wait and hope; he wished it might be given him to have and to believe.

Finally he had perceived an answer. It was a victorious and liberating answer to his mind because it did not merely grant a coming, a promised, day, something yet to be, but a redemption which was fulfilled even then—as it were, a Now. This answer became for him the end which meant everything because it contained everything: both that of which the mysteries of the nations had told him and that which the proclamations of his own Jewish people had said to him. Alongside the one God before whom the gods of the pagans were to vanish, it now placed the one redeemer, the one savior before whom the saviors of the nations could sink out of sight: it placed the oneness of the savior alongside the oneness of God. Thus he experienced it: paganism, with its deepest aspirations and thoughts, was led to Judaism; and Judaism, with its revelation and truth, was bestowed on the pagans, too.

Now everything seemed to fall into place. What his Judaism had let him find in the circle of those waiting, in the proclamation of the messianic faith, as the fulfillment and goal of all prophecy, this faith in the final answer, in the final certainty, in him who had come and would come—all this he discovered now in the quest of the pagans; all this he perceived when he contemplated the myth which the marvelous mysteries everywhere presented to the world. And where confused strains out of the pagan world had spoken to him of the mysterious tidings of grace, in which a whole world had created for itself the satisfaction of its yearnings, his own people's faith in a messiah now permitted him to comprehend quite clearly all that had till then seemed so dark. Now he grasped it: not Attis or Adonis, not Mithras or Serapis was the name of the resurrected, the savior, who became man and had been god, but his name was Jesus Christ. And the significance of Jesus, who had become the Christ of his people, could not be that he had become king of the Jews, their king by the grace of God, their admonisher, comforter, and helper; but his life and his power signified the one, the greatest, thing, that he was the resurrected, miracle-working, redeeming God, he that had been from eternity. And for all who owned him, who had faith in him and possessed him in sacrament and mystery, the day that was promised had become today, had been fulfilled. In him Jew and pagan were the new man, the true Israel, the true present.

The last veil now seemed to Paul to have been taken from his eyes, and he saw the hitherto divided world unified. In the messianic certainty of Judaism he now recognized the goal toward which the seeking and erring of the pagans had, in the depths of truth, always aspired; and in that which the pagans had wanted but not known, he now grasped the content and the answer which was spoken, which was promised to Judaism. Judaism and paganism had now become one for him; the one world had arrived which comprehended everything, the one body and the one spirit of all life. That Jewish and pagan wisdom meant, at bottom, the same thing, was one of the ideas of the age. Now it seemed to have become the truth. Now the Jews need no longer merely wait, as the community of the expectant, for the last day, which would then in turn become the first day, when the messiah would come or come again; in a mysterious sacrament, the fulfilled time in which everything has been accomplished, the goal of the longed-for redemption, was given to them even now, given in every hour. And now the pagans really could come to know him for whom they had from time immemorial looked, the named but unknown; and now they could comprehend the mystery which had since ancient times been present among them as their precious possession. Judaism and paganism were now reconciled, brought together in romanticism, in the world of the mystery, of myth, and of sacrament.

Precisely how this net of ideas took shape in the mind of Paul, how the different threads found each other and crossed each other, which idea came first and which one it then attracted—to ask about this would merely lead to vain and useless speculation. Beginning with his childhood, Paul had been confronted both with the possession of Judaism in the parental home and with the sight of the mystery cults in his homeland. In his consciousness both had their place, and they were woven together and became one. This union which was fashioned in him then emerged out of him into the world. And it became victorious in a world which had become weary and sentimental; it became the religion for all those whose faint, anxious minds had darted hither and thither to seek strength. It represented the completion of a long development.

For what had been most essential in the ancient mysteries is preserved in this Pauline religion. It, too, believed in the romantic fate of a god which reflects the inexorable lot of man and is the content of all life. What everything represents is not a creation of God and not an eternal moral order, but a process of salvation. In a heavenly-earthly drama, in the miraculous mystery that took shape between the here and the above, the meaning of world history and of the individual human life stands revealed. There is no other word but the definite word "myth," romantic myth, to characterize this form of faith. With this, Paul left Judaism; for there was no place in it for any myth that would be more than a parable —no more for the new sentimental one than for the old naïve myths of former times. This myth was the bridge on which Paul went over to romanticism. To be sure, this man had lived within Judaism deep down in his soul; and psychically he never quite got away from it. Even after his conversion to mystery and sacrament, he only too often found himself again on the old Jewish ways of thought, as though unconsciously and involuntarily; and the manifold contradictions between his sentences derive from this above all. The Jew that he remained in spite of everything, at the bottom of his soul, again and again fought with the romantic in him, whose moods and ideas were ever present to him. But in spite of this, if we are to label him as he stands before us, the apostle of a new outlook, then we can only call him a romantic. Trait for trait we recognize in his psychic type the features that distinguish the romantic.

Paul, too, sees everything—to use Schlegel's term—in the "phantastic form" in which the border lines of appearance and reality, of twilight and event, are lost; in which he sees images which the eye never saw and hears words which the ear never perceived; in which he can feel redeemed from this world and its harshness, from what is earthly in him and from what desires to cling to the soil of this earth. Thus he lives in the beyond which transcends all things, beyond the struggle between upward drive and gravity, beyond becoming and perishing, where only faith can reach and only miracles can take place. Therefore faith is everything to him. Faith is grace, faith is salvation, faith is life, faith is truth; faith is being, the ground and the goal, the beginning and the end; commencement and vocation meet in it. Faith is valid for faith's sake. One feels reminded of the modern slogan, *l'art pour l'art;* Pauline romanticism might be labeled correspondingly, *la foi pour la foi.*

This faith is so completely everything that down here nothing can be done for it and nothing may be done for it; all "willing or running" is nonsensical and useless. The salvation that comes through faith is in no sense earned, but wholly received; and it comes only to those for whom it was destined from the beginning. God effects it, as Luther later explained the words of Paul, "in us and without us."[1] Man is no more than the mere object of God's

[1] *in nobis et sine nobis.* Weimar ed., VI, 530 (*de capt. Babyl.*).

activity, of grace or of damnation; he does not recognize God, God merely recognizes him; he *becomes* a child of redemption or of destruction, "forced into disobedience" or raised up to salvation. He is the object of virtue and of sin—not its producer, its subject. One feels like saying: man does not live but is lived, and what remains to him is merely, to speak with Schleiermacher, "the taste of infinity," that is, the living experience; the mood and the emotional relation of one who knows himself to be wholly an object; the feeling of faith in which grace is present or the feeling of unbelief in which sin prevails.

The theory of original sin and election, which Paul formulated after the manner of the ancient mystery doctrine and then shrouded in a biblical-talmudic dress, serves only to demonstrate the completeness of that power which makes passivity—or, to say it again in the words of German romanticism, pure "helplessness" and "absolute dependence"—the lot of man. A supernatural destiny which, whether it be grace or damnation, is always a *fatum,* determines according to an inexorable law that a man should be thus or thus. He is pure object; fate alone is subject. In this way, religion becomes redemption from the will, liberation from the deed.

Later on, the Catholicism of the Middle Ages softened this conception and granted a certain amount of human participation. But Luther then returned to the purer romanticism of Paul with its motto, *sola fide,* through faith alone: "it must come from heaven and solely through grace." [2] The image which he supplies to illustrate this point is, quite in keeping with Luther's style, harsh in tone, and yet thoroughly Pauline in its meaning: *velut paralyticum,* "as one paralyzed," [3] man should wait for salvation and faith. The heteronomy of life is thus formulated: the life of man has its law and its content only outside itself.

This faith is therefore decidedly not the expression of a conviction obtained through struggle, or of a certainty grown out of search and inquiry. Seeking and inquiring is only "wisdom of the flesh" and the manner of "philosophers and rabbis." True knowledge is not worked out by man but worked in him; man cannot

[2] Weimar ed., XXIV, 244.

[3] *Ibid.,* II, 420: *oportet ergo hominem de suis operibus diffidere et velut paralyticum remissis manibus et pedibus gratiam operum artificem implorare.*

clear a way toward it; only the flood of grace brings it to him and gives him the quintessence of knowledge, the totality of insight. Knowledge here is not what instructs but what redeems, and it is not gained by thinking but given in faith; it goes with the consciousness of absolute dependence. "Do not seek, for to him who has faith all is given!" This is the new principle, the axiom of romantic truth; and all wrestling and striving for knowledge has thus lost its value and, what is more, its very meaning. There is no longer any place for the approximation of truth, step for step; there is no longer any middle ground between those who see everything and those who see nothing. Grace now gives complete light where up to now only darkness held the spirit in its embrace. Grace places man at the goal, and he is the perfect, the finished man.

The conception of the finished man which appears here—truly the brain child of romanticism for which truth is only a living experience—became one of the most effective ideas in the entire Pauline doctrine. It has again and again attracted and even permanently captivated those minds who would like so much to believe in their entire possession of the truth and who long for the rest which such complete possession would afford. Since the end of the ancient world, the intellectual life of the Occident has in many ways been determined by this notion. It has established that orientation in which the answer precedes every question, and every result comes before the task, and those appear who quite simply have what is wanted and who never want to become and grow.

The philosophy appropriate to this conception of the finished man is that doctrine which considers truth as given from the outset, that scholasticism which possesses and knows the whole truth, down to its ultimate ramifications, from the start and merely needs to proclaim it or to demonstrate it *ex post facto*. Most of the thought produced by the Catholic Middle Ages shows the influence of this conception. And Luther's world of thought is completely dominated by it; for Luther clings to the rigid faith in such possession and, in that sense, to the Middle Ages.

Only the age of the Enlightenment began to push the conception back, but it really made a beginning only. For when romanticism re-awakened in the last century, the conception returned with it, and it has survived together with romanticism. It has, indeed, created what might be called racial scholasticism, with its doctrine of salvation, with its system of grace, and with its faith that this grace works through the dark abysses of the blood—this modernized *pneuma*—and gives the chosen everything, so that the finished man is once again the goal of the creation. Wherever romanticism is found, this conception appears by its side.

The much quoted *credo quia absurdum*—"I believe because it is absurd"—is nothing but the ultimate formulation which results from this conception, almost as a matter of course. What confronts the inquiring spirit and his thinking as something opposed to reason, and unacceptable, may be the truth for the finished mind of the completed man, whether he owes his completion to grace or another source. To this faith knowledge must submit. Sooner or later, every romanticism demands the *sacrificium intellectus*, the sacrifice of the intellect. Here, too, the best commentary for Paul is found in Luther's words: "In all who have faith in Christ," he says, "reason shall be killed; else faith does not govern them; for reason fights against faith." [4]

Unquestionably, the romantic certainty which Paul proclaims is derived from an original psychic experience. When a strong idea emerges out of the hidden darkness of the unconscious, where it had slowly and silently taken shape, and all at once enters consciousness, it is always at first distinguished by the suddenness of the unexpected and seems to possess the power of a revelation. As if it had been fashioned by a miracle, as if the path of thought had not in this case been covered step by step, truth seems to confront the mind finished and completed; it appears to speak to him, and he feels that he does not have to do anything but listen; and the person who has this experience may have the feeling that grace has descended upon him and elected him. This is, after all, also one of the forms in which the seeking genius may find his solution; it is, in the words of a modern thinker, the romantic type of invention. And it is the same which confronts us in Goethe's epigram: "In very small matters, much depends on choice and will; the highest that we encounter comes who knows from where." Something universally human is expressed here.

[4] Erlangen ed., 44, 156 f.

Romanticism has had this experience very intensely—so intensely that this one thing has become everything for it. Romanticism considers this experience, in which man feels as if he were a mere instrument of a higher power, not merely a great experience, but the essence, the *whole* and the innermost content of our existence. Romanticism takes particularly the initial instant of reception, the power of that moment, for the quintessence and fulfillment of all humanity. Romantic magic becomes romantic truth.

The first moving impression with its mighty effect, with its suggestive capacity for multiple interpretations, here becomes everything, and there frequently remains no significance whatever for anything further, and especially for one's personal life's work. Instead of any positive judgment, there is merely hostile melancholy which accuses life for not continuously furnishing such high-pitched experiences. The relation is clear. Once the intoxication of this excitement has become the meaning of life, nothing remains, confronted with sober and harsh existence, except pessimism to which all reality becomes strange and hostile; *Welttrunkenheit* and *Weltschmerz,* this intoxication and this melancholy belong together.

This kind of absorption is dominant in every romanticism. Hence the jumpy and disconnected character of its thinking, the aphoristic, fragmentary style which is, for this reason, prominent in the Pauline exposition, too. And the stamp of this attitude which determines everything—this is a further misfortune implicit in it—can regrettably be of many different kinds: it can be ever so high and ever so shallow, most powerful or utterly hollow. It can be the strong impression of the hour, but also—much more frequently—a merely momentary, empty conceit of a mind eager, even greedy, for sensation. It can be genuine, but it can also be spurious; the psychic experience which overcomes a human being or the wish for artificial excitement with which those craving emotion spur on their feelings and senses. And here as there, this impression would count as everything and be received as a datum of faith, immune against doubt and rational examination.

It is the right of art to consider an impression valid simply as an impression and to accept it as something entire and complete without critical scrutiny. Art is, as Schopenhauer puts it, "everywhere at its goal." But for life, and hence surely also for religion, there is a danger, the romantic danger, in making the impression of an experience all-important. For then the sense for the content and commandment of life must all too soon evaporate together with any sense for reality with its definite tasks; and the place of all aspiration and exertion will be taken over by the sole dominion of the mood of faith which simply feels itself, and then finds it easy to deem itself, complete. This is faith for faith's sake.

For the romantic, the impression, the mood, that which comes over the human being, is everything. This determines his artistic bent, too. In the Pauline, as in any romantic religion we can clearly observe it. The component of faith and revelation, of transport and ecstasy—that which is, as it were, a psychic reception of religion, a religious consecration or even seizure—is here taken for the fulfillment of religion, for ultimate truth and perfection. No religion will want to do without openness to the profound, the hidden, the secret, the miracle of revelation, the experience of faith; this is the mystery of religion, that in it which gives birth. But for all it suggests and proclaims and bestows—and often this function could be found nowhere else—it still is not all of religion or even all of religiosity, any more than it is all there is to prayer, any more than mood as such supplies content, any more than birth is equivalent to life. The romantically pious, however, finds this sufficient and considers it everything. For he is a man of lofty sentiment who is capable of feeling and knows how to pray, but often does not get beyond feeling and prayer; the type which so easily remains on the threshold to receive everything there. His whole religion is merely a receiving; and therefore he finds it always so easy to think that he has finished his task. His faith remains purely passive; it is not faith in the challenging, commanding law of God, but merely in the gift of divine grace. Activity fights for everything; passivity has everything. There demands are made; here everything is given; even the love of man which is glorified in romantic religion is merely the gift of grace which is the share of those who have faith. The only activity of the genuine romantic is self-congratulation on his state of grace.

One might characterize the Pauline religion in sharp juxtapositions: absolute dependence as opposed to the commandment, the task, of achieving freedom; leaning as opposed to self-affirmation and self-development; quietism as opposed to dynamism. There the human being is the subject; here, in romantic religion, the object. The freedom of which it likes so much to speak is merely a freedom received as a gift, the granting of salvation as a fact, not a goal to be fought for. It is the faith that does not go beyond itself, that is not the task of life; only a "thou hast" and not a "thou shalt." In classical religion, man is to become free through the commandment; in romantic religion he has become free through grace.

Martin Buber

Martin Buber was born in Vienna in 1878, enrolled in the faculty of philosophy at the University of Vienna in 1896, and taught Jewish philosophy of religion at the University of Frankfort from 1923 to 1933. In 1938 he left Germany for Israel, where he has since lived. He is the author of over thirty books dealing with problems of Jewish theology and philosophy.

The following essay by Buber was translated for this volume by William Hallo. At Buber's request, this special introductory note has been provided for this essay by Maurice Friedman, a close friend of Buber's and author of *Martin Buber: the Life of Dialogue.*

"This essay must be understood in two contexts at once. One of these is that of Buber's fifty-year task of translating and interpreting the Hebrew Bible and of the dialogue between Judaism and Christianity that has grown out of that task. 'Professor Buber,' writes the Old Testament scholar J. Coert Rylaarsdam, 'is in a unique way the agent through whom, in our day, Judaism and Christianity have met and enriched one another.'

"The other context is that of the Nazi persecution of the Jews which had begun in 1933—the very year in which this dialogue between Martin Buber and Karl Ludwig Schmidt took place. This context adds a dimension of terror and greatness to this Jewish-Christian interchange, touching as it does on the common Biblical inheritance of the two faiths but also on the religious roots of anti-semitism in Christianity, which the Nazi exploited to the full. It was with this second context in mind that Professor Buber wrote me on October 28, 1963: 'I have no objection to including the translation of "Kirche, Staat, Volk, Judentum" in a volume prepared by McGraw-Hill Paperbacks, but it must be prefaced by some sentences on the circumstances under which that public dialogue was held. The reader must understand that the atmosphere was that of an impending crisis.' The very book in which this essay was published, *Die Stunde und die Erkenntnis* ('The Hour and Its Knowledge'), is made up of talks and addresses permeated by this crisis and by the 'spiritual war against Nazism' which Buber has spoken of as the endeavor of the German Jewish community of which he was one of the great spiritual leaders at that time."

CHURCH, STATE, NATION, JEWRY *

First Response When Karl Ludwig Schmidt and I exchanged letters in preparation for this dialogue, we were first of all obliged to come to an understanding about the formulation of the topic. He proposed "Church, State, Nationhood, Synagogue." I declined this, in the first place because I did not feel myself empowered to speak for a "synagogue," but more than this because I consider "synagogue" to be an unauthentic designation and not one with which to address a Jew in a manner enabling him to answer. Instead I accepted the designation "Jewry," although I do not consider this entirely correct either. Rather, I regard that designation as correct which Schmidt himself used with emphasis—so that we have already gained common ground by virtue of this word—this name, the name "Israel."

Israel is not something about which we possess only a Biblical report, something with which, thanks to this report, we Jews feel a history-laden connection. Rather Israel is something existing—something once and for all, unique, unclassifiable by either category or concept. Every pigeonhole of world history defies attempts at subsuming it. Israel is that which, to this day, amidst various distortions, dissimilations, destructions, still hides within this "Juda-

* German *Volk*. Buber seems to use this term in the sense of "people" as well as "nation." I have tried to translate by "people" when it clearly applied to Israel, by "nation" when clearly applied to political entities. I have used "Jewry" rather than "Judaism" in the light of what follows; both meanings are contained in the word *Judentum*. Translator.

ism" something peculiarly its own, something which continues to live within it as a concealed reality. Only from within this reality can we Jews address Christians; only from there have we the existential possibility of a response. And the more truly we are addressed as Israel, the more legitimate is the dialogue.

Karl Ludwig Schmidt has acknowledged that Israel is something unique, something unclassifiable. Israel exists for the Church in the Church's legitimate existence, and Israel exists for us in *our* legitimate existence. Both of us, Church and Israel, know "concerning" Israel. But we know one another in fundamentally different ways —a fundamental difference which is radically other than a mere difference of opinions such as one may express in order to try to harmonize them with each other. That is impossible here; for we are dealing here with a fundamental difference of perception or intellection. For like Israel, the Church too claims to know. This knowledge of the Church concerning Israel confronts Israel's knowledge concerning itself in a manner more strictly irreconcilable than a merely logical contradiction. The Church perceives Israel as a reality *rejected* by God. This condition of rejection necessarily follows from the claim of the Church to be the true Israel. Those of Israel have, according to this view, forfeited *their* claim because they did not recognize Jesus as the Messiah.

Christians believe that they have received this "being Israel," —the office, dignity, and election of Israel—from God. The certitude of their belief on this point is unassailable. We have no means of opposing this knowledge of the Church concerning Israel which could serve as more than an argument. We, however, who know concerning Israel from within, in the darkness of a knowing from within, in the light of a knowing from within, know otherwise concerning Israel. (I cannot even speak of "perceiving" here any more, for we know it from within, and we know it, not with the "eye of the spirit," but with our very lives.) We who have sinned against God a thousand times, who have turned our backs on God a thousand times, who have experienced throughout these millennia a divine dispensation which it would be too simple to call punishment (for it is greater than punishment)—we know that nonetheless we have not been repudiated. We know that this dispensation is an event, not in the conditionality of the world, but in the reality of the space between God and ourselves. And we know that precisely here, in this reality, we have not been repudiated by God, that in this discipline and chastisement, God's hand holds on to us and does not let go, holds us into this fire and does not let us fall.

Such knowledge is fundamentally and irreconcilably different. I would not dare to call ours a "claim." That is too human, too arrogant a term for our situation. We do not have a claim at all. We have only our poor but exceedingly factual knowledge concerning our existence in the hands of God. However, this fundamental difference cannot be resolved from the side of men, by human undertaking, by human speech, by human willingness to come to terms, no matter how comradely. But if we "wait patiently," it is for what cannot come to us from man but only from God; we await a unification which cannot be constructed by men, which, indeed, contemporary man is utterly incapable of conceiving in concrete terms.

Paul's dictum regarding the resolution of differences in the world of the Christian event has already been noted; however, we are incapable of sensing this resolution. We feel ourselves, in fact find ourselves, in a world where differences are unresolved and appear by their nature to be irresolvable. To be sure, however, we also feel something else. We feel that the "Spirit"—a term of belief which we have in common with Christians, although they call it *pneuma hagion* (holy spirit) and we *ruach ha-kodesh* (spirit of sanctification or of holiness)—is itself not bound by this differentiation. We feel that the Spirit alone wafts over our irresolvable differences, that though it does not bridge them, it nevertheless gives assurance of unity, assurance in the experienced moment of unity for the communality of even Christians and Jews.

In this sense I would like to understand that Jewish dictum which I set opposite that of Paul.[1] True, it is more reserved, but it radiates a factuality which can be experienced, it seems to me, by every man. It is a dictum from an ancient book dealing with matters taught in the "School of Elijah" after his assumption: "I invoke heaven and earth as witness: whether one be of the

[1] Schmidt quoted Galatians 3:28: "Here is neither Jew nor Greek, here is neither slave nor free, here is neither male nor female."

Gentiles or of Israel, whether man or woman, man-servant or maid-servant—only according to the deed which he does will the Spirit of Sanctification descend upon him." This is no resolution of differences, but rather a distribution of the Spirit to humanity as it is, in the fragmentation in which it stands, in such a way, however, that humanity as a whole, from whatever side, can look upon that which descends on men, no matter how different their point of departure or their very certitude of belief may be.

We, Israel, confront the Church's rejection of our knowledge concerning ourselves. The Church can perhaps say to us: "You who feel yourselves sustained by God, not abandoned, not spurned, still existing in the Presence—what you call actually experienced self-knowledge is an illusion prompted by your instinct for self-preservation." What then if the certitude of one side is thus rejected by the other, as final eschatological reality? [2] I believe that this is one of those decisive points at which we human beings have to acknowledge the genuine teaching of what human existence means, that hard and salutary teaching. We have to deal with each other in the diversity of the human, and we see how deep such diversity can go, even to the ultimate roots of belief. What then shall we do?

We can try to do something extremely difficult, something which is extremely difficult for the religiously oriented person, something which runs counter to his orientation and relationships or, rather, seems to run counter to them, something which seems to run counter to his relationship with God. We can acknowledge as a mystery that which, notwithstanding our existence and self-knowledge, others confess as their reality of belief. We are not in a position to appraise the meaning of their confession because we do not know it from within as we know *ourselves* from within.

Karl Ludwig Schmidt justifiably put the question of the Messiah, the Christological question, at the center of his observations.

If we wish to reduce the schism between Jews and Christians, between Israel and the Church, to a formula, we can say: "The Church stands on the belief in the 'having come' of Christ as the God-given redemption of man. We, Israel, are *incapable* of believing this."

[2] A different passage to render in English. The German is *von einem Letzten her, als Letzes.*

The Church views our declaration either as a case of not wanting to believe, as a very questionable sort of obduracy, or else as a kind of curse, as a basic limitation on the ability to recognize reality, as the blinding of Israel which prevents it from seeing the light.

We, Israel, understand in another fashion our inability to accept that gospel. We understand the Christology of Christianity entirely as a substantive occurrence between the Above and the Below. We view Christianity as something whose spread over the world of nations we are in no position to penetrate. But we also know that universal history has not been rent to its foundations, that the world has not yet been redeemed. We know it as surely as we know that the air which we breathe exists, that the space in which we move exists. We know it more deeply, more authentically. We apprehend the unredeemedness of the world.

The Church may or must understand precisely this sensation of ours as the consciousness of *our* unredeemedness. But we know it otherwise.

For us, the redemption of the world is indivisibly equated with the completion of creation, with the erection of a unity no longer hindered by anything, no longer suffering any contradiction, realized in all the multiplicy of the world, equated, in short, with the fulfillment of the Kingdom of God. We are incapable of comprehending anticipation of the *consummate* redemption of the world in any partial respect, such as the soul's already being redeemed, however much redeeming and becoming redeemed manifest themselves to us too in our mortal hours.

We are not aware of a caesura in history. We know no midpoint of history, only a goal, the goal of the way of God who does not pause on his way.

We are incapable of holding God to any one manner of revelation. We are prevented from regarding any unique event as a definitive revelation of God, prevented by that word from the burning bush: "I will be what I will be"; (Exodus 4:14) i.e., I will exist as I will exist at any given time. It is not as though we were able to declare anything about God's ability or inability to reveal himself. I am referring precisely to the fact that we are incapable of affirming anything absolute about all the revelations concerning which we know. We do not say: "God cannot reveal himself this way." It is only that we do not attribute unsurpassability, the character of an incarnation, to any revelations. That futuristic dictum of the Lord points unconditionally beyond each and every moment of occurred time. God is utterly superior to every one of his manifestations.

I have already stated: what joins Jews and Christians together is their knowledge concerning one uniqueness. And we can also confront this most profoundly divisive factor from the same vantage point. Every authentic sanctuary can acknowledge the mystery of every other authentic sanctuary. The mystery of the other one is internal to the latter and cannot be perceived from without. No one outside Israel knows concerning the mystery of Israel. And no one outside Christendom knows concerning the mystery of Christendom. But for all this ignorance, they can acknowledge each other in the mystery. How is it possible for the mysteries to exist side by side? That is God's mystery. How is it possible for a world to exist as a house in which these mysteries dwell together? That is God's affair, for the world is a house of God. We serve, separately and yet all together, not by each one of us shirking his reality of belief nor by surreptitiously seeking a togetherness despite our difference, but rather when, acknowledging our fundamental difference, we impart to each other in unreserved confidence what we know of the unity of this house, a unity which we hope one day to feel surrounding us without partitions. We serve thus, till one day we may be united in the common service, till we shall all become, as the Jewish prayer on the festival of the New Year puts it: "a single brotherhood for doing his will."

I repeat: that Israel exists is something unique, outside all categories. This name, bestowed by God, not by father and mother, marks the community as one which cannot be comprehended by the categories of ethnology and sociology. We fail to do Israel justice whenever we apply such a category to it. What this uniqueness of Israel is based on is declared in the Bible. It makes the origin of this community identical, historically and episodically, with the religious experience and the religious behavior of a human multitude in its decisive hour.

The human multitude of Israel experiences something which happens to it as a believing multitude, as a multitude united by belief, not as so many believing individuals but rather as a believing community. As such it hears and it responds. In this process of being addressed and answering, it is constituted in that very hour into what we call a people. It becomes something which endures henceforth in a closed circle of generations and births. This differentiates Israel for all time from nation-states and religions.

We deal here with a unity of belief and people which is unique. To regard its uniqueness as incidental implies incredulity vis-à-vis history as it has occurred. Its origin is designated as a covenant between the divine and the human.

This is a unique royal covenant: God says to a people (Exodus 19:6) that he takes it to himself as his immediate royal realm, and a people says of God (Exodus 15:18) that he will remain its king "forever and ever." To understand such a covenant as a privilege, however, is fundamentally mistaken. To be sure, the popular side of this people again and again succumbs to the temptation to do this.

Against such misconstruction there stands the great phenomenon of prophecy, which repeatedly reminds the people that it is nothing more than, so to speak, an experiment of God. Genesis recounts how God first attempted such an experiment with a mankind which failed. Only then did he attempt to cultivate a people for himself as the beginning of a mankind, the beginning of the realization of his Kingdom. God calls it the "beginning of his harvest." (Jeremiah 2:3)

This Israel, which is at once nation and religion and yet neither of these, is exposed to all the temptations of nations and religions. It would like to rest within itself; it would like to feel itself, by God's grace, as an end unto itself. But its leaders censure it for any sense of security: it exists as a people only because "peoplehood" is the presupposition of the *whole* human response to God.

There must be a people in order for the human response to fulfill itself in the whole of life, to which public life belongs. The whole life-response of man cannot be given to God by the individual person but only by the community in its plurality and unity, in the joint labors and the joint realization of its variously endowed and variously commissioned members. That is why there must be a people, why there must be an Israel. The community must endure as a presupposition of the fulfillment. If it wants to be otherwise, it must be sundered and renewed.

The knowledge concerning Israel can degenerate into the superstition that God is a purveyor of power. To counter this, the prophets point ever more clearly to the historical mystery. The way of God through history will not be represented schematically. God manifests himself as master of history, but not through bestowal of power and success. There is a covenant of God with suffering, with darkness, with concealment. In the prophetic dictum, the sinful people confronts God as one whom it can rejoin in darkness and suffering, not in power.

Ever since that time we have believed in this. It is again and again a contemporary concern that a people can sin by calling its obedience to self an obedience to God. Not until the Exile did Israel learn to disabuse itself of this sin.

With the Babylonian Exile, the conception of the "Servant of God" matures. It is a conception of the human type which ever and again appears on earth and effects what it has to effect, in suffering and in darkness, in the quiver of God: "He made me a polished arrow, in his quiver he hid me away." (Isaiah 49:2)

A suffering for God's sake, the concealed history of the arrows which God does not dispatch, which do his work in the darkness of the quiver: it is for this that we, as Israel, endure. Every struggle of ours can be understood only on this account.

According to our tradition, the destruction of Jerusalem took place because the community was not fulfilled, because there was a conflict in Israel which prevented the "beginning" from growing into a harvest. And not only do the Jews hence come among the nations: Israel too comes over the nations. That is, Jesus' gospel of the coming age as the triumphant revelation of the concealed universal history, which grew up in Israel, comes over the nations.

The concealed universal history seeks to ascend from the quiver and to manifest itself as the history—the way—of God. From a late, spiritualized form of theocracy, Jesus points back to the original certitude of the Kingdom of God and its fulfillment; he proclaims it by renewing and transforming the conception of the Servant. His gospel, however, reached the nations not in its authentic form but rather in a dichotomy which is alien to Jesus' gospel. We know this dichotomy most forcefully through Augustine, who surrendered the realms of the national community, of the state, who cut off this presupposition of the *whole* life-response of man from the domain of God. The dichotomy leads consequently to a separation of "religion" and "politics." Again and again some imperial concept attempts to surmount this duality, only to fail again and again.

The nations erected their concepts of empire as Christian nations. They accepted the Kingdom of God as their assigned task; they took it up and enunciated it as Christians. The nations' great imperial concepts all derive from the mission of Israel, but in such a way that, empowered by the Church, they declare Israel dismissed from its function, as no longer appointed to help build the godly community of mankind.

Thus the nations oppose Jewry in their concepts of empire. Jewry, however, confronts the nations in this way: it knows a Yea opposed to this Nay, a Yea which is neither light nor self-willed, but rather imposed and terribly hard to bear. It knows this precisely, in its pitiful way, but also immensely and inextinguishably.

The failure of the world of the nations truly to admit Jewry is connected with its opposition to Israel. Motivated by peasant traditions in the reality of its belief, Israel was excluded from agricultural production as early as the Middle Ages. It was denied participation in the creative life of the nations in whose midst it lived. The nations did not understand that what was addressed to them—indeed, enjoined upon them in their relationship to the resident alien, Israel—also is said of Israel's relationship to the resident alien: "So you shall divide this land among you according to the tribes of Israel. You shall allot it as an inheritance for yourselves and for the aliens who reside among you and have begotten children among you. They shall be to you as native-born sons of Israel; with you they shall be allotted an inheritance among the tribes of Israel." (Ezekiel 47:21 ff.) The nations made it impossible, thereby, for Israel to realize Jeremiah's principle for life in the Exile: "Build houses and live in them; plant gardens and eat their produce." (Jeremiah 29:5)

The nations of the Occident have from the first denied Israel participation in creative life. Even when they finally "emancipated" it, they did not admit it as Israel but rather as a plurality of individual Jews. Israel was not received as Israel by the Christians.

Some say that this is impossible. A believing person must not speak thus. He must not evade the fact that there is this Israel in the midst of the nations, that it has been dispatched into the midst of the nations. This prohibition applies to Israel as well as to the others. The uniqueness of Israel's situation corresponds to the uniqueness of Israel. But is it also properly a part of this uniqueness that that injunction to all nations with resident aliens in their midst still awaits its fulfillment; and that Israel still waits to be able to fulfill that dictum directed to it by Jeremiah?

Karl Ludwig Schmidt has asked me about Zionism. Certainly the concept of "peoplehood" has been emphasized and overemphasized in this. This has happened because, within an indissoluble union of peoplehood and belief, peoplehood had frequently been neglected in the period after the Emancipation. The attempt was made to allot Israel its place among the religions. Against this the caveat had to be expressed that Israel has no reality without its peoplehood. But today the time has come to replace national and religious concepts once more with the Israel properly so called, Israel in its unity and uniqueness. It is for the sake of this Israel that Zion must be built. And Zion cannot be solely a territorial concept, any more than Israel can be solely a national one.

Is an authentic acceptance of Israel possible?

This question seems to me to be connected in its very essence with that other question: is it possible for the Christian nations to behave according to the Bible?

I do not know what the situation is in this regard. Whether an authentic dialogue can exist between the Church, which does not know of the mission of Israel, and Israel, which knows of its mission, seems to me, however, to depend on what this situation is. In such a dialogue one will hardly come to an understanding with another, but one can understand the other for the sake of the one Existence which the several realities of belief imply.

My Christian partner in this conversation has applied the passage about the Servant of God to Israel's understanding of itself. This speaks for the possibility of such a dialogue. It touches the depths of Israel's self-knowledge concerning its mission. We are entitled, therefore, to hope that the possibility for an authentic acceptance of Israel exists in a common struggle, hard but blessed.

Finally, the question of the relationship of Israel to the state is determined by Israel's Messianic belief. This is the belief in a human community as the royal realm of God. Therefore, the question of the social and political structure of the effort to build the human community can never and nowhere be a matter of indifference to Israel. It is a matter of innermost moment to Israel, a part of its eternal mission, to take an interest in the striving of every political structure toward the Kingdom.

Seen from the perspective of Messianic belief, every political structure, no matter what its configuration, anticipates the Kingdom of God for Israel; it is a problematic model of that Kingdom which, however, points to its true form.

But at the same time, Israel knows, precisely in its Messianic belief, just how questionable are the realizations. Therefore, it senses unendingly the other side of the state. It senses that what we call a state is ever and again an index of how much willingness is available for community and, on the other hand, how much coercion is required to maintain here and now a minimum of honest human coexistence.

This twofold viewpoint of Israel's results in its twofold relationship to the state. Israel can never turn its back on the state; it can never disavow it. It must accept it, and it must long for that fulfillment of the state which is so inadequately intimated each time by its various manifestations.

The conservative and the revolutionary Jewish attitudes are both based on the same fundamental outlook.

Second Response I live a short distance from the city of Worms, to which I am also tied by ancestral tradition; and from time to time I visit there. When I do so, I always go first to the cathedral. It is a visible harmony of members, a whole in which no part deviates from the norm of perfection. I walk around the cathedral, gazing at it in perfect joy. Then I go to the Jewish cemetery. It consists of cracked and crooked stones without shape or direction. I enter the cemetery and look up from this disorder to the marvelous harmony of the cathedral, and it seems to me as if I were looking from Israel up to the Church. Here below there is no suggestion of form, only the stones and the ashes beneath the stones. The ashes are there, no matter how they have been scattered. The corporeality of human beings who have become ashes is there. It is there. It is there for me. It is there for me, not as corporeality within the space of this planet, but as corporeality deep in my own memories, back into the depths of history, back as far as Sinai.

I have stood there; I have been united with the ashes and through them with the patriarchs. That is a remembrance of the divine-human encounter which is granted to all Jews. The perfection of the Christian God-space cannot divert me from this; nothing can divert me from the God-time of Israel.

I have stood there and I have experienced everything myself. I have experienced all the death that was before me; all the ashes, all the desolation, and all the noiseless wailings become mine. But the covenant has not been withdrawn for me. I lie on the ground, prostrate like these stones. But it has not been withdrawn for me.

The cathedral is as it is. The cemetery is as it is. But nothing has been withdrawn for us.

If the Church were more Christian, if Christians were more fulfilled, if they did not have to dispute with each other as much as they do, Karl Ludwig Schmidt holds that there would be a keener debate between Christians and ourselves.

Were Jewry once more to become Israel, were the sacred countenance to appear once more from behind the mask, then, I would counter, the separation would remain unbridged, but there would not be a more bitter argument between us and the Church, but rather something wholly different, which today is still inexpressible.

In conclusion I ask you to listen to two quotations which appear to contradict each other but do not contradict each other.

The Talmud (Yebamoth 47a) teaches:

> If in this day and age a convert comes in order to be received into Judaism let him be told: "What have you seen in us, that you wish to be converted? Do you know that the people of Israel are at this time tortured, battered, buffeted, driven about, that suffering has overtaken them?" If he says: "I know, and I am not worthy," then let him at once be received.

This might seem to be Jewish arrogance. It is not. It is nothing other than the public declaration of that which cannot be dismissed. The distress is a real distress, and the disgrace is real disgrace. But there is a divine meaning in it which assures us that as God has promised us (Isaiah 54:10), he will never let us fall from his hands.

And the Midrash says (Exodus Rabba XIX, Sifra on Leviticus 18:5):

> The Holy One, blessed be he, declares no creature unworthy, rather he receives every one. The gates are opened at every hour, and whoever seeks to enter, will enter. And thus He says (Isaiah 26:2): "Open ye the gates, that the righteous nation (*goy zaddik*) that keepeth faithfulness may enter in." It is not written: That priests may enter in, that Levites may enter in, that Israelites may enter in. Rather is written: That a *goy zaddik* may enter in.

The first quotation dealt with converts, but not this quotation: it deals with all mankind. The gates of God are open to all. The Christian need not go via Judaism, nor the Jew via Christianity, in order to enter in to God.

Franz Rosenzweig

Franz Rosenzweig was born on December 25, 1886, in Cassel, Germany. From 1907 to 1912 he studied history and philosophy at the Universities of Berlin and Freisburg. One year later he met Eugen Rosenstock-Huessy, with whom he discussed religion and particularly Christianity; for several months Rosenzweig intended to convert to Christianity, but after attending an Atonement Day service in Berlin, he decided to remain a Jew. He died in 1929 leaving behind many essays, a brilliant correspondence, and the book-length works "Hegel and the State" (two volumes) and "Star of Redemption" (three parts).

The following selection (translated from "Star of Redemption" expressly for this anthology) was chosen at the suggestion of Nahum N. Glatzer, professor of Jewish history at Brandeis University. Professor Glatzer says: "Rosenzweig used the 'Star' (the Shield of David) for which the book is named as representation of the three 'elements' (upper triangle) and their corresponding 'paths' (lower triangle): a symbol of the ultimate perfection. The cross, its beams pointing into all directions, symbolizes the Christian mission in historic space and time. . . .

"Rosenzweig's work is the first attempt in Jewish theological thought to understand Judaism and Christianity as equally valid views of reality. In his view, both will exist, or, rather, are destined to exist to the 'end.' Yet forever will the Christian who is eternally on the way through history resent the Jew to whom it is granted to realize eternity in time, in a metahistorical existence."

THE WAY THROUGH TIME: CHRISTIAN HISTORY *

The rays shoot forth from the fiery nucleus of the Star. They seek out a way through the long night of the times. It must be an eternal way, not a temporary one, even though it leads through time. Not that it may deny time—after all, it is meant to carry [the world] through time—but time must not gain power over it. On the other hand, it must not create its own time after the fashion of the eternal people, continually reproducing itself in itself, and thus liberate itself from time. Thus only one thing remains for it: it must master time. But how could that happen? How could a way which runs through time partition time instead of being itself partitioned by time?

Epoch The question already embraces the answer. After all, the tempo of time determines everything occurring in it only because time is both older and younger than everything that occurs. Were an occurrence with a beginning and an end outside it to confront it, then the pulse of this occurrence could regulate the hours of the world clock. Such an occurrence would have to originate beyond time and run its course in a temporal beyond. True, an occurrence would be within time in any present; but knowing itself independent of time in its past and in its future, it feels itself strong against time. Its present stands between past and future.

* From Franz Rosenzweig, *The Star of Redemption,* part three, book 2, pp. 98-112. Translated by William W. Hallo.

The moment, however, does not stand; rather, it vanishes with the speed of an arrow. As a result it is never "between" its past and its future: it has vanished before it could be between anything. The course of the world knows a between only in the past. Only the point in past time is a point in time, an epoch, a stop. Living time knows of no points; as fast as it begins to be traversed with the speed of a flying arrow by the moment, every point is already traversed. But in the past the hours stand in that motionless juxtaposition. Here there are epochs, stations in time. These epochs may be recognized by the fact that time precedes them and time follows them. They are between time and time.

Time, however, attains gravity only as a between. Now it can no longer vanish like an arrow. The epoch no longer passes before I become aware of it nor transforms itself before I notice it. Rather it signifies something. Something: in other words, it is like a thing. In the past the course of the world assumes the form of immovable "things," of eras, epochs, great moments. And this it can do only because in the past the vanishing moments are captured as stops, held between a before and an after. As a between they can no longer escape; as a between they have stability, they stand still like hours. Time has lost its power over the past, which consists entirely of betweens. It can still add to the past, but it can no longer change the past except, at the most, through what it adds. Time can no longer play a part in the inner structure of the past, for that is fixed, point by integrated point. The measured cadence of the years may appear to dominate the present so thoroughly that the impatience of a world reformer, the lament of one haplessly aware of his turn of fate, bridles against it in vain. In the past, however, this cadence loses its power. In the past, events dominate time, and not vice versa. An epoch is that which stands—stands still—between its before and after. It little cares how many years it is assigned by the chronicle; every epoch weighs the same, whether it lasts centuries or decades or only years. Here events rule time by marking in their notches. Yet the event exists only within the epoch; the event stands between before and after. And a stationary between exists only in the past. If the present were also to be elevated to the mastery of time, it too would have to be a between. The present—every present—would have to become "epoch-making." And time as a whole would have to become the hour, this temporality. As such it would have to be yoked into eternity, with eternity its beginning, eternity its end, and all of time but the between between that beginning and that end.

Christian Chronology Thus it is Christianity that has made an epoch out of the present. Only the time before Christ's birth is now still past. All the time that succeeds, from Christ's earthly sojourn to his second coming, is now that sole great present, that epoch, that standstill, that suspension of the times over which time has lost its power. Time is now mere temporality. As such it may be surveyed in its entirety from any one of its points, for beginning and end are equidistant from each of its points. Time has become a single way, but a way whose beginning and end lie beyond time, and thus an eternal way. On ways which originate in time and lead into time, by contrast, only the next piece can ever be surveyed. Every point on the eternal way, moreover, is a midpoint, since beginning and end are, after all, equidistant, no matter how time advances. It is a midpoint not because it is, at the precise moment, the present point—not at all, for then it would only be a midpoint for one moment and already in the next instant no longer midpoint. That would amount to the kind of vitality with which time rewards a life that submits to it: a purely temporal vitality. It is the vitality of a life in the moment to be life in time, to let itself be carried off by the past, to summon up the future. Men and nations live thus. God withdrew the Jew from this life by arching the bridge of his law high above the current of time, which henceforth and to all eternity rushes powerlessly along beneath its arches.

The Christian, however, takes up the contest with the current. He lays the track of his eternal way alongside of it. He who travels this road gauges the spot of the river which he is just looking at only by its distance from the points of departure and destination. He himself is ever and only en route. His real concern is only that he is still and yet on the way, still and yet between departure and goal. As often as he glances out the window, the current of time, ever yet passing by outside, tells him this and nothing more. He who travels the current itself can only see from one bend to the next. For him who travels the iron way, the current as a whole is but a sign that he is still en route, only a sign of the between. Beholding the current, he can never forget that the place whence he comes and the place whither he travels lie beyond the current's territory. If he asks himself where he may be now, at this moment, the current gives him no answer, while the answer which he gives himself is never anything but "en route." As long as the current of this temporality still runs at all, he is at every moment midway between beginning and end of his course. Beginning and end are both equally near to him at every moment, for both are in the eternal, and it is only thereby that he knows himself as midpoint at every moment—as midpoint, not of a horizon which he surveys, but of a stretch which consists entirely of midpoint, which is, indeed, all middle, all between, all way. He can and must sense every point along this path as a midpoint only *because* his path is all middle and because he knows this. The entire stretch, by consisting entirely of midpoints, is in short but a single midpoint. "Were Christ born a thousand times in Bethlehem and it is not also within you—you would still be lost"—this dictum of Angelus Silesius' *Cherubinic Wanderer* is for the Christian a paradox only in the bold pregnancy of its expression, not in its spirit. For the Christian, the moment becomes the representative of eternity not as moment but as midpoint of the Christian world-time. And since it stays and does not perish, this world-time consists entirely of such "midpoints." Every event stands midway between beginning and end of the eternal way and, by virtue of this central position in the temporal middle realm of eternity, every event is itself eternal.

Thus Christianity gains mastery over time by making of the moment the epoch-making epoch. From Christ's birth on, there is henceforth only the present. Time does not bounce off Christianity as it does off the Jewish people; to Christianity time which is only transitory is banned and must serve as a captive slave. Past, present, and future—once perpetually interpenetrating each other, perpetually transforming themselves—are now become figures at rest, paintings on the walls and vaults of the chapel. Henceforth all that preceded the birth of Christ, prophets and Sibylline oracles included, is past history, arrested once and for all. And the future, impending hesitantly yet inescapably attracted, is the last judgment. The Christian world-time stands in between this past and this future as a single hour, a single day; in it, all is middle, all equally bright as day. Thus the three periods of time have separated into eternal beginning, eternal middle, and eternal end of the eternal way through this temporality. Temporality itself is disabused of its self-confidence and allows this form to be forced on it in the Christian chronology. It ceases to believe that it is older than Christianity and counts its years from the birthday of Christianity. It suffers all that preceded this to appear as negated time, as unreal time, so to speak. Hitherto it had re-counted the past by counting the years; now this counting becomes the prerogative of the present, of the ever-present way. And Christianity treads this way, treads it deliberately, certain of its own eternal presence, ever in the middle of the occurring world, ever in the event, ever *au courant*, ever with the imperious glance of the consciousness that it is the eternal way which it treads, on which time now follows merely as an obedient counter of its steps.

Christendom But what is Christendom if not people, successive generations, nations, states, persons differing in age, condition, sex, in color, education, breadth of vision, in endowments and capacities? And are these nevertheless to be henceforth at every moment one, gathered into a single midpoint and this midpoint in turn the midpoint of all other midpoints of this one great middle? This question touches on the formative element in this communion of Christendom. In the preceding book (*The Star of Redemption*, part three, book 1) we raised the question of the formative element in the communion of Judaism, which Jewish dogma might have answered with "the Torah." But we were not entitled to be satisfied with that answer, and the dogmatic answer "Christ" would avail us no more here. Rather, it is precisely the manner in which a communion founded on dogma gives itself reality which we wish to fathom. More exactly still—for we know it has to be an eternal communion—we ask again: how can a communion found itself for eternity? We fathomed this for the communion of the eternal life; now we ask it concerning the communion of the eternal way.

The difference cannot simply be found in the fact that at every point of the way there is a midpoint. After all, at every moment in the life of the Jewish people there was the whole life. God led every individual out of Egypt: "I make this covenant . . . not with you alone but both with those who are standing here with us this day . . . and with those who are not with us here this day." (Deuteronomy 29:13-14) Both the eternal life and the eternal way have this in common: they are eternal. Eternity is, after all, just this: that everything occurs at every point and at every moment. Thus the difference does not lie here. In the final analysis it must lie in that which is eternal, not in its eternal character. And so it is. Eternal life and eternal way are as different as the infinity of a point and the infinity of a line. The infinity of a point can only consist of the fact that it is never erased; thus it presents itself in the eternal self-preservation of procreative blood. The infinity of a line, however, ceases if it became [sic] impossible to extend it; it consists of the very possibility of unrestricted extension. Christianity, as the eternal way, has to spread ever further. Merely to preserve its status would mean for it renouncing its eternity and therewith death. Christianity must proselytize. This is just as essential to it as self-preservation through shutting the pure spring of blood off from foreign admixture is to the eternal people. Indeed, proselytizing is the veritable form of its self-preservation for Christianity. It propagates by spreading. Eternity becomes eternity of the way by making all the points of the way, one by one, into midpoints. Every point of the way must bear witness that it knows itself as midpoint of the eternal way. In the eternal people the carnal onward flow of the one blood bears witness to the ancestor in the engendered grandson. On the eternal way the outpouring of the spirit must establish the communion of testimony in the uninterrupted stream of baptismal water coursing on from each to another. Every point which this outpouring of the spirit reaches must be able to survey the whole way as an eternal communion of testimony. But the way can be surveyed only if it is itself the content of the testimony. In attesting the communion, the way must be attested at the same time. The communion becomes a single one through the attested belief. The belief is a belief in the way. Everyone in the communion knows that there is no eternal way other than the way which he is going. Only he belongs to

Christendom who knows his own life to be on the way which leads from Christ come to Christ coming.

Belief This knowledge is belief—belief as the content of testimony. It is belief in something. That is exactly the opposite of the belief of the Jew. His belief is not the content of testimony. The Jew, engendered as such, attests his belief by continuing to procreate the Jewish people. His belief is not in something; he is himself the belief. He is believing in an immediacy which no Christian dogmatist can ever attain for himself. This belief cares little for its dogmatic fixation; it has existence, and that is worth more than words. But the world is entitled to words. A belief which seeks to win the world must be a belief in something. Even the tiniest union formed to win a piece of the world requires a common belief, a watchword by which those united can recognize each other. Anyone who wants to create a piece of way of his own in the world must believe in something. Merely to believe would never allow him to attain to something in the world. Only he who believes in something can conquer something—namely, what he believes in. And it is exactly so with Christian belief. It is dogmatic in the highest sense, and must be so. It may not dispense with words. On the contrary: it simply cannot have enough of words, it cannot make enough words. It really would have to have a thousand tongues. It would have to speak all languages. For it has to wish that everything would become its own. And so the something in which it believes must be—not a something but everything. For this very reason it is the belief in the way. By believing in the way, Christian belief paves the way for the way in the world.

The Church Thus Christian belief, the witness to the eternal way, is creative in the world. It unites those who bear witness into a union in the world. It unites them as individuals, for bearing witness is always an individual matter. Here, moreover, the individual is supposed to bear witness concerning his attitude toward an individual, for the testimony, after all, concerns Christ. Christ is the common content of all testimonies of belief. But though they were united as individuals, belief now directs them toward common action in the world. For the paving of the way is the common labor of all the individuals. Each individual can, after all, set foot on only one point of the eternal way—his point—and make of it what the whole way must become in order to be the eternal way: the middle. And thus belief establishes that union of individuals, *as* individuals, for common labor which rightfully bears the name of ecclesia. For this original name of the church is taken from the life of the ancient city-states, and designates the citizens assembled for common deliberation. The people of God designated its festivals as "sacred convocations" with what was essentially a similar term. But for itself it used words, like people or congregation, which once designated the people in arms—that entity, in other words, in which the people appears as the self-contained whole into which the individuals have dissolved. In the ecclesia, however, the individual is and remains an individual, and only its resolve is common and becomes—*res publica.*

Christ Now Christianity gives itself precisely this name of ecclesia, the name of an assembly of individuals for common labor. Still, the labor only comes to pass by virtue of each one dealing in his place as an individual. In the assembly, similarly, the common resolve emerges only by virtue of the fact that each expresses his opinion and votes as a whole individual. Thus, too, the community of the church presupposes the personality and integrity—we may safely say the soul—of its members. Paul's analogy of the congregation as the body of Christ does not imply some kind of division of labor like, say, the famous analogy of stomach and limbs by Menenius Agrippa. Rather, it alludes precisely to this perfect freedom of each individual in the church. It is illuminated by the great "For though everything belongs to you . . . yet you belong to Christ." (I Corinthians 3:21-23) Everything is subservient to Christianity on its way, and on the way of every Christian within it, from the crucified one. Every Christian is privileged to know himself on the way, not merely at some arbitrary point, but rather at the absolute middle of the way which, after all, is itself wholly middle, wholly between. But while Christianity and the individual still await the second coming, those who have just been liberated as lords of all things at once know themselves again as everyman's slave. For what they do to the least of his brothers, that they do to him who will return to judge the world (cf. Matthew 25:40).

How then will the ecclesia constitute itself on the basis of that freedom and integrity of individuals which must be preserved? How is the bond which connects each to each within it to look? It must, after all, leave the individuals free while it binds them; indeed, in truth, it must first make them free. It must leave everyone as it finds him, man as man, woman as woman, the aged old, the youths young, the master as master, the slave as slave, the wealthy rich, the paupers poor, the sage wise and the fool foolish, the Roman a Roman and the barbarian a barbarian. The bond must not place anyone in the status of another, and yet it must cover over the cleft between man and wife, between parents and child, between master and slave, between rich and poor, sage and fool, Roman and barbarian. It must free each one in his own being, in all his natural and God-given dependencies with which he stands in the world of creation. It must set him on the middle of that way which leads from eternity to eternity.

It is the bond of brotherliness which thus takes men as it finds them and yet binds them together across the differences of sex, age, class, and race. Brotherliness connects people in all given circumstances—independently of the circumstances, which simply continue to exist—as equals, as brothers "in the Lord." From being men they become brothers, and the common belief in the common way is the content of this belief. In this Christian covenant of brotherhood, Christ is both beginning and end of the way, and thereby content and goal, originator and master of the covenant, as well as the middle of the way, and therefore present wherever two have met together in his name (cf. Matthew 18:20). Wherever two have met together in his name, there is the middle of the way. There the whole way may be surveyed. There beginning and end are equidistant because he who is beginning and end is dwelling in the midst of those assembled here. Thus in the middle of the way Christ is neither establisher nor master of his church, but rather a member of it, himself a brother of his covenant. As such he can also be with the individual; in brotherliness even the individual—and not only two who have met together—already knows himself as Christian. Though seemingly alone with himself, he yet knows himself as member of the church because this solitude is togetherness with Christ.

Christ is near to this individual in that form to which his brotherly feelings can most readily direct themselves. The individual is, after all, to remain what he is: the man a man, the woman a woman, the child a child. Thus Christ is a friend to the man, to the woman a spiritual bridegroom, to the child a holy infant. Tied to the historical Jesus, Christ may forego this identification with the familiar figure of the neighbor, the object of brotherly love; but then the saints make their appearance in Christ's own stead. At least they do so in the Petrine church of love, the church which holds its believers most ardently to the way and allows them to remember less of its beginning and end. There man is privileged to love Mary as the pure virgin, and woman to love her as the divine sister, and each to love the saint of his class and nation from within his class and nation. Indeed, everyone is there privileged to love his saintly namesake as a brother from within the narrowest confines of the self as it is contained within his Christian name. This church of love is even more intrinsically a church of the way than the others. And in it the figure of the living wanderer on earth pushes itself ahead even of the deceased God on the cross; in it—more than in the sister churches—this wanderer becomes an example to be followed like an exemplary human brother; in it, at the same time, the whole crowd of saints, interceding for their frail brothers and sisters, surges before the judge of the last judgment, where the way reaches its goal.

The Christian Act Thus brotherliness weaves its bond among men of whom none equal each other. Nor is this brotherliness by any means identity of everything with human countenance but rather the harmony precisely of men of the most diverse countenances. One thing is necessary, of course, but only one: that men have some countenance altogether, that they see each other. The church is the communion of all those who see each other. It joins men as coevals, as contemporaries at disparate loci of the ample space. Contemporaneity is something which in temporality does not even exist. In temporality there is only before and after. The moment in which one catches sight of oneself can only precede or follow the moment in which one catches sight of another. Simultaneously to catch sight of oneself and of another at the same moment is impossible. That is the profoundest reason for the impossibility of loving one's neighbor as oneself in the heathen world which is, after all, precisely temporality. In eternity, however, there is also contemporaneity. It goes without saying that, seen from its shore, all time is simultaneous. But that time too which, as eternal way, leads from eternity to eternity admits of simultaneity. For only insofar as it is middle between eternity and eternity is it possible for people to meet on it. Thus he who catches sight of himself on the way is on the same point—that is on the exact midpoint—of time. It is brotherliness which transports men into this midpoint. Time, already overcome, is placed at its feet; it is left for love only to traverse the separating space. And thus it traverses in its flight the hostility of nations as well as the cruelty of generations, the jealousy of class as well as the limits of age. Thus it permits all the hostile, cruel, jealous, limited ones to regard each other as brothers in one and the same central moment of time.

The Jewish Deed The contemporaries catch sight of each other in the middle of time. At the boundaries of time, similarly, those had encountered each other for whom the differences of the space did not mean a separation that first had to be overcome. For there these differences had already been overcome to begin with, in the innate communion of the people. There the labor of love—both of divine love for men and of human love for each other—had to be directed solely toward the preservation of this communion through time, toward the creation of contemporaneity of the sequences of generations separated in temporality. That is the league between descendant and ancestor. By virtue of this league the people becomes an eternal people. For in catching sight of each other, descendant and ancestor catch sight in one another at the same moment of the last descendant and the first ancestor. Descendant and ancestor are thus the true incarnation of the eternal people, both of them for each other and both together for him who stands between them, just as the fellow man become brother is the church incarnate for the Christian. We experience our Judaism with immediacy in elders and children. The Christian experiences his

Christianity in the sensation of that moment which leads the brother to him at the height of the eternal way. For him, all of Christianity seems to crowd together there. It stands where he stands, he stands where it stands: at the middle of time between eternity and eternity. We too are shown eternity by the moment, but differently: not in the brother who stands closest to us but rather in those who stand furthest from us in time, in the oldest and the youngest, in the elder who admonishes, in the lad who asks, in the ancestor who blesses and in the grandson who receives the blessing. It is thus that the bridge of eternity does its spanning for us: from the starry heaven of the promise which arches over that mount of revelation whence sprang the river of our eternal life, unto the limitless sands of the promise washed by the sea into which every river empties, the sea out of which will one day rise the Star of redemption when once the earth froths over, like its flood tides, with the knowledge of the Lord.

Cross and Star In the final analysis, then, that tension of beginning and end withal strives mightily toward the end. Though as tension it can originate only in both, it finally gathers after all at one point, namely at the end. The child with its question is in the final analysis still and all a more powerful admonisher than the elder, no matter how we may perpetually draw nourishment from the inexhaustible treasure of the elder's inspired life, no matter how we may maintain and fortify ourselves on the merit of the fathers: the elder turns into a memory, the child alone compels. God establishes his kingdom only "out of the mouths of babes and sucklings." (Psalm 8:2) In the final analysis the tension after all concentrates itself entirely at the end, on the latest sprout at last, on the Messiah whom we await. So too the Christian agglomeration at the midpoint at long last does not remain glued to that spot after all. Let the Christian discern Christ in his brother: in the final analysis he is driven beyond the brother to Christ himself, without mediation. Let the middle be but middle between beginning and end: it gravitates, for all that, toward the beginning. Let man discern cross and last judgment alike from the middle of the way in eternal proximity: he cannot let that satisfy him; he steps directly under the cross, and will not rest till the image of the crucified one cover all the world for him. In thus turning to the cross alone, he may forget the last judgment: he remains on the way for all that. For though it still belongs to the eternal beginning of the way, the cross is after all no longer the first beginning; it is itself already on the way, and whoever steps under it thus stands at its middle and beginning at the same time. Thus Christian consciousness, all steeped in belief, presses toward the beginning of the way, to the first Christian, the crucified one, just as Jewish consciousness, all gathered up in hope, presses toward the man of the end of time, to David's royal sprout (cf. Isaiah 11:1). Belief can renew itself eternally at its beginning, just as the arms of the cross can be extended to infinity. Hope, however, eternally unites itself out of all the multiplicity of time in the one near and far moment in space of the end, just as the Star on the shield of David gathers all into the fiery nucleus. Rootedness in the profoundest self—that had been the secret of the eternity of the [Jewish] people. Diffusion throughout all that is outside—this is the secret of the eternity of the [Christian] way.

Arthur A. Cohen

Arthur A. Cohen was born in New York City in 1928, graduated from the University of Chicago in 1946, and from 1951 to 1953 was Fellow in Medieval Jewish Philosophy at the Jewish Theological Seminary of America; during this period he continued studies in philosophy and religion at Union Theological Seminary and Columbia University. He is a member of the editorial advisory board of the Jewish Publication Society of America, and the editorial board of the theological quarterly "Judaism."

Mr. Cohen's writings have appeared in many journals and he is the author of "Martin Buber" and "The Natural and the Supernatural Jew." Work in progress includes "The Myth of the Judeo-Christian Tradition."

In addition to his work as philosopher and theologian, Mr. Cohen is editor-in-chief of the trade department at the publishing firm of Holt, Rinehart and Winston.

THE TEMPER OF JEWISH ANTI-CHRISTIANITY: A THEOLOGICAL STATEMENT *

The relations of Judaism and Christianity from the end of the fourth century, which saw the completion of Jerome's monumental translation of the Hebrew Bible into Latin, until the renewal of Jewish-Christian communication during the nineteenth century were those of compounded ignorance. What had commenced as a struggle in the interest of revealed truth—the quality of that truth and the magnanimity of that revelation—had declined into what can only be regarded as the inheritance, transmission, and renovation of ignorance, each generation forgetting something more about the other, each generation finding in the continued witness of the other some further confirmation for uncharity, suspicion, and hatred. It cannot be denied that my sympathies are with the ignorance which my fellow Jews conserved toward Christianity; however, my sympathies are those of a creature for his fellow creatures, creatures to whom he is bound by the nexus of shared misfortune, for the historical destiny of the nation and people of Israel, construed independently of any role which they may be said to play in the order of salvation, can be only a misfortune. (Would any say that there is human glory in having delivered to death

* This essay is a revised and expanded version of a lecture delivered in a Jewish-Protestant Colloquium sponsored by the Divinity School of the University of Chicago and the Anti-Defamation League of B'nai B'rith in April, 1963.

at the hands of tyrants and fanatics in the course of two thousand years perhaps as many Jews as are alive today?) On the other hand, if it were my persuasion that my nexus with my fellow Jews were but the impulsion of historical necessity and unavoidable complicity in their fate, I should be persuaded by reason and good sense to avoid their society and detach myself from their fate. That I might fail in such an undertaking—that, indeed, the likelihood that I would fail may be presumed—would not, of itself, persuade my reason or sway my will not to make the effort. There is, then, no argument from history which would prevent the dissimulation of my origins—my assimilation to anonymity in the Gentile world.

The only grounds on which I may take my stand as a Jew before man and history is that I have been granted no option by God to do otherwise. Though I may elect to be quits with him, to be released from the covenant of my ancestors, it is a release and severance which can follow only from a radical autonomy of will, a suspension of historical realism, a denial of all that in the past which has formed the actual creature who says no. To say no to God—recognizing that it is God to whom one says no—is a fatal contradiction. It is to nullify that which cannot be nullified. The consequence of such an ontologically self-contradictory undertaking is to nullify not God but oneself. If it may be argued that there is no escape possible from the historical condition of the Jew—as a natural-historical phenomenon—it may equally be said that there is no theological exit for the Jew who admits the reality of the God whose very existence authenticates theology. The Jew cannot escape himself. He cannot escape history by entering and disappearing into it. He cannot escape God, for God does not free him. The Jew has no choice but to endure God. It is no less onerous for God to endure the Jew. But it is true, is it not, that a covenant is a covenant. I am therefore obliged as a Jew to situate myself within a curious history—a history which has been secularized by Christians, although ostensibly redeemed by Christ; a history in which, as a son of the covenant, I can have no part in its categories, intentions, fascinations, which are those against which my ancestors struggled in order to become a Holy People. In short, the history of times and predicaments, solutions and provisional medicaments is a history in which I participate only to the extent that

I am a man, not to the extent that I am a Jew. To the extent that I am a Jew all history is an ironic charade or a filmy gauze through which I dimly see the unfolding of a drama. I do not comprehend history in my Jewish soul, but I must bear both its transitory reality and my incomprehension.

The Disunion of Judaism and Christianity It is inappropriate for one such as myself to list the items of convergence or similarity which might mark the renewal of Jewish-Christian fraternity. Any such dossier of compatibilities would be essentially unreal, abstract, and hypostatic, encompassing as they would but the smallest portion of our historical being—for what we share with Christianity is only our beginnings. It is, however, what we have built upon our beginnings that describes our disunion; for Judaism, in contrast to Biblical religion, begins at that moment in which Christianity announces its death, and Christianity emerges at that moment in which the history of the Gospels is transformed into the rich categories of Paul the Apostle. The Jew, upon whom the pagan Christian comes to depend for his first knowledge of God, is no longer the lonely, passionate, longing lyricist who is the paradigmatic Jew of the "Old Testament." [1] He has become, by 70 C.E., certainly by 200 C.E., when Judah the Prince redacts the Mishnah, and surely by the end of the Gaonic era in the tenth century, a creature intent upon sustaining a vision which is finally indifferent to the thrusts and challenges of historical adversaries. The Jew of that advanced time has long since rejected any Jesus who might be the Anointed. The Christian, moreover, is no longer expectant of an imminent parousia. He is, as Eugen Rosenstock-Huessy so tellingly observed to Franz Rosenzweig, no longer in need of any "Old Testament," for after the period of the Councils and the definition of the Creeds and the elaboration of the structure of the Church, the living Christian recalls not the "dead" Jew and his, indeed, "*Old* Testa-

[1] Throughout this essay I have avoided such commonplace references as Old Testament and the honorific Saint in order to underscore the seriousness of the Jewish-Christian disunion. Moreover, such devices for marking the passage of time in the measurements of Christian anticipation and retrospection are replaced by the usual Jewish nomenclature of C.E. (Common Era) and B.C.E. (Before the Common Era). This is all symbolic usage, but rhetorically suitable to the volume in which this essay appears.

ment," but the traditions and witnesses of the early Church which are become his old, that is to say, his historically past, witness to the Christ.

The Jew and the Christian, as historical creatures, it would appear, have nothing to say to one another, except insofar as they speak beyond and in spite of faith. But is this really so? Do we not ontologize history too severely by such an affirmation—for if it were true that we have no cause to regard one another, then our continuous historical collision would become more horrendously irrational and our historical alienation even greater cause for despair. Rather, it is the case that we may adduce our continuous historical collision as evidence that we are unable to avoid one another that our endurance before each other is proof of our interconnection, that in some obscure and indefinite way we are for each other an obligatory testimony.

The vivid presence of Christian to Jew and Jew to Christian is, of course, not reflected in the ballooning expansion of Christianity which transforms it from the faith of individuals redeemed in Jesus Christ into a world-wide institution, which knows few if any of its ancient opponents.

The "foolishness" of the Gospel in the sight of the pagan will pass as the Greek in man languishes before the public and interior victories of the Church.

The pagan may remain unbaptized, but he will no longer be scoffingly indifferent; he will succumb, as do men of the East in our time, to the wisdom of the Gospels, though not yet persuaded of its ultimacy or superiority. But of the stumbling block which the Gospels remain to Israel there can be no alteration, for the imagination of Israel is not peopled with many gods that we should regard the pagan's acknowledgment of Jesus Christ as extraordinary (although we might share with Franz Rosenzweig, to whom we are indebted for this moment of our exegesis, the question of why Jesus Christ and not, as seems often more appropriate, Goethe, Hegel, or Jung). For the pagan, such folly is easily and advantageously remedied; but for Israel that knows from its birth only a single God, to multiply and proliferate him is not only a stumbling block but a meaningless unreality. A messiah, to be sure; a Son of God, hopeless!

The face that Christianity turns toward the world of today is already radiant with triumph. However much it may be subtly corroded by the opposing principalities of state, secular knowledge, and unbelief, it knows that it takes to itself the whole world, that it is in itself the universality which history seeks. The Jew of today, moreover, is no longer the Jew of old, for he is no longer without a shared history, without a participation in the movements and currents of a larger secularity which overwhelm his classic categories of aloofness and incapsulation.

The Jew whose rhythm of time was once marked by a sacral procession of ahistorical events (which were but apparently historical, being in fact the consciously apprehended structures of providence) has disappeared. The Jew of today is permanently post-emancipation; he can never again return completely to the precincts of his ancient law. The vast Church and the broken Synagogue—like the figures confronting one another in the façade of the cathedral at Strasbourg—are in our time monuments that become increasingly empty and meaningless, for it matters little whether the Church is vast and universal if Christians have not yet come to the Father, and it does not demean the Synagogue if it is empty as long as there are still Jews frozen in its doorway, seeking to return. Ultimately only individual Christians and individual Jews will form the new community of Church and Synagogue. Divested as we are by history of all that which enabled our participation in a community that could do the will of God with a whole heart, now and for the immediate future, it will only be individual Christians and individual Jews who, in remembrance and recall of their origins, will begin the renewal.

The Church, triumphant over history in the universality of the Johannine Gospel, is victorious and loser, for its commitment to historical structures and inherited dominions makes it partner to precisely the history which it seeks to annihilate. The Jew, the victim of history, renounces the eternity he carries within him in order that he may share, not the universality of world history, but the *worldliness* of world history in the renascent nationalism of the Jewish people. In sum, therefore, it may be said that the externally apprehended Jew provided the occasion and the rationalization for the attachment of Christian faith to precisely that history which, in its origins, it was obliged to refuse; and the conduct of the Christian toward the Jew provided the occasion for the Jewish refusal of its vocation to the Christian—the rejection of the Christ by the Jews compelling Christianity into world history and consecrating it to the often bloody task of "saving" whole nations and peoples; the persecution of the Jew forcing Judaism to seek the succor and favor of any and all neutral and antipathetic powers of this world by which to mitigate and contain the enmity of Christianity.

Our historical collision is therefore the consequence of defective understanding, a default of mutuality, a refusal to acknowledge that though the Father may be One and solitary, his providence remains a mystery, perhaps the only authentic mystery for time and history.

The Jew and Jesus as the Christ We return, as we must, to the primary question: what does the Jew say of Jesus as the Christ? For, indeed, what I have observed above would not have come to be if the Jews in the time of Jesus of Nazareth had acknowledged his messiahship.

We shall not rehearse the narrative of historical events—that but a small number of Jews knew of Jesus' claim to be the Christ; that Judaism was already by the time of Jesus a religion diffused throughout the Roman world, numbering one in ten Roman citizens as full or partial converts; that Jewish leadership, extraordinarily harassed as it was by Roman authority, behaved, in spite of the trial and condemnation of Jesus, with remarkable indifference toward him, regarding him less as a falsely intentioned insurrectionist than as another of the pretender messiahs of whom tradition records that seventy appeared and seventy were condemned and executed; that Jewish messianism, although profound, was heavily scarred by mythological construction, being imprecise, vague, and fundamentally undisciplined. It might be said that Jesus was, so far as the Palestinian Judaism of the first century is concerned, a religious eccentric whose doctrine and practice had politically debilitating side effects. He was paid little attention by the Jews of his day; and, given the unremitting efforts of Christendom for two millennia to enforce the attention of the Jew, it must be remarkable and disconcerting to Christian missionaries to observe how little attention he is paid by Jews even today.

Such historical derogation, however accurate it might be for the brief period which encloses the actual life of Jesus of Nazareth, is immediately transformed by the events which succeed his death. It is one thing to judge in the moment of happening the truth or untruth of a historical person, to condemn or acquit, to praise or to curse; it is quite another when the generations which succeed such persons insist upon recalling, remembering, testifying, and transmitting the knowledge of their life, works, and death. At such moments memory transforms historical persons, informing them with a context and association which indeed they may not have enjoyed, adjudicating and appraising their significance, radiating their influence into cultures and societies of which they knew nothing, connecting and relating what they said in some isolated sector of the world to all that the world was saying at that moment. How much more so is the case when the memory conserves, not individual persons, but prophets or saints, crystallizing and freezing events of the life past into examples and testimonies for the instruction of the future; and how much more still, how unbelievably much more when a few disciples incorporate every word, every gesture, every activity of the person and elevate these into no less than a God who assumed the aspect of mortality and a mortal who was himself the perfect incarnation of God. When such happens—and it has happened but once—the past is discarded and sundered from that moment of his contemporaneity and the future is become like to nothing which has been or could be before. This, in essence, is what has been accomplished by the Synoptic Gospels. But it was not sufficient. The Petrine Church, the community of Jewish Christians, who were knowing and obedient to the Torah, might well have come to be regarded by regnant Jewry as heresy and schism to be calmly fought and as calmly returned in penitence to the Synagogue—for the Pharisees were not unsympathetic to the advent of the messiah, and they were familiar with the passion to consummation which seethed in their own time. That they judged Jesus to be false was inescapable; but that his disciples judged Jesus—in spite of continued eschatological disappointment and postponement—to be still true, is yet (however much a misjudgment in my sight) a continuing source of wonder and bafflement, as it is that in the years following his death there should arise one who, persuaded to belief, turned the entire force of his intellectual skill to the creation of a theology to interpret disappointment, a theology which at the same time could address the anguish of the pagan in terms which made the disappointment of the parousia not only believable but its chief power and strength.

It is therefore, for me, a Jew, as much a mystery that Christianity survived and triumphed as it is a mystery for Christianity that the unconverted Jew persists, not only in his unbelief but in the confident assertion that he is still chosen by God, covenanted to him, and patient before his ultimate discretion.

Toward a Jewish Theology of Jewish Unbelief Even if the death of Jesus of Nazareth shall be without significance for Israel in its own understanding of salvation, the fact remains that as long as history accounts that death as being more, as the death not of a carpenter from Nazareth but of Jesus the Christ, then Israel cannot but entertain that historical fact as though it were *more* than history. Believing it, however, to be no more than history and knowing it as history, Israel must conjure with what this means for those who affirm it as an action and as a grace of God, that is, as a fact whose meaning exceeds the plane of the historical. Israel must soften its heart before the historical happening of the life and death of Jesus for the sake of those who affirm it to be more than history; but likewise those who believe in Jesus as the Christ and in their belief know its truth for themselves, must understand what is affirmed in Jewish unbelief. For the unbelief of Israel, as it regards Jesus Christ, is the belief of Israel in God who himself is, does, and works all things. That we do not believe in Jesus as the Christ is for the fact that we believe; and were it that we believe not in our true belief, surely then we could not believe in him who is believed by Christians to come from God himself. Therefore the unbelief of Israel in Jesus as the Christ is not unbelief in God (for God could have worked in Jesus of Nazareth, all things being possible to God), but that the Jew—who is saved by God himself, being with him from his own birth—is not saved by him who came after for the sake of those who were born after, for Israel was with God from the beginning and will be with him until the end. Israel's belief makes possible that the nations shall believe in Jesus

Christ, but that Jesus Christ shall save them is only for the fact that Israel is not yet saved. In that consummate time all men shall be saved in fact, whereas now we are but saved in that we believe in God and in believing do his *mitzvot* (commandments) and in doing his *mitzvot* obey his will. And our obedience is to the Law of God, whether that Law be for the Gentiles in Jesus Christ or in the Torah of Israel.

A Polemic with Thomas Aquinas Having affirmed the historical disjunction of Jew and Christian, we are still obliged to address ourselves to the vastly more thorny issue, not of Jewish rejection in the time of Jesus Christ or the formation of a theology by which rejection and unbelief are transformed into service and fidelity, but rather of how, in the face of history, Jewish rejection has not only continued but strengthened and become emboldened.

I shall not examine the fundamental opposition of Torah and Jesus Christ, for that issue, central though it is to my thought, requires a different approach independent of the one we have defined. Let me present my view rather by responding to two passages in which Thomas Aquinas expands on Paul's Epistle to the Romans (chapter 3).[2]

> The New Law is not disjunct from the Old Law, because they have both the same end, namely, man's subjection to God; and there is but one God of the New and the Old Testaments, according to Romans 3:29-31: "Or is God the God of Jews only? Is he not the God of Gentiles also? Yes, of Gentiles also, since God is one; and he will justify the circumcised on the ground of their faith and the uncircumcised through their faith. Do we then overthrow the law by this faith? By no means! On the contrary, we uphold the Law." The unity of faith under both Testaments witnesses to the unity of end. . . . Yet faith had a different state in the Old and New Law, since what they believed as future, we believe as fact.

Comment One In Romans 3:9, Paul affirms that all men, both Jews and Greeks, are under the power of sin. If all men are equally condemned before God, then surely there can be no difference between the Torah and Jesus Christ other than that the Torah

[2] *Summa Theologiae*, parts i, ii, qu. 107, art. 1; qu. 104, art. 2, Reply to Second Objection.

promises the inheritance of the future, while the Christian acclaims salvation as accomplished. The ransom from sin which the Christ affords is given, but the "ransom" which the Torah affords becomes illusory. Before the judgment of God, imminent as it is, no man can be patient. While the Torah is turned to the future, damnation is at hand. This is a persuasive rhetoric to unhappy Romans who knew not what it was the Torah promised but knew too well what it was their hour demanded.

The critical misapprehension is that the Law does not promise salvation, nor was it ever thought to promise it. The Law is but the Way to the Father; it is the structure which allows disordered life to be educated. The Law is holy culture (and thus, as Denis de Rougemont noted, impoverished in all the familiar artifices of culture),[3] but culture is not and never was a substitute for the messiah. The Law is propaedeutic to redemption but is no substitute for it. It is the container and corrective to sin; it does not ransom from sin. It is the inspiriter and director of right action, but it is not righteousness itself. The radicalization of alternatives before the common human condition of sinfulness is one upon which Paul capitalizes in his witness to the pagan. It is irrelevant to the Jew.

Comment Two The mystery of Israel to the nations is that it regards the gift of the Anointed to the pagan as a fortuity in no way integral to the life of Israel. This position is logically comprehensible and meaningful only if the messianism of Israel is tied to the End, the real End. For Israel there can be no penultimates. If there are penultimate ends, caesuras and breaks in the unfolding of history toward salvation, then our first rejection of Jesus as Christ shall have been as much an error as would be our rejection of a second or a third or an indefinite number of messiahs, with whose advent there is no End. If the Christ returns and the End is not with his coming, then surely Israel is justified in its first refusal; but if he comes again and with his coming there is the true and consummate End and Israel again refuses, then surely Israel is condemned, for what is presently futurity and expectation in our sight becomes at

[3] Denis de Rougemont, "The Vocation and Destiny of Israel," *The Christian Opportunity*, Holt, Rinehart and Winston, Inc., New York, 1963, p. 59 f.

that time the reckless refusal of salvation. We shall not, I pray, refuse to believe then, at that distant moment to come, for in believing *then* amid the conclusion of history, we shall have justified our unbelief past, and if we do not believe at the true End, we shall have demonstrated that our earlier unbelief was already our condemnation. This judgment is to God alone and neither to us nor to the Paul of Romans 3.

> The Jewish People were chosen by God that the Christ might be born of them. Consequently the entire state of that people had to be prophetic and figurative, as Augustine states. For this reason even the judicial precepts that were given to this people were more figurative than those which were given to other nations. Thus, too, the wars and deeds of this people are expounded in the mystical sense; but not the wars and deeds of the Assyrians and Romans, although the latter are more famous in the eyes of men.

It is hopeless to expect that this view of Thomas Aquinas, a view already well expounded by Paul, should be received by Jewish tradition with anything more than uncomprehending anger or amazement. Indeed, Jewish reaction could be no less conclusive than that of Nietzsche when he observed in his *Morgenrote:* "The Christians gave themselves up to a passion for reinterpretation and substitution—a process which cannot possibly have been compatible with good conscience. However much Jewish scholars protested, it was affirmed that everywhere in the Old Testament the theme was Christ and only Christ." It must be acknowledged, however, that strictures against the Pauline typological construction of the Hebrew Bible are legitimated only on the presumption that Jesus is not the Christ. The violence which Paul does to the scriptural narrative of the life of Abraham, or the person of Moses, or to the prophecies of Isaiah and Jeremiah is violence in two senses. First, the exegetic rendering is a forcing and misconstruction of the actual text (that is to say, it is a literary mishandling of text whose Jewish principles of exegesis, always more explicit and reasonable in its use of *peshat*, *derash*, *remez* and *sod*[4] are to be deplored).

[4] The traditional modes of rabbinic exegesis are *peshat* as the simple, literal meaning of a word or passage; *derash* as the exegesis by homiletic parallelism and analogy; *remez* as symbolic meaning; *sod* as mystical exegesis.

Second, his notion of divine foreshadowing and divine concealment by which the Hebrew Bible does become, indeed, the "old" and the past covenant preparing man and history for the new is a violence to the reality of Jewish faith.

Let us grant the exigencies which compelled Paul to this exegetic turn: the necessity of bringing the promise of salvation to the Gentiles, the equivalence which he felt obliged to establish between the Gentile in Christ and the born Jew, and finally the confirmation of the rejection of the Jewish people, the Torah, and the modalities of Jewish redemption in order that the missionary appeal of Judaism to the pagan world be blunted and the superiority of Christianity be defined. All Pauline judgments are understandable if the situation of the young Church amid the Gentiles and the conflict of the Church of the Gentiles with the Jerusalem Church and with the rather appealing views of the Ebionites are regarded as the background of Paul's typological derogation of Judaism. Paul was waging a struggle within the Church; and the more intense the struggle became, the more radical became his polarization of the Torah, Judaism, Israel, and the Christ.

On any objective grounds it is hopeless to inquire whether Paul reads the Bible correctly: he reads it correctly if one is a Christian who may say in faith that all is possible to God, even the use of the generations from Adam to Abraham to Jesus the Christ as preliminary and preparatory to the regeneration and salvation of man. To the Jew, however, what Thomas Aquinas takes for granted is senseless.

Comment One If the Jew is without faith in that which is prefigured in his Bible but believes rather that what he is given in Scripture is to be understood as God speaks it and gives it, then to make retrospectively of God a figural revealer is to seal into the faith of the Christian and the responding faith of the Jew an abiding and immutable incomprehension.

The true speech between Christian and Jew, the only speech possible against the background of figural, allegorical, and typological exegesis, is that of the masked dialogue in which each word spoken can be understood only as its opposite; for that which the Christian speaks of the Jew, the Christian speaks literally (since he, in fact, speaks of the Christ come in whom he believes), while the Jew hears such speech figurally as the anticipation of him who is yet to come. When the Jew, on the other hand, speaks to the Christian of the Torah, meaning that this Torah is the Way before the future, the Christian hears the Law figurally as the incompleteness and adumbration of him who has come.

In effect, the Christian reads futurity back into the past, and the Jew ontologizes the past before the future. The Christian, from his perspective, cannot help but mythologize a reality which in its *real* existence is prophecy outlined, consummated, and thereby petrified if it survives beyond its fulfillment; for that reality is to the Christian the old covenant which has indeed ended and, moreover, never really existed as the Jews believe it to exist, since its function was always prophetic and thus always a future for the present, a future event even at the moment of the giving of the Law, the building of the Temple, or the instruction of the prophets.

The movement from Paul's epistolary halfway house for Israel, to the Letter of Barnabas in which the existence of any covenant between God and Israel is repudiated, to the doctrine of Marcion that the God of the Jews is "an alien God" is henceforward a reasonably easy one. Paul takes Israel seriously, but it is an Israel in which no Jew believed. The Israel of Paul is a theological construction and a theological necessity; it is an intermediate device which must be employed that the pagan world be redeemed in Christ—at which point, hopefully, in the spirit of Romans God might return to graft on once more the broken shoots of the old stock of Israel. Israel is for Paul and for the Christian the first thought and the last, but the middle is all of Christ. Such a use of the presence of Israel cannot be less than a falsehood in our sight.

Comment Two The requirement of Pauline eschatology, implicit in the observation of Thomas Aquinas, is that the Jew is become a chimera, a substantial chimera but nonetheless a shadow creature enduring a shadow history. If the Jew endures beyond the fulfillment of his own prophecy, then his perduration can only be construed as a divine witness of judgment. God preserves the

Jew as threat to the Christian and testimony to the bankruptcy of the Jew. The Jew becomes a myth insofar as any reality he enjoys unto himself becomes irrelevant. What comes to count is his hypostatic, exemplary existence as a dismembered, dispersed, and condemned people. But such a view has serious consequences for the manner in which Jew and Christian, Synagogue and Church view one another now, nearly two millennia after the fact, when we are become no longer dogmatic enemies but common seekers of the truth.

The Christian has been obliged by his tradition either to naturalize or demonize the Jew: to naturalize him insofar as the Jew no longer resembles the Jew of the myth, to demonize him insofar as the Jew continues to resemble the Jew of the myth. The Jew, on the other hand, either naturalizes or demonizes the power of the Church: naturalizing it insofar as its power is regarded as no different than any other center of authority in a secular society; demonizing it insofar as the Church, in fidelity to its theological origins in Paul, must regard the Jew as continuing testimony to its own, the Church's failure. There is, however, a deeper level to the mutual mythologies which we entertain. Christian and Jew cannot avoid mythologizing each other because each can only know the external function the other performs within the closed system of his truth. Can I, for example, regard the Christian as other than an errant, misguided believer—a believer who believes within a universe that rebukes the substance of his belief? (For my eyes, in my unbelief, cannot see the redemption which he sees; and his eyes, in his belief, cannot know the quality of continuing unredeemedness.) The Jew mythologizes the *goy* (the Gentile, the individual among the nations who knows not the God of Israel), for he cannot help but regard his supernatural vocation in the Church as but a mask for the palpable unfulfillment and incompletion of Christianity; for the Christ did not yet return, as he believed in the infancy of his faith he would, and the objective time and history which we share as Christian and Jew is unredeemed. Similarly, the Christian mythologizes the Jew either by declining to regard his existence beyond 70 C.E. as other than a fortuity, *or* as a mystery by which God declines, for reasons inscrutable, to consummate his promise in Jesus Christ by ending history and converting the Jews, *or* as a historical scandal to the Church, for the continuance of the Jew is mute testimony that the Christ has not yet come for all the universe, that the pagan is not yet ransomed from his superstition, and that the Jews—not a remnant, not the witness of a handful, but a whole community—persist in its way, ignoring the Church of Christ.

Does it not finally seem, therefore, insofar as the parousia is still before us, that Christian eschatology is unfulfilled, that Jewish eschatology is yet unrealized, that we are, both Jew and Christian, in the same human and historical predicament? Our common promise is behind us; our common hope is before us. There is no difference between the Jesus of the Gentiles and the Torah of the Jews—no functional difference as regards the End—although there are crucial and decisive differences which emerge relative to our distance from the End.

A Summary of Divisions But having affirmed, rather incompletely and obliquely, I am afraid, the utter divergence of the view of Israel and the view of the Church regarding the event of Jesus as Christ, we are still confronted by the fact that we are nevertheless obliged by both history and faith to live with one another in the same world. How can it be, we may ask, that God apparently cherishes our disagreement? For we would not have endured in separateness for two millennia, preserving as we do the distinctive modes of our existence before each other and before the rest of the world, had it not been that he finds a use in our encounter. Part of the answer is surely that the End has not come, that history is not yet perfected into the Kingdom and beneath the Kingship of God, that mankind is still suffering from the bite of that primordial serpent, the tempter and the adversary of God.

We are removed from one another in faith: our putative Pelagianism affirms that all is in the hand of heaven, but the fear of heaven is surely removed from the Christian view that the endowments of faith are the gift of God. *We are surely removed in practice:* though Judaism always runs the risk of decaying into a foolish formalism, it *does* still believe that God has vouchsafed us an instruction by which to make ourselves fearers and lovers of his person (the Law in this regard being viewed by innumerable rabbinic sources as the *via media* which nourishes and guides and directs our natural knowledge of God into our supernatural awe and love); the Christian holds that the Law is only a substitute for the *Kyrios Christos*, a preparatory stage to be transcended and abrogated. For us our works count before God—not the stated commandments only (for the commandments explicate what we might not have known to do without revelation), but the commandments which all of the literature of Israel regards as being written in the heart of man; for the Christian, works tend to count for rather less than faith—and I might well sympathize with such a heterodox emphasis, for I find the articles of Christian faith so scandalously demanding that, not unlike Paul judging that the Law cannot be kept, I wonder at the extent and perfectness of any possible Christian faith. *We are removed from one another in our understanding of divinity:* for us there is but God alone and he is unique, capable of all those works of charity, grace, and redemption for which the Christian requires the mediation of the Incarnation. Can a Jew ever understand the Incarnation other than as a typology in reverse—as an analogy wherewith to instruct the Gentiles by vivid image and living symbol what it is that Torah asks of man? *We are distant from one another in our view of man:* we regard him as the creature of his Creator, distant and near to him, imperfect before a criterion of perfection which is the Image in which he was created, victim of temptation and impulse, victor in that he subdues and orders his passion, neither evil beyond measure nor good beyond credibility; man, the general order of man to whom Torah is given, is the *benoni*, the man who is neither saint nor monster, and it is for him that the world is sometimes thought to have been created. Such a view of man (a realistic humanism, I believe) is at odds with the radical human predicament which Paul and later Marcionite tendencies (never properly or successfully overcome within the Church) describe. Man had to be uncompromisingly in bondage to sin that the extraordinary challenge of the Christ might seem appropriate; moreover, he had to pass through aeons of regeneration before Christ could return in order that the fact that he did not return could be sustained. The anthropology of Christianity is, I fear, an anthropology which unless corrected—and I believe profoundly corrected—by Biblical humanism cannot but fail, for it was an anthropology appropriate to the period immediately succeeding the death of Jesus, but is hopeless for a humanity that has none of the chiliastic opportunities of the monk, solitary, or ascetic in which to withdraw, but must—like the Jew—maintain the whole of the religious life while earning bread, raising a family, building a home, and waiting for the Messiah.

No Tradition, Only Nexus We are left with a perplexity. I have virtually stated throughout that I do not believe in the Judeo-Christian tradition. I regard this conception as an ideologizing of a fundamental and irreconcilable disagreement. There is a Jewish-Christian nexus; there is a Jew for the Christian and there is a Christian for the Jew, but the reciprocity of their relation arises, not from the assumption of their communality, but from the assumption of their difference. The nexus is that Christian and Jew divide before the same Lord; it is the sameness of the Lord which establishes our connection, but it is the breach of our understanding of him that makes all use of the significant word "tradition" hopelessly irrelevant.

There is indeed a "carrying over" from Jew to Christian; in that sense there is a Judeo-Christian tradition, a tradition determined by the Christian's dependence upon the Jew for his past. But this hyphenated tradition is not reversible. There is no Christo-Jewish tradition, no passage backwards, no return into us except in the fullness of days. It is not incorrect to say that to the extent that we begin in this time to communicate anew with Christians as believers who believe differently, but seek to learn from us in truth what it is that has sustained us during the centuries that have elapsed since the time the Church cut us off in our living members and refashioned us as a Christian myth, we may be beginning the joint work of coredemption to which I have alluded.

Confessional conversation between Jew and Christian only takes place when two persons who are really connected address each other, when they acknowledge their sharing of a history but believe it to signify different truths, when both direct their energies to the transformation of the same humanity and the same past. In this sense Jew and Christian are empirically equals, although their equality under nature and history is differently quantified by the roles and attitudes and postures which their historical past has enforced upon their contemporary views of each other. But they also meet each other at a different plane, for when they eliminate from their views the mockeries of history—when the Christian overcomes his terrestrial fear of the Jew and when the Jew deadens the pain of his historical encounter with Christendom—then there is the possibility of asking what claim each makes upon the other. I do not mean the claim of each turned outward to the world but looking back over the shoulder toward the other; rather, what claim each directly make upon the other, and is it a significant claim?

The Christian is present for the Jew only as a reminder of that which the Jew must expect and as a witness to what he has been allowed to forego in order that the pagan world might be redeemed. The Christian is the visible testimony for the Jew of his messianic vocation, that he never be permitted to throw off what only he, as Jew, can do, which is to affirm that amid the cry of all, there is still no peace—even more, that there is no *shlamut*, no perfection until Christianity is reunited with Israel, until it has learned to transcend the Son to the Father, until it too shall have learned to say Lord and Lord alone, having been instructed to do so by the Son.

We await patiently the return of Christendom to the Synagogue, as we await patiently the coming of the messianic herald of the End; but we do so not with the trumpet of the missionary nor the timbrel of the tract—for it is a requirement that the only proselyte who comes wholly within our gate be one who has learned of his own to love and fear God, and loving and fearing him seeks then to serve him. So we are patient before the reunion. Can we be more than patient before the reunion? What more has Israel to offer the world than an eternal patience?

Islam

Maulavi Saiyid Amir Ali

Amir Ali was born in 1849, graduated from Calcutta University in 1867, and soon after became Judge of the Calcutta High Court. In 1885 he went to England where he was appointed to the Judicial Committee of the Privy Council. He died in England in 1928.

Among his many articles and books dealing with legal issues, "The Legal Position of Women in Islam" and "Mohammedan Law" have been the most widely received. He has written "A Short History of the Saracens," "A Critical Examination of the Life and Teachings of Mohammed," and "Persian Cultures." In addition to these works, Amir Ali is the author of perhaps the most significant study of Islam to have appeared from the Moslem world in modern history, "The Spirit of Islam." It deals with the fundamental problems of religious revival and intellectual revival in Moslem theology. W. Montgomary Watt, in reviewing similar studies in his Islamic Philosophy and Theology, *refers to Amir Ali's as "the most noteworthy."*

*CHRISTIANITY FROM THE ISLÂMIC STANDPOINT**

Ever since it seated itself on the throne of the Cæsars, Christianity has claimed to exercise, and has in fact exercised, a potent influence over large masses of mankind. Within certain limits it has furthered civilisation and the development of humanitarian ideas. And although its humanity has been at all times of an exclusive character, even in its mediæval phase it produced many generous and noble natures. Whilst it burnt, regardless of age and sex, witches and heretics, it gave birth to a Las Casas and a St. Xavier. In spite of the inroads of science and freethought into the domains of orthodoxy, its demand to be regarded as the sole means of salvation is great and persistent. How its principles, tenets, and doctrines appeal to the religious consciousness of outsiders must always form an interesting subject of study.

I propose, therefore, to examine the dogmas and ethics of Christianity from the standpoint of a cognate religion. The following pages give frank expression to the Islâmic views, without implying the smallest disparagement or disrespect to the Christian faith or its professors. In common with all Moslems, I entertain the profoundest veneration for the Prophet of Nazareth, and I should be grieved if my remarks were taken in a spirit other than philosophical, having for its sole object the eludication of the thesis entrusted to me.

* M. Amir Ali, "Christianity from the Islâmic Standpoint," *Hibbert Journal*, London, 1905.

Both Islâm and Christianity have identical aims and ideals; both agree in their general principles. Even in matters of dogma the agreement is often astonishing. The belief in "one living and true God, everlasting, without body, parts or passions, of infinite wisdom and goodness, the Maker of all things visible and invisible," is common to both; they are agreed that the immutable laws which regulate human relations emanate from a divine source. The orthodox Moslem, like the orthodox Christian, accepts Jesus as the Messiah of the Jews, and even designates him as "the Spirit of God." And what is most noteworthy is that they both believe in the mystery of the "Immaculate Conception." And yet an impassable gulf, as it seems, of bitterness and misunderstanding divides the two religions so closely allied to each other, and makes all communion in the work of humanitarian development well-nigh impossible.

To the question what can be the cause of this divergence, the answer is not difficult. It consists primarily in the Christian dogma of the Sonship of Jesus—that he was "the only begotten Son of God."

The Moslem denies that there is any warrant for this doctrine in the teachings of the Nazarene Prophet. He asserts that the idea is borrowed from foreign sources and interpolated with his sayings. The Arabian Prophet regards the very notion as preposterous, that Jesus claimed divine worship: "It beseemeth not a man," warns the Koran, "that God should give him the Scriptures and the wisdom and the gift of prophecy, and then he should say to his followers, 'Be ye worshippers of mine as well as of God,' but rather be ye perfect in things pertaining to God, since ye know the Scriptures and have studied deep." (Koran 3:7) The conception that God should have issue is viewed with a feeling akin to horror. "They say the God of mercy hath begotten a son. Now have ye uttered a grievous thing; and it wanteth but little that the heavens should be torn open and the earth cleave asunder, and the mountains fall down, for that they attribute children unto the Merciful; whereas it is not meet for God to have children. Verily there is none in heaven or earth but shall approach the Merciful as His servant." (Koran 19:91-94)

It is an article of faith among Moslems of all shades of opinion that the Christian Gospels in their present shape give an imperfect and erroneous view of the life and preachings of Jesus, and that his sayings have been garbled and tampered with according to the idiosyncrasies of individual compilers or the environments of the times and the requirements of factions and sects. That this view is not altogether unwarranted is amply borne out by the results of modern Biblical criticism, which shows how age after age everything human, everything not purely ideal, has been smoothed away from the adored image of an incarnate God, "the essentially pathetic story of Jesus has been converted into a fairy-tale," and his life so surrounded with myths that it is now impossible for us to know what he really was and did.

The religious consciousness of the Islâmist repels all idea of associating another in the worship of God. "Your God is one God, there is no God but He, the Most Merciful. In the creation of heaven and earth and the alternation of night and day, and in the ship which saileth on the sea . . . and in the rain which God sendeth from heaven, quickening again the dead earth . . . and in the change of winds and the clouds balanced between heaven and earth, are signs to people of understanding." (Koran 3:158-160) "God, there is no God but He, the Living, the Eternal. . . . Whatever is in heaven or earth is His. Who can intercede with Him but by His own permission? . . . He alone is God, God the Eternal. He begetteth not and He is not begotten; there is none like unto Him." (Koran 122)

Again, the idea of an "Intercessor" between God and man, either to purge him of his sins or to reconcile him to an angry Deity, is repugnant to the Islâmic conception. The relations between the Creator and His creatures are such that all human beings can obtain "nearness" to Him by the practice of self-sacrifice, self-denial, and obedience to His commands. If they sin, they can obtain forgiveness by appealing direct to Him and by "*abandoning their evil ways.*"

Nor can the Moslem reconcile the humility of spirit which pervades most of the sayings of Jesus, even as they have reached us, with the pretensions that are often attributed to him. Whilst Islâm accepts Jesus as one of the greatest teachers of the world, the Messiah of the Jews, sent to regenerate and reform a backsliding race, it regards him strictly as a human personality. The "Immaculate Conception" is the only mystery it recognises.

The attitude of the Moslem mind towards the central doctrine of orthodox Christianity can hardly be appreciated without an understanding of the Islâmic view concerning the Hebrew traditions, which sometimes run parallel with the Moslem traditions, at other times diverge widely.

The Hebrew prophets occupy an important place in Moslem hagiology, but their utterances are construed on a historical and rational basis. Like the Moslem dervishes, they entered, or attempted to enter, into communion with the Deity by the mortification of the senses and the cultivation of an inner spirit. Like them also, these holy men often worked themselves up to the highest pitch of exaltation, when they saw visions of the past, frequently of the future. They brooded over the sufferings of their nation, and naturally poured forth lamentations for the sins of Israel. At the same time they were full of hope that the Almighty would redeem His "chosen people" and restore their glory. In this they voiced the national sentiment. Their outpourings, full of imagery and replete with exhortations, breathe the most passionate anticipation of a time when Israel, freed of its burdens and rid of its enemies, would enjoy peace and prosperity in abundance. The Messianic prophecies thus pervade the Hebrew traditions from the earliest times, and furnish the keynote to the whole Jewish history. Like the Jew, the Moslem believes that the "predictions" refer to a human Messiah. Among the neighbouring nations, whose religion and philosophy so largely influenced Jewish conceptions, and, in later times, Christian thought, the idea of a Deliverer took a different shape. The Mago-Zoroastrian believed in an Angel-Messiah who became incarnate in a virgin and revealed "the Word"; the Buddhist, in a divine being who was born, in the flesh, of a virgin queen, lived as a man, and after death returned to heaven. These conceptions, engrafted on Jewish traditions, gave birth to the doctrine of Sonship.

With regard to the mystery of the Annunciation, the divergence between the Christian and Moslem traditions is not great. To the Moslem, however, Jesus is the "unbegotten" son of Mary.

According to the Moslem traditions, Jesus performed "miracles" even in infancy. According to the Christian traditions, "the child waxed strong, filled with wisdom." An incident in his early life which is so human and natural that it may be regarded as authentic, shows his thoughtful and mystical nature and the keen desire to learn the law of his people. At the age of twelve, journeying back from Jerusalem, after the Passover festival, he was lost in the crowd. When his distracted parents discovered him later, he was found seated in the Temple listening to the rabbis, asking them questions and "amazing them by his understanding and answers." The rest of the story is peculiarly pathetic. "And his mother said to him, Son, why hast thou thus dealt with us? Behold, thy father and I sought thee sorrowing. And he said unto them, How is it that ye sought me? Wist ye not that I must be in my Father's house? And he went down with them and came to Nazareth, and he was subject unto them. And Jesus advanced in wisdom and stature and in favour with God and man."

Thoroughly acquainted with the poet-prophets, whom he frequently quotes, Jesus was naturally imbued with the Messianic hopes and aspirations which filled the air in which he lived and moved. The "visions" of Daniel and the preachings of Yahya (John), his immediate predecessor, could not but make a deep impression on a sensitive and mystical mind. The whole atmosphere was charged with the expectation of the coming Messiah, and all the conditions, social and political, inspired the Teacher with the faith that he was destined to fulfil in his person the presagings of the nation's seers. Thus does the voice of God speak to the souls of His servants.

There is ample warrant for the Islâmic belief that Jesus considered hmiself as the Messiah of his people, and his answer to the piteous appeal of the Canaanite woman would indicate that he regarded his mission as exclusively confined to the Jews. But it is by no means proven that he ever *claimed* to be the "Son of God"; whilst the discrepancy between the statements of Matthew and Mark regarding the answer of Peter to the question put by Jesus in the neighbourhood of Cæsarea Philippi suggest a doubt if the apostle ever called him "the son of the living God."

According to Islâm, the conception of Jesus as to his own personality, when divested of the "Aberglaube" of his followers, was singularly free from exaggeration.[1] His idea of the "Fatherhood" of God embraced all humanity. Even if it were assumed that he made use of the expressions attributed to him, do they prove that he claimed to be "the only begotten Son of the Father"?

The holy men of the East, in spiritual exaltation, have often claimed affinity with God. Hussain bin Mansur al-Hallâj, "a man of pure life, who had no equal in his time either in the East or in the West," had in an ecstatic mood called himself "The Truth," and, like the ancient Sanhedrim, the Mussulman divines (with some notable dissents) pronounced him guilty of blasphemy and sentenced him to death. Al-Hallâj, the mystic martyr who also suffered on the cross the extreme penalty of the law, has now a recognised place in Moslem hagiology as one of the holiest of saints. The lovable and enthusiastic character of Jesus, with its earnestness and mysticism, its "passionate pity for the poor," finds an echo in Shams-i-Tabriz, "the Sun of Tabriz," who suffered the same fate for claiming to be part of the Divinity. One would hardly be justified in concluding that they meant to represent themselves as the Deity incarnate.

It is not the "unique life of Jesus" which makes him, in the Moslem mind, one of the greatest landmarks in the history of religious development. It is the message he brought to humanity —the message the Almighty entrusts to His chosen ones only at intervals, to recall mankind from the worship of their passions, symbolised in the idols of their infancy.

The Moslem belief probably is in accord with that of the primitive Christians—of the Ebionites, "the sect of the poor," to whom Jesus had preached and among whom he had lived. It has nothing in common with Pauline Christianity. To Paul, Jew by birth, Greek by education, who had never felt the influence of the great Prophet, is due the present divergence between Islâm and Christianity.[2] He took up the idea of the man at whose martyrdom he had assisted, and spread it abroad. The educated classes had been

[1] When a man called him "Good Master," Jesus replied, "Why dost thou call me good? None is good save one, even God." This is an instance of his conception regarding his own personality, that he was no more than a man.

[2] "And straightway he preached Christ in the synagogues, that he is the Son of God." (Acts 9:20)

trained by Alexandrian philosophy to the conception of a Demiurgus between God and man; Syria and Palestine were permeated by the Essenic doctrine of the Angel-Messiah borrowed from the further East; the blood of Stephen the martyr blossomed into the faith of Christianity, and his defence before the "council" became the fountain of Pauline inspiration.

So far from being an angel or the Son of God, the great Teacher, in the sublimity of his character, like all prophets, was eminently human. His *humanity* was one of the most attractive features of his character. He was neither free from the human frailty of anger,[3] nor that excess of religious zeal which borders on exclusiveness.

Although the Moslem does not accept the doctrine of "Sonship," his veneration for the mother of Jesus is profound. She is regarded as one of the purest and holiest of women, only two others taking rank with her—Khadîja, the wife of the Prophet of Islâm, and Fâtima, his daughter, "the mother of the Syeds," the nobility of Islâm.

This veneration for Mary is carried so far, that the Mogul sovereigns of India, in speaking of their deceased ancestresses, often applied to them the expression *Mariam-Makâni,* "occupying the abode of Mary (in heaven)"; whilst a noble and virtuous woman is frequently described as *Mariam-sifat,* "one endowed with the virtues of Mary."

The Moslems, in common with the Docetic Christians, do not believe that Jesus died on the cross. The Docetic belief regarding his disappearance is more consistent with his Sonship than the orthodox doctrine. For it seems somewhat difficult to understand that the Father would allow his beloved Son to die on the cross without bringing about a convulsion of nature. "These Christians believe that the man who suffered on the cross was a different person from the divine Christ, who escaped from the hands of his persecutors, and went away to the regions whence he had come."[4] According to the Moslem traditions, the Jewish Messiah was at the last moment saved by divine agency from an ignominious death.

[3] His anger with the Pharisees and Sadducees who had come to ask for a "sign" was not without cause; but the curse on the fig-tree seems strange.

[4] Syed Ameer Ali, *The Spirit of Islam,* London, 1922, p. 57.

The orthodox belief is that he was translated to heaven, whilst the rationalist explains the disappearance on more intelligible hypotheses.

The story relating to the crucifixion and resurrection of Jesus in the Christian Gospels is poetical but hardly convincing. It reads more like a myth than a historical account. We know of the intense desire of Pilate, whom Tertullian calls a Christian at heart, to save Jesus; we know that outside the circle of his disciples he had many sympathisers; we are told also that a preternatural gloom overshadowed the earth at the most awful part of the drama. There is no inherent improbability in the belief that the innocent escaped and the guilty suffered. And this probability grows into a conviction when we consider the circumstantial account given in the Gospel of Luke, how after the Resurrection Jesus called for and partook of food. "And as they thus spake," says the chronicler, "Jesus himself stood in the midst of them, and saith unto them, Peace be unto you. But they were terrified and affrighted, and supposed that they had seen a spirit. And he said unto them, Why are ye troubled? and why do thoughts arise in your hearts? Behold my hands and my feet, that it is myself: handle me, and see; for a spirit hath not flesh and bones, as ye see me have. And when he had thus spoken, he showed them his hands and his feet. And while they yet believed not for joy, and wondered, he said unto them, Have ye here any meat? And they gave him a piece of a broiled fish, and of an honeycomb. And he took it, and did eat before them." From this it is quite clear that "the Resurrection" was corporeal. Then, the Moslems asks, what became of the wounds Jesus is said to have received on the cross, which caused his death?

The accounts in the several chronicles regarding "the Resurrection" are so discrepant that they may safely be treated as "unhistorical," and the stories of the women relating what they saw at the tomb, as the Apostles treated them, "idle tales" (Luke 24:11).

The rationalistic Moslem belief that Jesus was rescued, if not by his lukewarm disciples, by persons who were in sympathy with him and revered his character, is based on some solid facts. He was apparently kept concealed for a time from his enemies. But the atmosphere of Jerusalem was fraught with the greatest danger. Accordingly, after giving his final instructions, the Prophet betook himself to the regions of the East, where, safe from Jewish persecution, he could peacefully pursue his great mission, and where he eventually died.[5]

In order to reconcile the two conflicting theories—the Sonship of Jesus with his death on the cross—Pauline Christianity formulated the doctrine of Atonement, which again is based on the dogma that "mankind sinned in Adam." (Romans 5:12) Islâm absolutely repudiates the doctrine of original sin. Hereditary depravity and "natural sinfulness" are emphatically denied. Every child of man is born pure; every departure in after life from the path of truth and rectitude is due to education. "Every child of man," declared the Prophet of Islâm, "is born religiously constituted; it is his parents who make him afterwards a Jew, a Christian, or a Sabean. . . . Every human being has two inclinations—one prompting him to good and impelling him thereto, and the other prompting him to evil, and thereto impelling him"; but "the Godly assistance is nigh, and he who asks for the help of God in contending with the evil promptings of his own heart obtains it." The Moslem cannot naturally conceive that the Almighty Creator of the universe, the All-good, the All-wise, should create a world abounding in sin; that, not successful in rooting it out, He should send His "sole begotten Son" to offer himself as a sacrifice to save mankind from eternal perdition. It seems somewhat absurd that, because the first man was unreasonable or disobedient enough to eat the forbidden fruit of the tree of knowledge, he should not only be expelled from the Garden of Eden, but an awful doom should be passed on all his posterity, from which they would not be extricated until the Son of God should sacrifice himself.[6] To the

[5] A recent Moslem writer asserts that the tomb of a prophet called Nabi Isa is still pointed out in the country north of Cashmere.

[6] The writer is aware that many modern Christians do not hold these doctrines in the form described above. At the same time, these doctrines remain unaltered in the official formularies of the Christian religion, and so long as they remain there, Moslems will be justified in taking them as truly representative of Christianity.

Moslem mind, it is incomprehensible that, if the Father accepted the life of the Son as a forfeit for the sins of mankind, the bulk of humanity should still not be exempt from divine wrath, nor those who believe in the Son be free from sin.

The Moslem believes that the idea of atonement in Christianity is a survival of the conception which prevailed among all the nations of antiquity, and which is in vogue even now among some races, that an angry God can only be appeased by the "sacrifice" of human beings, particularly someone especially dear or especially precious. The Islâmist does not believe that Jesus ever wished his followers to understand his death as a sacrificial offering for the sins of mankind in general or *their* sins in particular. The enthusiasm with which the common folk had welcomed him unto Jerusalem had already died out; whilst the bitterness and alarm of the priests and rabbis had increased. As the dream of an immediate advent of the kingdom of heaven faded away, the heart was filled with forebodings of betrayal and death. And these forebodings naturally found expression at the Last Supper—the Passover feast which the Prophet shared for the last time with his disciples. It was then that he invited them on all such occasions to remember him and the tidings he had brought. The old message was dead in the hearts of men; the new, fresh with hope and charity, had broken the rigorous bonds of the Levitical Law. It was the beginning of a new era—a new life; and he naturally called upon them to forget the old associations, and not, in future, to connect the Passover feast with the deliverance from Egypt, but to remember it in his personality as a memorial of their liberation from the shackles of a lifeless formalism. To accentuate his advice, and to impress on them his earnestness, it is possible he told them, when partaking on the paschal meal, to look upon the bread they ate as his flesh, and the wine they drank as his blood. The Moslems think this to be a more natural explanation of his words—if he ever used them—than to suppose he meant to convey, mystically disguised, an unnatural idea, which does not commend itself to reason.

Among the Jews the paschal lamb was killed on the day of the Passover (Leviticus 23:5) merely as a memorial (Exodus 11:4) of the deliverance from Pharaonic bondage. The Essenes, however, observed the day of slaying the paschal lamb as a day for purification and the purging of sins. The blood of the paschal lamb sprinkled over the lintels and side-posts of the doors of the Israelites had enabled God to distinguish their houses from those of the Egyptians, and thus spared their first-born from being smitten. With the belief that Jesus had died on the cross, it was easy for Paul to evolve the idea that, as the blood of the paschal lamb had saved the first-born of the Israelites, the blood of Jesus had saved mankind. To Paul, then, Christianity owes the doctrine of Real Presence (I Corinthians 23:29) which is repugnant to the religious consciousness of Moslems; nor do they believe there is any justification for it in the teachings of Jesus.

The belief in a certain spirit-power in man which enables him to do acts out of the ordinary course of nature has existed among all races of mankind. It exists even now, although under other names, amongst the most advanced communities. In ancient times the person endowed with this spirit was believed capable of peering into futurity, diving into the mysteries of the unseen world, and performing "miracles." In the Eastern world the dervishes are still believed to exercise that power, and their "miracles" are called *Karâmât*, as distinguished from the *Mujaza* of the Prophet.[7] Then as now men tried to liberate themselves from the bondage of the flesh by self-mortification, and to obtain communion with God by the practice of self-denial and asceticism. According to the Moslem belief, the spirit of God, in a greater or less degree, is in all mankind; the voice of God speaks to every human soul. To the soul of the prophet it comes in mighty waves; to the humbler folk it speaks in whispers. Jesus declared that the Spirit of God dwelt in all human beings. So far Islâm is in accord with the teachings of Christianity. But it does not accept the doctrine "of the effusion of the Holy Ghost," by which it is said "the Spirit of God" made its appearance like a dove or a flame, and gave the Apostles the power of tongues. This is regarded as a palpable fable.

The doctrine of "justification by faith," an important feature in Protestantism, may be said to derive support from the sayings of Jesus as reported in the Christian Gospels. Literally construed, they would convey the idea that, so long as people believe in him,

[7] Shams-i-Tabriz is believed by his disciples to have raised the dead, and healed incurables by a mere word.

conduct is immaterial. And this view Paul has interwoven into his system as an integral part of Christianity.[8]

The Prophet of Islâm declared the present life to be a seed-ground of the future. To work in all humility of spirit for the human good, to strive with all energy to approach the perfection of the All-perfect, is the essential principle of Islâm. Each man will be judged at the Great Account by the work he has done in this life. "Verily those who believe (Moslems) and those who are Jews, Christians or Sabeans, whoever hath faith in God and the last day, and *worketh that which is right and good,* for them shall be the reward with their Lord." (Koran 5:73)

"To every man we have given a law and way . . . and if God had pleased He would have made you all one people (people of one religion). But He hath done otherwise that He might try you in that which He hath severally given unto you; wherefore strive in good works. Unto God shall ye return, and He will tell that concerning which ye disagree." "There is no piety in turning the face to the east or the west, but in placing trust in God and in *doing good.*" The Moslem naturally regards the doctrine of "justification by faith" as disastrous to human morality.

In this connection arises the question, what did Jesus actually teach? The Islâmic belief is that his mission, like that of Mohammed, was to re-enunciate the eternal truths of God, and to recall humanity to the inevitable track of spiritual evolution. His ethical precepts, whether direct in form or dressed in parables, are thus common to all higher religions. There is no question of borrowing from one source or another, for God imparts His truths to all He chooses for His work. Jesus was thus not the first to impress on the conscience of mankind the duties of self-sacrifice, self-abnegation, devotion to God, love of humanity. There were others before him, as others after him, to preach the practice of peace, humility, charity, good works, submission to God's will, forgiveness of injuries, and the denial of self. Among the many maxims of the famous Rabbi Hillel occur the following: "Do not to others what you would not others should do to you"; "Thou shalt love thy neighbour as thyself"; "Judge not, that ye may not be judged"; "He that

[8] "But to him that worketh not, but believeth on him that justifieth the ungodly, his faith is reckoned for righteousness." (Romans 4:5)

exalteth himself shall be abased." These precepts are found also in the sayings of Jesus. It does not follow, however, that he borrowed them from Hillel; they were God's direct gift to him, as were the enunciations of the Prophet of Islâm: "Adhere to those who forsake you; speak truth to your own heart; do good to everyone that does ill to you." "Blessed are they who are constant in their charity, who guard their chastity, and who observe their trust and covenants; verily God bids you do justice and good, and give kindred their due, and He forbids you to sin and to do wrong and oppress."

Buddha had preached in the East that a perfect life could only be acquired by "abandoning the world." Jesus, accustomed from childhood to connect wealth with oppression, and its acquisition with corruption and deceit, naturally believed that holiness could only be attained through poverty and asceticism. The Essenes and Ebionites insisted on their members leading a life of absolute self-denial. The Essenian hermits, clad in tattered garments, living on meagre fare, moved among the humble denizens of the countryside, and preached that the favoured of God were the poor, the lowly, the downtrodden, the merciful, and the peaceful. The preachings of these pietists found an echo in the teachings of Jesus. Like them, he went among the poor and distressed, bringing them solace and healing their physical ills; like them, he enjoined his disciples to practise humility and self-denial. To him poverty was a passport to heaven, and the abandonment of the world the sole means of obtaining merit. "It was easier for a camel to enter through a needle's eye, than for a rich man to enter into the kingdom of God." (Mark 10:25) The ascetic spirit—the spirit of absolute disregard of all the natural dictates of human love and family affection—burns throughout his preachings. Mere doing of duty to God and man was not sufficient to "inherit eternal life"; he who seeks it must forsake all whom he holds most dear on earth (Mark 10:17-22), leave the revered dead unburied, must not even say a farewell to them he leaves behind, but must follow the preacher.

The sacrifices insisted on by the Nazarene Prophet, though explicable by his environment, are not accepted by the religious consciousness of Islâm as furnishing permanent guides to human conduct, nor have they been recognised or generally acted upon in Christendom. Islâm does not condemn the rich because of their riches. Their wealth carries with it the obligation of helping the needy, supporting the orphan, ransoming the captive. They are enjoined not to make a show of their piety or to walk proudly on earth, to abstain from vanities and the indulgence of their passions, to give alms, offer prayers, and tend well their trusts.

With these precepts in his mind, the Islâmist considers the stern ascetism of the Nazarene Prophet, so alien to his other precepts of love and charity, as an accident. Again, filial devotion and reverence to parents are inculcated in the strongest terms in the Koran. "Defer humbly to your parents; with humility and tenderness say: O Lord, be merciful to them even as they brought me up when I was helpless." "Moreover, we have enjoined on man to show kindness to his parents. With pain his mother beareth him; with pain she bringeth him forth; and he saith: O my Lord! stir me up to be grateful for thy favours wherewith thou hast favoured me and my parents, and to do good works which shall please thee, and prosper me in my offspring: for to thee am I turned, and am resigned to thy will."

To the Moslem, therefore, the attitude of Jesus towards his mother—the mother who had so tenderly watched over him in infancy and youth, and whose maternal devotion shone forth at the last crisis of his life—when she, accompanied by his brothers, came to see him (Matthew 12:46-50), is utterly incomprehensible, and only explainable by an exalted enthusiasm in his own mission.

Predestinarianism, which in a more or less pronounced form runs through Christianity in all its phases, and which was a dominant factor in the religious thought of England during one of the greatest crises of English history, may be said to be a reflex of the dominating idea of the Teacher. The doom foreshadowed for those who did not accept him as the Messiah carries the suggestion of pre-ordination, whilst his quietism in the early part of his prophetic career, and his direction to the disciples not to make public his character as "the Christ," are explainable only on the hypothesis that he firmly believed in the immediate advent of the kingdom of God, when his Messianic character would be revealed and established by divine agency. Fully conscious of the dangers that surrounded him in the stronghold of Jewish fanaticism, he proceeds there—as in Jerusalem alone was the Messianic prophecy to be fulfilled. All his words and acts during the last phase of his mission show that he anticipated a speedy change in the political conditions. His pathetic words before his rescue—"Lord, Lord, why hast thou forsaken me?"—indicate the firmness of conviction with which he looked forward to divine interference. The Moslems hold that God did not forsake him!

Again, the speech of Peter to the Jews brings prominently to view the strong belief held by the disciples that everything that had happened—and, by implication, was to happen—was due to "the determinate counsel of God." (Acts 2:23)

Withal, the Moslems regard Jesus as one of the greatest moral teachers of the world, and love and revere him as such. The Jews had turned the Levitical law, with all its minutiæ, into a fetish: Jesus redeemed them from its bondage. He was the first among his nation to teach in the truest sense that the kernel was of greater value than the shell, the spirit than the letter. In an age when hardness of heart was a virtue, and poverty a crime, he preached charity and love, compassion to the poor, pity for the orphan. He taught the sacredness of truth, justice and purity, the blessedness of humility. He widened the narrow horizon of Judaism, and raised its ideal. His messengership was essentially a link in the chain of man's spiritual development. But Jesus had appeared in the midst of an organised society subject to one of the most civilised governments of antiquity. His precepts were, therefore, of a general character, naturally wanting in that definiteness which alone makes them of practical value to the uncultured and undisciplined mind. *Principles*, inculcated by revelation or philosophy, are sufficient for the higher natures: a Marcus Aurelius could exist independently of Christianity or Islâm. But for lower minds, positive rules are essential, and where religion does not supply them, its deficiency must needs be supplemented by the secular law. A religion without rules acceptable to the conscience of all humanity is mere philosophy, which leaves untouched both the heart and mind of the ordinary man. The lives of the ministers, often elevating in their example—the weekly sermons, eloquent and appealing—act but as a ripple on the surface. The worshipper carries into his home little of what he hears. The terrible crimes against women and children which one shudders to read of daily, the savagery with which parents maltreat, nay, murder, their own offspring, are all due to one cause—the absence of positive prescriptions. The natural man is a savage; drink, lust, or greed turns him into a veritable beast.

Religion has to elevate him towards humanity. To effect that purpose, to humanise the home, to regulate the domestic relations, to make the parents remember that children are a sacred trust from God, it must be directory—like the secular law, in the outward dealings of man to man. Rules against drunkenness, rules prescribing cleanliness, charity, devotion, duty towards the bondspeople, pity for the dumb creation, form thus the very essence of an effective moral religion aiming at universality. Why has Christianity, which appears so largely to satisfy the spiritual aspirations of many cultured minds in the Western world, failed in its work of amelioration with lower natures and lower races? Because, devoid of positive prescriptions, though idealistic and elevated in its conceptions, it does not appeal to the intelligence or heart of the natural man.

In view of the denunciations of the Nazarene Prophet against the rich, and the promise of the kingdom of heaven to the poor and the humble, the Moslem fails to understand the feverish pursuit of wealth in the Western world, the devotion to luxury, the unregulated dispensing of charity, the callousness to distress and suffering, the contempt for the virtues which Jesus inculcated—patience, meekness, and humility of spirit; or why the system which styled its founder "the Prince of Peace" should not be able to suppress war and rapine among his followers. The fanaticism which threw its dark shadow over the whole of Europe for centuries, and made holocausts of innumerable beings, was not inconsistent with the religious sentiment of the times. How is it, asks the Moslem, that modern Christianity, with its philosophic ideals, cannot root out the evil of racial exclusiveness?

Islâm makes charity a part of the obligatory rules. In the Christian system, this is left to individual sentiment. Here and there it finds practical expression in a Barnardo or a Booth; but unless the suffering is forcibly visible or offensive to the æsthetic sense, much that might relieve poignant distress at home is diverted to the making of distant and doubtful converts.

The key to the problem may perhaps be found in the saying of Jesus that he had come "to fulfil and not to destroy." Did he intend that his precepts were to be taken as supplementary to the Mosaic Law? If that was the meaning, it had become impossible, for the world had moved on and made difficult the observance of the old directions, even with the solvent of Christian doctrines. If his teachings constitute a new system, then it is permissible for the Moslem to think that the great Prophet left it incomplete, and that his holy work remained unfulfilled until another Master with a larger grasp of human needs and human limitations arose to convey afresh to mankind the message of God.

Moslems do not recognise that modern Christianity, overladen with Greek philosophy and Pauline mysticism, represents the religion Jesus in fact taught. They consider that Islâm represents true Christianity. They do not think that Jesus, who prayed in the wilderness and on the hillside in the huts of the peasants, in the humble abodes of the fishermen, furnished any warrant for the gorgeousness of modern Christian worship, with all the accessories which beguile the mind, mystify the intellect, and thus divert the human heart from the worship of the great God towards a symbol and a type.

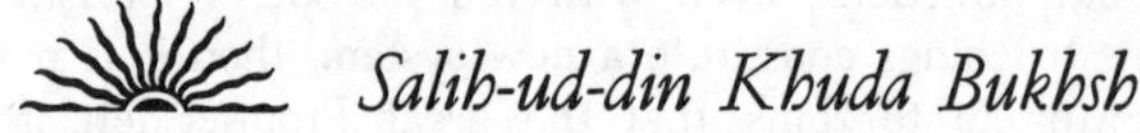

Salih-ud-din Khuda Bukhsh

S. Khuda Bukhsh was born in Calcutta in 1877. After graduating from Calcutta University, he became a lecturer there and a professor at the University Law College. He died in 1931.

S. Khuda Bukhsh regarded himself as primarily a scholar and lawyer, but he was also a productive author. Among his most important works are "Contributions to the History of Islamic Civilization," "History of the Islamic Peoples," "Politics in Islam," "The Arab Civilization," and "Essays: Indian and Islamic." The essay which follows was written at the request of A. S. Peake and R. G. Parsons, editors of the five-volume "Outline of Christianity"; S. Khuda Bukhsh's essay appeared in the last volume, "Christianity Today and Tomorrow."

A MOHAMMEDAN VIEW OF CHRISTENDOM *

Closely related, as they are, Islam and Christianity should be carefully studied, not to accentuate differences, but to emphasize the points on which they agree; for on their mutual good-will in large measure depends the future of Asia, if not of the whole world. On the whole happy and harmonious until about 1000 A.D., their relations were then affected by mutual suspicion; the seeds were then sown of a hostility which has not yet quite ceased to bear poisonous fruit. We will not pause to inquire here into the nature of those suspicions, which were partly political, partly religious. The spirit of hostility which marked the writings of early European scholars curiously continued in all its fanatical fervour till 1829, the date of the appearance of "Mahometanism Unveiled," by Charles Foster.

But things are changing to-day, and happily for the better. Mohammed is no longer deemed an impostor, but a reformer of world-wide importance; Islam is no longer regarded merely as a religion propagated at the point of the sword; Islamic culture is no longer considered a curse; but a stage in human progress for a great portion of the human race. This change is very gratifying, welcome, and reassuring. And, indeed, when we consider the many similarities subsisting between the true Islam and true Christianity,

* **K. Bukhsh, "A Mohammedan View of Christendom," Waverley Book Company, Ltd., London, 1932, pp. 245-255.**

we fail to see (now that "Arabism" is of the past) why there should be any hostility, or even estrangement, between the two cults.

For what else is Islam but a revised edition of Judaism and Christianity? Mohammed never claimed originality. He insisted, he emphasized, in season and out, that his mission was but to rid Judaism and Christianity of what he regarded as life-destroying accretions—to proclaim their pristine purity—to enthrone in the hearts of men the *din*[1] of Abraham, in its undimmed excellence! Did it not set itself against paganism, with its gross fetishism, hideous morality, narrow outlook, cruelty, barbarism, the cult of the family and the tribe? Eclectic was Mohammed's religion. He took from all, and freely—from Judaism, Christianity, Parsiism.

It was not first-hand information that Mohammed had, either of Judaism or of Christianity. The stories told by him are anything but correctly recounted. They abundantly prove that they were drawn from traditions and hearsay and little talks with men at home and abroad. The Koran teems with such stories; and Moslem religious institutions, too, are full of such extraneous influences. A mere glance will suffice. In Islam, by far the most important biblical character is Abraham. Mohammed makes him the builder of the Kạba, and therefore the founder of Mecca, and sees in him his predecessor and model. As regards New Testament characters, Mohammed seems to have had some acquaintance with the history of John the Baptist, and the life of Jesus. John, we are told, is a prophet, and like the prophets, receives a book, i.e., Revelation. Zachariah, his father, is also once mentioned in the list of prophets. Elsewhere he comes in incidentally in connexion with the birth of his son. Zachariah's prayer and its answer are related at some length, following, in the main, the narrative of Luke. As for Jesus, He is always mentioned in connexion with Mary—in fact, there is a tendency to exalt Mary as the chief character. Nor is this altogether surprising, for in Arabia the Collyridians invested her with the name and honours of a goddess. But, quite in keeping with his views regarding Mary, is Mohammed's idea of the Trinity. It is made up, according to him, of Father, Son and Mary. No less in contrast with the Christian record is his version of the Crucifixion and the Redemption through the cross. Mohammed rejects them

[1] *Din* probably means here "faith" or "belief." Editor.

both. He denies the crucifixion of the Christ, and teaches that Judas was substituted for Him and nailed to the cross, while the Christ himself ascended direct to heaven.

But, whatever the divergences, Islam and Christianity are akin in their veneration for Jesus. Mohammed acknowledges Him as a prophet, and the Moslems never mention his name without the formula "Peace be on Him!" Indian *Shiahs* believe in the reappearance of Christ simultaneously with the last of their twelve *Imams,* and look forward to the amalgamation of the two creeds.

And what is the attitude which the Koran takes up? "Dispute not against those who have received the Scriptures, that is, Jews and Christians, except with gentleness; but say unto them 'We believe in the revelation which hath been sent down to us, and also in that which hath been sent down to you; and our God and your God is one.'" And again in another place: "Verily the Believers, and those who are Jews, those who are Christians and Sabeans, whoever believeth in God, and the last day, and doeth that which is right, they shall have their reward with their Lord, there shall come no fear upon them neither shall they be grieved." And a still more striking passage: "Unto every one have we given a law and a way. Now, if God had pleased, He would surely have made you one people; but He hath made you differ, that He might try you in that which He hath given to each; therefore strive to excel each other in good works. Unto God shall ye all return, and He will tell you that concerning which you have disagreed." Such is the spirit of the Koran—the Bible of Islam.

If the influence of Christianity is profound, no less profound too is the influence of Judaism and Parsiism and Hellenism on Islam. Nowhere was the unity of God so emphatically insisted upon, at the time of the Prophet, as in Judaism, and it is therefore impossible to hold that this fundamental doctrine of Islam came from any other source. Equally striking are other importations from Judaism, but it would take us far afield to deal with them all. Jewish ideas penetrated into Islam in two ways; directly, and through the channel of Christianity. The spirit of Judaism is present, says Becker, either directly or working through Christianity, as an influence, wherever Islam accommodated itself to the new intellectual and spiritual life it had encountered.

But traces of Greek and Persian culture too are discernible in the infant Islam. Whence come they? Through the Semitic dialect known as Aramaic, of course. The Greek and Persian cultures were transmitted to the Arabs through this medium even before the rise of Islam, and the history of Islam shows how potent was this influence about this time.

Islam freely accepted light from many quarters. It modelled its faith on what had gone before it. We find in Islam precisely the same framework as in Judaism and Christianity: prayer, purification, solemn festivals, scriptures, and prophets. The idea of the Sabbath was accepted in principle, but, instead of Sunday, Friday was chosen. Here palpable is the Parsi influence, which robs the Sabbath of its character as a day of rest. From Parsiism Islam has taken both directly and indirectly. A number of obviously Parsi ideas have passed into Islam through the channel of Jewish books, notably the Talmud. The fast of Ramadhan seems to be an imitation of the Christian Lent; while prostration is apparently an importation from a Judæo-Christian sect. *Sujud* (prostration) was never in vogue among the Arabs.

The process of borrowing continued after the death of the Prophet, and, indeed, on a much grander scale. This was only to be expected. Persia, Syria, Egypt and Asia Minor became provinces of the Moslem Empire, with the result that the entire culture of the subject-races lay before the Moslems to absorb and make their own. In Greek, Syriac, Coptic, and Persian garbs we encounter a definite intellectual movement, which perhaps we may best designate Christo-Hellenism. Decisive, alike for Islam and Hellenism, was the incorporation of this culture into the youthful Arab Empire. The Hellenistic culture was revived, reanimated by changed circumstances, by contact with Arabism, by an intellectual clash with a new religion—akin in thought and tendencies. Islam and Arabism, on the other hand, after a century of wrestling and combat, were taken captive by the superior culture of the conquered races. To Hellenism, Arabism furnished its language, and supplied opportunities for wide diffusion; whereas Hellenism repaid its debt to Islam with its wealth of science and art. The clash of mind with mind, the impact of a superior foreign culture, the resulting scepticism and free-thinking, and, consequent upon it, a broad and broadening spirit of toleration—these led to peaceful exchange of ideas between Moslems and Christians, to the advantage of both.

At Damascus, through one portal, both Moslems and Christians passed to perform their devotions. Christians had not merely free entry at the court of the Caliph, but were entrusted with the most important posts of confidence. Sergius, the father of John of Damascus, enjoyed at the court of Abdul Malik the place of first councillor, and after his death his son was given the same position. A Christian—Al-Akhtal—was even the official court-poet of the Omayyads. So favourable, indeed, was the position of the Christians, that they were even allowed to enter the mosques unmolested, and go about in public adorned with the golden cross. The toleration accorded to the Christians by the Caliphs must, of necessity, have encouraged frequent intercourse with Moslems.

By associating with Greek theologians, disciplined in the art of dialectics, the Arabs first learnt philosophical reasoning, which later on they prized so highly. It was from the Greeks again that they received their first lesson in dogmatic subtleties—an art in which Byzantine scholarship revelled. Foremost is the inquiry into the essence and attributes of God, which fills the first place in the writings both of the Greek Fathers and of the oldest Arab theologians. The oldest Moslem theologians, just as much as the Fathers of the Greek Church, busy themselves with discussions about fate and free-will. In opposition to the Western Church, the Fathers of the Greek Church declare themselves against the "eternity of the punishment of Hell," and the very same view was taken by the oldest theological school of Islam, known as the Murjiah. Nor is the Christian idea of penance absent in Islamism. The more we carefully examine this subject, the more we find the pervading influence of Christianity on Islam. Its founder freely made use of Christianity, and the example set by him was followed by his votaries.

Amazing is the influence which the didactic utterances to be met with in the Gospels exercised on the development of Moslem precepts as unfolded in the literature connected with the *Hadith* (the body of traditions relating to Mohammed). Among those whom God will protect with His shadow on the Day of Judgment is mentioned "The man who does good but keeps it a secret, so that his left hand knows not what his right hand has done." We also come across, in the Moslem tradition, a paraphrase of the saying, "Render unto Cæsar the things which are Cæsar's." The passages in the New Testament relating to the beatitude of the poor and their advantage over the rich, and the obstacles of the latter to entering the kingdom of heaven, an idea quite opposed to the Arab conception of life, find continual echo in the speeches of Mohammed and those of the oldest Moslem theologians. "I stood (said the Prophet) at the gate of paradise, and observed that the majority of those who found admission there were poor; while the people of wealth were kept away from it."

Handhalah-al-Abshami relates: Never a company meets, and mentions the name of God, but a voice from heaven calls out to it: "Rise, for I have forgiven you and converted your evil into good deeds." We cannot fail to notice the influence of Matthew 9:2-7 on this saying. Similarly the glorification of the "poor in spirit" (Matthew 5:3) is found in the Moslem saying, "the simple (the innocent) will form the largest portion of the inhabitants of paradise." In close relation to Matthew 10:16 stands the saying reported by the companions of the Prophet, "Be innocent like doves." Of obvious and unmistakably biblical origin is the use which is made in the *Hadith* of the Paternoster. The Prophet is reported by Abu Darda, the first *Kadhi* of Damascus, to have said: "If anybody suffers, or if anyone's brother suffers, let him say 'Our Lord God who art in Heaven, hallowed be Thy name, Thy kingdom is in Heaven and on Earth; just as Thy mercy reigns in Heaven, so show Thy mercy on Earth; forgive us our faults and our sins. Thou art the God of the virtuous. Send down (a portion) of Thy mercy and Thy healing power on this pain, so that it may be healed.'"

Not only the ideas, but even instances of New Testament phraseology, are to be found in the religious language of the Moslems. Very early did the expression occurring in Matthew 7:5, "mote and beam," pass into Moslem literature. Even Matthew 5:13 passed in an apocryphal tradition as a saying of the Prophet about his companions: "My companions bear the same relation to my community as salt does to food, for without salt food is no good." Similarly, Matthew 7:6 is echoed in the saying, "He who wastes learning upon people who are unworthy of it resembles one who casts pearls before swine."

Though Islam resisted the creation of a priesthood, yet to Christian influence we must ascribe the gradual growth and establishment of a sacerdotal class in Islam—the exponents of moral principles and legal theories. In course of time they assumed an importance not unlike the scribes under Judaism or the clergy in the Christian Church. They professed themselves the custodians of religion and censors of thought. The *Sunna*—obedience—the imitation of Mohammed—the desire to emulate him in the smallest details of life, reproduces in Islam the Christian practice of gaining eternal life by following Christ. Nor does the parallel break down in the sphere of politics. According to an Arab proverb, religion and kingship are twin-born. This feature of the Islamic state, Ibn Khaldun, the great Arab historian, emphasizes by saying that the spiritual and temporal power, here, are one and indivisible. The idea of a divine polity is thus an idea at once common to Islam and Christianity. Both of these religions disapproved of a State independent of religion, both sought to effect the union of the two, with enormous differences.

We must now pass on to the influence of Islam upon Christendom. Very early, says Haines, did Spain "gain a reputation for introducing innovations into the doctrines and practices of the true faith, and even of priding itself on its ingenuity in this way, 'Let us, now, take the several heresies which bear traces of Islam.'" During the eighth century a heresy is said to have arisen in Septimania (Gothic Gaul) which denied the need of confession to a priest, on the ground that men ought to confess to God alone. This heresy is clearly traceable to Islamic ideas, which the Christians of Septimania could not have escaped. Islam admits no priest, and hence no confession, save to God. But this heresy is small and negligible compared to the view of the Trinity held by Migetus (*circa* 750 A.D.), who denied the divinity of the Word—thereby making an approach to Islam. But both these are cast into the shade by the adoptionist heresy, in which the influence of Islam is not only obvious but is even acknowledged by eminent writers on Church history. Mariana, the Spanish historian, and Baronius, the apologist of the Roman Church, held that the object of the new heresiarchs was "by lowering the character of Christ, to pave the way for a union between Christians and Mohammedans." Nor can the Iconoclastic movement, fraught as it was with ominous consequences to the Byzantine Empire, be said to have been free from Islamic influences. To mention but one fact—Claudius, the Bishop of Turin (appointed in 828), who set to work to deface, burn, destroy all images and crosses in his bishopric, was born and bred in Moslem Spain. This Claudius—so his opponents tell us—saw much in Islam and the Moslems to appreciate and admire. Their verdict is: "The Jews praised him and called him the wisest among the Christians, and he, on his part, highly commended them and the Saracens."

Islam is said by some to be hide-bound, narrow, averse from advancing with the times. No charge could be less in accord with the judgment of history. It is not only now that Islam has been accommodating itself to the needs of the times. There has been age-long war between the party of acceleration and the reactionaries—the party calling for the brake. But the liberal exponents—throughout Islamic history—have invariably won the day. Islam, as understood and interpreted by its liberal exponents, has never stood in the way of necessary changes to meet changed conditions. In the course of centuries, like other religions, Islam has yielded to the pressure of progressive ideas. But, in effecting these changes, Islam adopted a method which was exclusively its own.

The old Arabs had a body of inherited views and practices which were the universally accepted standard of good or evil. Conformity to them was a duty; deviation from them a crime. We can imagine what hold such a heritage had on the Arab mind by the incontestible fact that the main ground of opposition to the Prophet's teachings was that he defied inherited views and challenged established practices. His teachings were not condemned on their merits. With the triumph of Islam the old *Sunna* of the Arabs was changed for the new *Sunna* of the conquering faith. This new *Sunna*—though widely differing from its predecessor—was like it in one respect—its universally binding force. The ideals and usages of the Prophet and his companions henceforward became the standard of excellence, the rule of conduct, the kindly light of guidance. The result was that all views and practices not strictly in accordance with the *Sunna* were regarded as *Bid'a*—innovation—and, as such, were to be ruled out by the faithful. This rigid principle, so fatal to progress, could not long endure unbroken; and, as a matter of fact, it was broken in upon at an early date.

After the victories of Islam and the establishment of the Moslem Empire, new needs arose, new problems called for solution, fresh administrative measures forced themselves upon the attention of the conquerors. All had to be faced and met. The *Sunna,* as it lay to hand, forged amid simple conditions of life, could not, in the nature of things, deal with the complex situation that had now arisen. The difficulty was solved in a practical way. Moslem jurists and statesmen—always fertile in resources to meet the exigencies of the times—put forward the theory that, in certain circumstances, *Bid'a* was permissible. This opened the door for reform; this led to the path of progress. The rigidity of orthodoxy could always be softened, or even, as was actually the case, circumvented, by this all-powerful theory, sanctioning innovation in certain circumstances. The channel through which it was effected was *Ijma*—consensus of opinion. It was laid down that long-standing usage legalized a practice, though not in conformity with, nay, even in opposition to, the practices of an earlier age. To such a practice *Ijma* gave a prescriptive title, an authority, a binding force, which could not be assailed or called in question.

The necessity for conforming to altered conditions became clearer and clearer and more and more insistent as the years went by, until popular opinion accepted the view that departures from *Sunna,* to suit the needs of the times, were in no way inconsistent with Islam. This was a long step forward. In one of the four orthodox sects, the one linked with the name of Malik Ibn Anas, the *Maslaha, utilitas publica,* or the common interest, was recognized as the normal point of view in the application of law. It was permitted to deviate from the normal law if it could be shown that the interest of the community demanded a different decision from that given in the law, corresponding to the principle of *corrigere jus propter utilitatem publicam* in Roman Law. This liberty, to be sure, is restricted to each case as it arises, and does not carry with it a definite setting aside of the law. But the principle involved is, in itself, an indication of willingness to make concessions within the law.

But the modern world has witnessed, and is actually witnessing to-day, most amazing developments in Islam. Western influences have powerfully leavened Moslem thought, just as Christian thought influenced Islam at its birth and during its adolescence. This for two reasons: Western influences do not, in any way, affect the central unity of Moslem thought; and, again, in Islam there is no opposing force, such as an Œcumenical Council, to combat or thwart such influences. The unity of Moslem thought consists in the belief that there is one God, and that Mohammed is His apostle. The rest does not count, or counts very little. Coupled with this is the absence of any recognized ecclesiastical authority, to call a halt to the advance of modernism, or to punish departures from the path of strict orthodoxy. The cries of "Heresy," not infrequently heard, soon die away. The heretic of one age is the apostle of the next. Was not Sir Syed Ahmad of Aligarh such a one? Western civilization has shaken Moslems out of their slumber. Everywhere —in India, in Egypt, in Persia, in Turkey—wheresoever we turn, Moslems are pulsing with new life, viewing problems from the modern standpoint, forging fresh rules of religious interpretation, reconciling the needs of the hour with their allegiance to the past, justifying modern institutions by appeals to the Koran and the traditions of the Prophet, striving to close the breach between the two great sects which divide the Islamic world.

Tremendous changes are being introduced into Islam. Basing themselves on an independent interpretation of the Koran, eminent Moslem scholars are making strenuous efforts to liberate Islam from the fetters of authority, from the dead hand of past ages. Concession to the demands of the times being admitted, these concessions are justified by appeals to the Koran and the traditions of the Prophet. Whether the appeal be real or illusory, the fact of the appeal is one more instance of the utility of legal fiction in the history of human development.

By a special Fatwa the Egyptian *Mufti*, Shaikh Mohammed Abduh (d. 1905), sanctioned the establishment of Savings Banks and the distribution of dividends; and by a similar process, his colleagues in Constantinople enabled the Ottoman Government to issue interest-bearing State bonds. Of a piece with these is the legalization of insurance policies, which the ancient Moslem law, if interpreted strictly, does not appear to permit.

Like the demands for the furtherance of cultural and economic progress, those for modern forms of government are similarly supported through the Koran and the traditions. In politics, too, the justification for parliamentary government is found in the Koran, and the Shiite Mullahs base the claims of the revolutionists on the doctrine of the hidden Imam. But yet wider movements are the flower and fruit of Western culture in Eastern lands.

Look at the Babi movement in Persia! What else is that but a war-cry against the petrified theology and outworn legal conceptions of the Mullahs? What else but an attack upon their hypocrisy and worldliness? What else but an attempt to establish a more equitable social order? The founder of Babiism combines Pythagorean subtleties with a distinctly modern point of view.

Bahaism, an offshoot of Babiism, takes us a step further on the path of liberalism. "While Bab, at bottom," says Goldziher, "was only a reformer of Islam, Baha advanced to the larger conception of a world-religion which was to unite all mankind in a religious brotherhood. As, in his political teachings, he professes cosmopolitanism—emphasizing that there is no preference to be given to him who loves his country over him who loves humanity—his religion in this matter was stripped of all narrow sectarianism."

Nor is India behindhand. Here, too, Mirza Gholam Ahmad of Qadian has inaugurated a religious movement of tremendous force and potency. He condemns fanaticism, advocates peace and tolerance; seeks to create an atmosphere favourable to culture; and stresses the necessity of the ethical virtues for Moslems. It were idle to deny the great gifts made to the East by Christendom. As a civilization, it has permeated Eastern life through and through in all its phases and aspects, social, intellectual, economic, religious. It has taught the spirit of compromise, and the necessity for concession to modern thought. It has weakened the force of merely inherited ideas and customs. It has slackened the hold of unreasoning orthodoxy, and driven home the need for a critical differentiation between fundamental principles and mere fleeting accretions. It has helped the faithful to realize that their paradise can be found as assuredly on this earth as it is said to await them in the life beyond the grave.

True Islam and true Christianity are akin; the mission of each is fundamentally identical. Let, then, Islam and Christianity be henceforward faithful allies in the liberation of humanity.

Muhammad Kamel Hussein

Kamel Hussein is one of the most distinguished intellectuals in Egypt, a renowned surgeon and an educator whose interests have carried him into literature and philosophy. He has also written on ancient Egyptian medicine, including a translation of an old treatise from hieroglyphics. He is a former president of Ibrahim University in Cairo and a member of the Arab Academy.

In the only fictional work to be included here, the author, in a postscript to "City of Wrong," explains that the idea for this novel came to him on reading Freud's "Moses and Monotheism." Extracting Freud's major premise that nations, races, religions, and cultural groups can be the subject of psychological complexes, Kamel Hussein analyzes Judaism from the point of view of the Exodus. He refers to this event as "a major psychological stress (or Trauma) occurring in the infancy of the race." In seeking a similarly crucial occurrence in the history of Christianity, Hussein turned to the day of Crucifixion for what he considers to the "failure" of the Apostles and consequently, the failure of Christianity.

CITY OF WRONG *

The disciples came together that night to consider what action ought to be taken now that the people of Israel and the Romans had agreed to crucify Christ. There was no more high-souled or great-hearted group of men on the face of the earth than they, and none more well intentioned. They talked together of how they could uphold what was indubitably right and how they could obviate gross and undoubted wrong. They were in no sense feeble in their conviction or irresolute. Nor were they intimidated by danger. They were not given to unruly passion nor to the self-will that might have diverted them from the path of right. On the contrary, they were motivated by strong, pure, disinterested love. In the long debates in which they engaged argument was sharp among them as they exchanged mutual recriminations, of which, God knows, they were innocent. Indeed, only their strength of faith and sincerity of purpose had preserved them from intrusive hatreds. Sharp differences of view arose despite their piety and devotion, their self-sacrifice and high dedication.

Perhaps in that circumstance there is ground to make us pause critically over the view that to bring together a group of people with the same outlook necessarily creates among them a common front or mutual cohesion and shared reactions such as to ensure common attitudes. And it is all the same whether those assemblies consist of disciples, or idolaters, learned doctors or ignorant folk,

* K. Hussein, *City of Wrong*, Kenneth Cragg, trans., Djambatan N. V., Amsterdam, 1959, pp. 101-121.

criminals or men of piety. It is not long before they give evidence of being the same mixture, some enterprising and lethargic, adventurous and cautious, advocates of boldness and advocates of prudence, some given to haste, others to long range plans, near-sighted and far-sighted. You have all these disparities whatever be the theme of debate. Agreement is not readily reached on the part of people like these, unless it be of a precarious sort.

There were ten disciples in the meeting. The traitor had departed and the beloved disciple was absent because they had sent him to the master to bring back word of him and to ascertain his wishes. They had with them one of the Magi whom they knew well and greatly esteemed. He was one of the three who had come to Bethlehem at the birth of Christ, following a star to which their knowledge guided them as it shone in the heavens, until it directed them to his birthplace. Then they observed that the star increased in brilliance reaching its brightest on the day of the sermon on the mount. Two of the Magi were present then. As thereafter the star grew dim they knew that Christ's sojourn on the earth was nearing its end. The youngest of the three remained to witness the final eclipse of the light which for so long had guided him.

The disciples spent more than a little time going to and fro in their minds over all that had happened. They were in the deepest distress, each in his own mind brooding over their sorrow and desperation or turning it over in debate with one another. Yet no line of thought emerged clearly before them and no line of action found formulation.

Then the doyen of them, the bearer of the keys, spoke up and said:

"We are today confronting the sorest trial we have ever undergone. The turmoil of grief and sorrow that has seized you will avail nothing in this catastrophe. Those things will get us nowhere. I fear for you unless remorse and regret give way to resolve and action. A man can be troubled in soul to such a point that he has no strength left when his conscience summons him to serious action. When that happens his staying power will fail him and his mind will be incapable of seeing the true shape of his duty, of facing things decisively and resolving on a clear course of action. Then he will find peace for his spirit, however fraught with danger his decision may be and however exacting his undertaking. So I bid you rid yourselves of your present frame of mind and think calmly about what action we ought to take tomorrow. Irresolution and perplexity take a greater toll of mental and inward balance than does the worst exposure to physical dangers."

There was silence for a while as they got into a quieter frame of mind. Then one of them said:

"The sin that is to be done tomorrow is the foulest ever to be committed by man in all his sin-laden history. People have never been so far from the right as they are in this. They have confused the best of men with the worst and made prophets equal with brigands. This is a dastardly deed. But it cannot be laid at the door of one group only or of one particular community. The guilt of it falls upon everybody. If we deliver the Lord Christ we shall be delivering humanity as a whole from a burden under which it would groan to all eternity."

Another disciple said:

"It were good indeed for us to deliver him, and all humanity with him, from an unparalleled crime. But even more is it incumbent upon us to rescue him, out of sheer love for him. He who does not offer his life in the cause of the one he loves has no love at all for him. And any one who has no love is not one of us. Nor is he of our company whose faith does not override a mere desire for security. I am going to intervene between him and his unjust oppressors. They are not to be compared with the thongs of his shoes. I will challenge the forces that are set to do him evil. Either I save him from them, or they destroy me. If I die I will be content to do so. If I save him, what bliss, now and hereafter."

Another said:

"But do you not think that it would be equally fitting we should save and defend even an ordinary person from so foul a deed being perpetrated on him? It is the evident enormity of the thing itself about which our conscience refuses to be silent. If we are not passionate about justice anywhere what is the point of talking about right and wrong and justice? Unless we repel the detestable thing with hand and tongue, it doesn't help anyone that we repudiate it in our hearts. Love of justice, and that alone, lays on us the solemn duty of making our indignation effective on behalf of him who is oppressed, whatever his status among men and however virulently men hate him. If this is so, how much more then when the victim of foul wrong is the best of all humanity, the dearest and most beloved to our hearts? If you want your faith in truth and justice to have any meaning you must defend him against the evil of the men of iniquity. In default of such action you pronounce judgement on your own selves that your creed is a delusion and your faith a wisp."

Yet another said:

"I am with you, in your passionate zeal for him, for humanity and for justice. But you have forgotten that the primary consideration making his deliverance our duty is our obligation to be vigilant and jealous for the religion he inaugurated. There is not one of us who can preach it after him as he does. Men will not follow any of us as they follow him. There cannot be the least doubt that if these blood-shedding rulers destroy him they will wipe out this precious religion. Our shame before men when they see our failure to defend our prophet will further increase our incapacity to proclaim his message. His life in itself alone is more competent to bring about the fulfilment of the peace for which the world yearns and for its guidance than the lives of all of us without him."

And another disciple said:

"This is undoubtedly right and well said. But I would go further and add that if you are concerned to safeguard the religion, the plan should certainly be to do so by delivering the master forcibly. Persuasion and petitioning for mercy, talk about justice and love, are not the way. Already we have been a heavy drawback to him in his mission. Have not people said that if he were any good he would have had other followers than the riff-raff of our society? We are already quite despicable enough in men's eyes. Did they not dub us the dregs of the population and say that God does not guide the people of Israel by means of a gang of fishermen from Galilee?

"As long as we were with him people could say what they liked about us. His presence among us was enough to make us a match for the whole world. But if he is no longer in our midst we will never succeed after him, unless people are assured that we were acting submissively, before, only out of deference to his authority;

and that, acknowledging no other lordship, we then held off from resisting them, not out of fear or cowardice but out of identification with him and out of rejection for his sake of the world's ways, and in loyalty to the religion in which he believed."

Another said:

"Strength and weakness in men's eyes really depend upon whether or not man is clearly willing to face death. Don't you agree that the reason why some rider to battle is so awe-inspiring that thousands of free men worship him is just that he alone is ready to die and by that circumstance contrives to lead them and escapes death into the bargain?

"Let no one on any account say that we are too weak to warrant any hope of success. If we shrink from defending him our enemies will take revenge on us and they'll leave us only the alternative of death or undying shame and disgrace. If they treat us leniently our life after that will be contemptible. Such capitulation on our part to falsehood will be unbelief. If we act boldly people will remember our action with pride and admiration, and if we die posterity will have us in honoured memory. Who has greater glory than the man who, despite his being aware of his weakness, is ready to be killed in the cause of truth and justice?"

Their corporate enthusiasm grew to a high pitch and the weight of despair was lifted from their spirits. Their hearts beat high with courage and they rejoiced in their new found resolve after the bitter taste of vacillation and perplexity. They were of one mind to take every possible means to save him.

After a silent pause one of them declared:

"My proposal is that we snatch him tonight from prison. The guards are not numerous and it will not be difficult to overpower them even if one or two who challenge us are killed. Or it may be a better idea to wait until the soldiery goes up the mountain and attack them then. We shall get away with him quite easily."

Naturally there was an intoxicating feeling in the desire for bold action after they had spent so much time in inactivity, preoccupied with matters of dogma and belief. It was natural too that they should have sensed the need to demonstrate their strength and tenacity. For these hitherto had not been conspicuous. It was natural too that they should have in common a longing to be rid of their past—a thing which is not always easy for men. To resolve on active and decisive steps was a source of real satisfaction to them. None of them doubted that, resorting as they would to force, they might well be obliged in doing so to face death and what to them was worse than death, namely the killing of innocent men among their adversaries.

Their arguments came thick and fast and with increasing force. They followed each other in a sort of mounting crescendo, just as waves, though they be weak ones, gather increasing strength if they move rhythmically and steadily, whereas even high waves diminish and weaken when they beat hither and thither. In a community like theirs the points of debate interacted sharply, the weak arguments gathering strength by their sheer accumulation and strong arguments losing force when they did not sustain each other.

So their determination to give battle and to resist by force increased, to the point where it became difficult for any one of them to counter and oppose it in its full tide. They were almost in a fever of excitement. Some of them imagined themselves arming with swords and rubbed their hands as if warming up for the fight.

At this point one of them spoke up, in some fear:

"You know well enough that I am not a craven-hearted fellow or lustful to live. Nor do I doubt that what we have said tonight is true and right. But while our master is alive among us I do not want to contravene a command of his. My faith in him is all I have in this world. I would not wish to die having gone counter to him in anything, great or small. I cannot be guided in any matter whatsoever except by him. You know well that when the armed guards came out to take him and the people clamoured against him he commanded us not to resist them or harm them. You remember too how he remonstrated with one of us who drew his sword and struck the ear of one of the soldiers. His command to us then was crystal clear. However right any action seems to me I will never go ahead with it unless you bring me authorisation from him. If he is no longer with us tomorrow, tomorrow I will then allow myself to determine things by my reason, on condition that I do not go against conscience. But today he remains both my reason and my conscience. If you are wanting me to set our ideas above his commandments, I would in that case be giving my reason precedence over my religion and that is something I cannot countenance."

Another disciple rebutted him saying:

"Do you want him to have to say to us: Die to defend me? That is what emperors and other stony-hearted men will say. It is not likely that he, with his tender heart of compassion, will order us to die on his behalf, even when we are well assured that we are in the right and they in the wrong. It isn't our job to consent cheerfully to shame and perfidy. We are not bound to obey him on the question of whether he should be rescued. To deliver him is an absolute good that nothing can disqualify."

"I would be opposed to rescuing him if that should involve us in the use of force. For that is the very thing he has forbidden us. My view is that our religion has not given to conscience unlimited authority but authorises us to act as reason indicates while remaining within the limits that conscience does cover, however desirable it may seem to be to transgress them. Religion has to do with limits and prohibitions rather than with right guidance and positive commands."

"This notion of yours is weak to the point of near treachery. It is open to such vacillation that it is almost stupid. Would not a successful outcome for us be also the victory of religion? What then is the point of your impeding a religious victory in the name of religion?"

"I have no desire to perpetrate a crime for the sake of making religion secure. Religion has a Lord Who is well able to secure it, and has no need to require a transgression on my part in the worthy cause. Such fantasies are the product of the feeble in faith who are half-baked in their religiosity."

"God makes us factors in the execution of His will. It is up to us to guard jealously the security of religion."

"Are we more concerned for religion than he is? Do you know better what befits the spread of his gospel than he does? You look upon his being taken from us as destructive of religion. That is what we think. It may or may not be so. But to use violence is a plain rebellion against his word. This is a matter of conscience and Divinely decreed. To defy it is in my view the worst presumption."

"Of course it is permissible to depart from religious principles for the sake of defending religion itself. There is, for example, no alternative but to destroy false belief by death, if such false belief is seditious. Sedition is a worse evil than killing."

"Well, alleged heresy may or may not be heresy: but murder is a definite transgression of religion which no exegesis can sustain. It is not a matter of differing opinions. Doubtless action aimed at the destruction of the faith is a worse evil than death. But it must in truth be action destructive of the faith, and that is precisely what it is so difficult to be sure about. Killing, however, is an evil about which there's no uncertainty once it has been done. You consider that leaving him to his fate would be a flagrant dereliction of duty. But is it not possible that our abstaining from his rescue today is one of the fundamental principles of religion, having to do with atonement for sins? Conspiracy against the faith is truly worse than killing, if the conspiracy is established. But establishing it requires proof and it is just there that one can be right or wrong. But there are no two ways about killing and violence. They are incontrovertibly evil and neither probable good nor anticipated evil justify them as a policy to follow."

"Religion in no way enjoins us to ignore our reason to that extent."

"Religion commands you to obey your reason unless your conscience tells you to desist. When your conscience says: 'Stop' there is no option but to obey. Our master, who is our conscience, has forbidden us to use force, even in the interests of his victory or the victory of the faith."

"But Moses killed people and did so in order to bring them into religion and truth."

"Moses fought to safeguard his nation from the hostility of their enemies. It may be that this hostility derived from religious otherness. But it was at all events hostility. Self-defense is permissible if there is verified hostility, on condition that you are not yourself the originator of the enmity in precaution against some anticipated ill-will. Moses, however, did not make war to propagate religion nor to resist deviations from the faith. He only slew the worshippers of the calf because they violated the law and flouted his authority, he being a ruler; and rulers have the right to require obedience. Once in control again, he did not let his enmity against them enter into the religious realm. The rest of the prophets who took up the sword resembled him in this. They only took it up in self-protection and to safeguard their people from their enemies. None of the prophets compelled any community into embracing faith by dint of the sword, for there can be no forcible recruitment into religion."

"We today have nothing to do with this exegetical discussion. The point is that if we refrain from delivering him, it will be a catastrophe for him, for us and for religion."

"Is there no way open to us of saving him without resort to force?"

"Do you remember the Roman soldier who attended our sessions? It was clear that he knew the difference between good and evil and that he believed in peace. Can we not seek out his help to prevent his brother soldiers of Rome from perpetrating this foul deed, or at least to persuade them to leave him in our hands to flee, he and we, from this city of wrong?"

"That would be a treachery to his nation which I would not wish us to ask of him. I am terribly afraid that we are slipping into the depths of sin. When we reach the lowest point we will find no easy way back to salvation."

"I heard that some time ago he was accused of betraying his army and his nation on the field of battle, and that he will be condemned today. Most people think he will be put to death in the most fearful manner as a penalty for his treachery."

Their enthusiasm ebbed away and they were back again in their old state of hesitation and distress. Gone was the exultation they had felt when they agreed to take definite action to resist the monstrous wrong. They were angry with those who had kindled these new doubts after they had brought themselves to the point of being assured that it was right to take up the fight. If the arguments calling for brave action were in need of going over again in order that they might be sharpened and corroborated, did not those advocating inaction decline all too readily into the abyss of total negation?

The summons to positive action is always easier for the advocate than the summons to reflection, even if, at the hour of actual translation into fulfilment, the former is more difficult. The call to abstain from action is harder to advocate but easier to obey. A positive line of action makes the spirit more assured: and brings a psychological satisfaction which controversy only intensifies. For this reason such a policy is easier and more satisfying both for him who sponsors it and for those he calls upon to follow it. The negative or inactive approach, however, puts its advocate into a position where he is suspect.

Thus it requires courage and sincerity and yet offers no occasion for exuberance, since its implementation calls for no display of bravery whatsoever.

Men take a different attitude to duty when they are discussing it from when they are face to face with acting on their decision. The spokesman for a brave front may well be the least courageous of men when the time for action arrives, though the fact would argue no necessary cowardice or hypocrisy on his part. Similarly the protagonist of inaction may well be the bravest of men without his bravery amounting to any assured conviction about the rightness of what he does. It is simply a phenomenon that is in the nature of public gatherings where men come together for full discussion. It is most likely that the point of view demanding bold action, even if it be mistaken, will prevail over the view that calls for restraint, however right it be. And it will fall out so, irrespective of whether the partisans of bold action are actually by temperament resolute in action or not. Such is the nature of corporate consultation when it is worked out in this form in a great society. It would seem that there is no guarantee of valid ideas or of immunity from mistakes, even though the men who compose these bodies are the manner of men the disciples were, thoroughly well intentioned, sincerely religious and most zealous in faith. Yet despite all these qualities, when they consulted together they were in no way different from any other community council. Such bodies are not a means of neutralising wrong thinking.

Anger over the waverers prompted one of the disciples to resume the debate. He said:

"Who in any case is going to benefit from renunciation of force? The men most likely to use violence are the wicked doers and their violence and evil alike are only increased against good men when the latter affirm non-violence. In this manner they leave an open field for these criminals to despoil them with impunity, without fear of retaliation or of force to counter force. It is precisely the best of people who have no need of the gospel of non-violence. Force is something they will never misuse while non-violence is something the evil doers will never respond to. I can see nothing but danger in this absolute veto on the appeal to force."

"Well, I at least shall get from it the satisfaction of having obeyed God and having shunned what He has forbidden us. And more than this, as I see it, no man can desire."

"As if the only thing to be desired was to secret oneself in a monastery or live in a mountain and leave other men to do the sinning and the erring."

"Of course not. I want men to live together in communities, actively striving to bring their life and work as individuals within the limits of obedience toward God. And if they want to be sacrificial let them sacrifice themselves, not others."

"Were we not ashamed when the people saw us fleeing when he was arrested?"

Whereupon their leader spoke:

"I am indeed as much ashamed of that now as I would be of downright unbelief. I have never been so humiliated either in my own eyes or before men as I was then. I wanted to use my sword —though I am no swordsman. But I only made people laugh and failed miserably. Anybody attempting an unwonted task, even though it be a right one, is exposed to two dangers, the danger of false appearances and the danger of failure. Those among us who are not practised in taking the sword and in force and who are not temperamentally suited to doing battle with men had better steer well clear of what they are not good at. Being true, in the widest meanings of the term, namely the proper correspondence between man's life and the natural characteristics that make up his constitution, is the primary secret of a fine and happy life.

"I was almost stunned the day the master told me that I would deny him three times before the morning cock crew. I knew within myself that I would never deny him. But when it happened I discovered my inward frailty despite all my brave resolves. Talk and thought both lie but action does not. He who seeks to give an impression of courage when he is a coward ends up with two disappointments, one in himself and the other in what he does. Most of us are conscientious men of faith: we had better stick to our last, be what we were made to be, and not cross swords with those who are habitués of war with its alarums and excursions. I do not mind admitting to you that I, at all events, was not made for this sort of conflict, though I trust that God will grant me power to enable me to struggle in another way in His cause.

"Truly I find there is much weakness in me. Did not the master teach us to love our enemies? Perhaps in love of my enemies I have succeeded, but I find it difficult to love his enemies, those who treat him so wrongfully. But that I consider is a weakness. I think we are bound to obey him if his command to us is clear and altogether unambiguous. If he has forbidden us to use force to bring his cause to success it is incumbent on us not to transgress his prohibitions."

"I see between us no difference of view, except in regard to the means and the extent to which we concede to ourselves the right to use force. My opinion is that we should not let ourselves be mastered by anger and hatred. If we do so we will transgress our religion. Let us so order this issue that we do not involve ourselves in the sin of violence."

"All that is fine so long as it is not inspired by cowardice and weakness. If any of you senses that he holds this view out of fear or apprehension then it is the counsel of Satan. But if it issues from faith and conviction it is the counsel of God. For men may do the same things from two entirely contrasted impulses, the one the inspired revelation of God and the other the wily suggestiveness of Satan. Though there is of course a vast difference between their actions men may be aware of no difference at all."

"Are you of the opinion that we should take the line dictated by fear knowing that to be Satanic, if it coincides with what the prophet enjoined? Or should we abandon it as long as the incentive to it is an evil thing? Do I disobey the prophet in his good commandment, if I feel in the depth of my soul that I am only impelled to do so by hatred and spite?"

"It is your business to obey the prophet and to cleanse your soul from Satanic motives."

"What is the point of cleansing the motives so long as the action is one and the same?"

"The point is that motives have an abiding effect in the soul beyond the actual doing of the deed. From one and the same action you will find contrasted consequences in the soul, tending toward evil if the motives were evil and to good if they were good, all depending on the incentives in the heart."

The wise man who was their guest sat silently listening to their discussion without making his views known. But at this point he intervened to say, while they gave him close attention:

"Much of what I have heard has surprised me. I have been apprehensive to see how far short you come in fulfilling the sermon on the mount. We listened to it and understood its import and I thought that it had penetrated your innermost souls and purified your conscience. I was convinced none of you would take a course of action inconsistent with its principles. Now I realise that you still regard it only as a noble exhortation whose directives are to be followed only when feasible, and neglected when they conflict with the weakness and evil in man's nature.

"I have also noted in much of what you have said that the emotions actuating you are not such as the master commended to you. In other people who have not listened to the master or known his guiding word, they might well be the most lofty sentiments. But in your case, your motives must be absolutely irreproachable. Motives are worthy or detestable, according to whether they coincide with or contravene conscience. I have heard you argue that it is your love for the master Christ that compels you to take reprisals against those who wrong him. But the real truth is that what drives you to them is hatred of his foes, not love for him. These two are sharply contrasted, though it is often supposed that they are mutually necessary. In their confusion on this score, people imagine that love on their part for a friend can only be by dint of their hating his enemy. To love one's country, for example, means, on this view, hating its enemies. But in fact there is a vast difference between the two attitudes. Love never invites to evil. If I find love calling for evil-doing I know that in the heart of the person in question it has turned into hatred of his enemy. This is an error into which most people fall. You must be wary of it. So easy is the confusion that only a very fine sensitivity of conscience is aware of it, and is zealously vigilant for the good in all its purity.

"You have invoked also the principle of the triumph of the right through force. But what else is this on your part but a confusing of right with power? It is a delusion into which most people fall. Right recognises itself as bound by obligations; indeed it could be said in its very nature to be these limits. Force, however, in the nature of the case overreaches these limits as far as it can go. As and when proceeding together it is only temporarily so. Those who defend the right by force, only do so until they gain their end. Then force alone becomes their master passion. Claims about force as the means to right are usually short-lived claims. They last only a while. Then force, in full career, needs no sanction from right. All who have recourse to force as a means to the right soon discover that they have merely invoked the right as a means to force. So the idea that what is manifestly right should be defended by force should have no place in your motivation. Otherwise your fate will be that when you have righted the right you will be resting upon force alone. That is precisely what your religion forbids.

"You should realise that as long as the right is put in an inferior position it is all the same whether it be force or falsehood to which it is made subservient.

"Furthermore, I heard some of you remark that fear of what people say of you was a motive for action to be taken. It is true enough that there are those who believe that fear of this kind is a powerful factor in inducing people to do what is right. The error is very prevalent. Fear of being thought ill of is a very different thing from the desire after virtue. Such fear, as is the case with hatred, may sometimes lead to admirable actions and then quite soon after lead irretrievably to evil. It is in no way fitting that what you do should be motivated by fear.

"Then too I heard one of you taking pride in his bravery and readiness for sacrifice, out of his anxiety for a good reputation and prestige. One of you remarked that you would find a place in history and that posterity would hold you for ever in glorious remembrance. This is indeed a strange motive for action, though by many it is highly valued as an incentive to well-doing. But it is a pagan way of talking: it is the very sort of hollow vaunting and self-magnification the master forbade you. It is a stupid impulse by which only fools are guided. It has no validity as a motive for goodness, but is, in fact, very close to evil.

"I have no wish to summon you to any particular line of action or to urge any course upon you. You know better than I the issues before you and are more competent to decide them. But I warn you: watch yourselves, scrutinise the motives behind what you do. If they are evil you will ultimately land in evil, even though you have been motivated by immediate good. I warn you against force and where it may lead you. If you kill or harm anyone in going through with what force prescribes, you will thereby transgress the bounds of conscience. That is the supreme disloyalty to your religion, whatever justification you may think you have for it.

"On the point raised by some of you as to the role of that reason with which God has endowed us and the place of our freewill, if it is our job to ignore our reason in plain issues like this one, my view is that you should be guided by reason so long as it keeps within the limits of conscience. You must understand that there are laws which the soul must not transgress unless it is to suffer disease. For in that respect the soul resembles the body though, of course, the principles of soul health are more subtle and less easily understood. The harm too that results from flouting them is less evident than the diseases of the body and more far-reaching. The true unison of our powers of choice, the obligations under which we are laid by these laws of the soul and the behests of reason, is the problem of problems in the life of man. It may bring the problem home to our minds if we borrow the parable of a man in a boat. He has full freedom of movement and action, as his mind and his reason may determine, but always on condition that he stays within the boat and the limits of the laws of nature that relate to it. Otherwise he will drown."

At this point the disciple returned whom they had sent to the master to find out his mind and bring back to them his directions. They clamoured around him for news, each hoping that his opinion would be the one to be vindicated. The messenger said:

"He commands you to go aside for worship and prayer and to leave him until God fulfills His purpose for him. He bids you go abroad into the world calling men to his truth. He says he will meet you after three days in one of the villages of Galilee and that whatever be the suffering that befalls him on the morrow it is by the will of God and it is not for us to resist it. He warns you against violence and reproaches you for your attitudes at the time of his arrest."

When they knew that these were his definite instructions and that they were final, their minds were put to rest in that they had a directive they could not possibly transgress. But the decision threw them into profound sorrow, whether their policy had been action or inaction, violence or non-resistance. Equally hard on all was this call for surrender and acquiescence in the worst. Many of them wept.

They had no compensating satisfactions, such as come with decisive action—the thrill of sacrifice in the cause of truth and the lust of revenge on the enemies of religion. Faith and obedience—these only were left to them. They submitted to his command with sorrowing and despairing hearts. They made up their minds to leave Jerusalem, the city of wrong. But there was in their hearts an utter sadness, a regretful reproach, at being obliged to abandon their prophet to the clutches of evil men, who would wreak their will on him. They were wellnigh broken at the thought of this inescapable choice between tragic inaction and the violation of their prophet's will.

The messenger said to them:

"I paid the closest attention to what he said. My view is that we should occupy ourselves wholly in worship and prayer, however distraught by anxiety we may be. We must be led by that mountain sermon. It proved so grievous to us that we forgot it, or so exacting that we pretended to. Maybe it is well for us to heed the words of this wise man. He drank in that sermon and believed what it said with a far firmer faith than ours. It is duty to follow his advice and wisdom."

When they heard that, they clung all the more wistfully to this man of wisdom, so untroubled by doubt and distress or indecision. They clung as a drowning man might to his rescuer. They sensed that somehow his absolute faith would be their refuge, that they would find in him the inspiration to lighten, perhaps, the burden of grief during three long days. Through these they had to await their master's return, God having meanwhile raised him to Himself. They gave themselves to prayer and devotion seeking respite thus from the bitter weight of grief they bore.

There can be no doubt that the decision of the disciples was the right one, by the criteria of revelation and religion, and by reference to the things that transcend the capacity of the human mind fully to understand. Nor is there any doubt that they were mistaken in fearing the collapse of the Christian religion when their master was no more with them. In fact by this action of theirs in holding back from forcibly inducing his victory, they rendered a great service to the Christian message. In that day's events, the Christian religion defined its principles and formulated its philosophy. Its dominant characteristics were there and then fashioned. It was those events which gave rise to the most impressive of its tenets about forgiveness and redemption. From them came also that sadness which is a ruling element in the character of the greatest adherents of Christianity, their fear of sin, their love of self-reproach and abasement, their sense of the importance of the sin of Adam and their belief that it had to do with the anguish Christ underwent that mankind might be saved from its consequences. Perhaps all these hallmarks of Christianity are simply an echo of the great sin of the apostles' self-reproach, as if Christians are expiating this sin until the end of time.

But of all that the disciples knew nothing. And apart from revelation they could not know it.

From the purely human point of view, however, there is no doubt that what they did was wrong. They left the right in all its unmistakeability to suffer outrage. They exposed their religion to extinction, their prophet to foul wrong and themselves to destruction. Nobody knows what would have happened to Christianity had they succeeded in rescuing him by force. But the fact remains that without doubt the line of action their reason had approved and the guidance deriving from their reflection and their intuitions were alike invalid.

If then the disciples, though the finest of men, were not saved from error after consultation and debate and having to hand all that makes for right guidance, the people of Israel have some excuse also if they proved to be misguided. They took the Christian religion for a piece of sedition, which would quickly have destroyed the pillars of their religion, their law and their nation. They supposed that the man was a sorcerer and his followers criminals. They proceeded upon purely human and self-made criteria and from human emotions in no way stamped with that ardent faith that characterised the disciples. If both groups, disciples and Jews, erred and went astray, what can man do in his desire to avoid error, as long as he proceeds in what he does upon human reason alone?

To the present day, Christianity has not freed itself, and perhaps never will, from the entail of that sorrow and regret which haunted the souls of the disciples because of all that they were lacking in relationship to Christ at the time they held back from saving him. They have been destined to bear the reproach of the great sin—the sin of abandoning Christ to his foes, to his oppressors and persecutors. It seemed to them that they were only commanded to withhold themselves from rescuing their prophet because they did not deserve to be his witnesses.

And thus a dread of falling into sin, an apprehensiveness about evil-doing, has become a dominant feature of the Christian spirit. And so it will always remain. For Christians have no way of atoning for what happened on that day.

Mauliv Muhammad Ali

Mauliv Muhammad Ali was born in 1875 and died in 1951. He was cofounder of the Ahmadiya movement in Lahore, India, and became president of that group. The doctrines of the Ahmadiya deviate from the teachings of conventional Islam only in their relationship to Christology and to the djihad *(the holy war). They assume that Jesus did not die on the cross but that after his apparent death, he migrated to India where he preached the gospel until he died at the age of 120.*

The Lahore group of the Ahmadiya are missionary-minded, spreading propaganda throughout India, England, Germany, and other foreign countries. Mauliv Muhammad Ali published an English translation of the Koran, several biographies of Muhammad, "Religion of Islam," "The Living Thoughts of the Prophet Muhammad," and "A Manual of Hadith." He also wrote "The Anti-Christ" and "Muhammad and Christ," which are bitter attacks on orthodox Christianity. The selection which follows is taken from the latter.

MUHAMMAD AND CHRIST *

The Gospels are full of the stories of the miracles wrought by Jesus Christ and in them, as in nothing else, is thought to lie the argument of his Divinity. Even the central fact in the Christian religion is a miracle: if Jesus did not rise from among the dead, the Christian faith and the preaching of Christianity are in vain. Religious duties, moral teachings and spiritual awakening do not occupy the place which miracles do in the Gospels. The dead are made to rise from their graves, multitudes of the sick are healed, water is turned into wine, devils are cast out, and many other wonderful deeds are done. Suppose for the sake of argument that this record of the Gospels is literally true; what was the effect of this on the lives of those who witnessed these miracles? The miraculous in a prophet's life is needed to assure the people of the truth of his message and to convince the ordinary mind that being a possessor of extraordinary powers he must be followed in spiritual matters. The bringing about of a moral and spiritual transformation is admittedly the real object, the miraculous being only needed as a help towards the attainment of that object. The former at most may be looked upon as the means to an end, the latter is the end itself. The best evidence of miracles thus consists in the effect they produce, and the most important question for us therefore is that supposing Jesus wrought all the miracles recorded in the Gospels, what was the result? How great was the success he attained

* M. M. Ali, *Muhammad and Christ,* Ahmadia Anjuman, Lahore, India, 1921, pp. 18-40.

in bringing about a transformation? One Gospel tells us that Jesus was followed by multitudes of sick persons who were all healed; another says that many were healed. Now if either of these statements were true, not a single person should have been left in the land who should not have believed in Jesus. It is inconceivable that those who saw such extraordinary deeds done by Jesus Christ should have rejected him as a liar. They saw the sick healed and the dead raised to life and yet they all disbelieved in him as if not a single miracle had been wrought! And how strange that even the great multitudes that were healed do not seem to have been believers in Jesus, though the Gospels tell us that faith was a condition prior to being healed; for if even these multitudes had believed in Jesus he would have had a following at the time of his crucifixion far more numerous than he actually had, and sufficiently large to baffle the authorities. But what do we find? The following of Jesus is poor, not only as regards number, but also as regards its character. From among the five hundred that followed him he chose twelve who were to sit on twelve thrones, who were to be entrusted with the work after the Master, and these twelve showed a strange weakness of character, the greatest of them, Peter, denying Jesus thrice for fear of being treated harshly by the enemies, and not even hesitating to curse when he thought that a curse was the only means of escape. The others even durst not approach Jesus, while one of the chosen ones turned out to be a traitor. On an earlier occasion when Jesus asked them to pray for him, he found them all asleep. Often had he to rebuke them for having no faith. Who was it in the world on whom the miraculous deeds of Jesus, if they were ever done, made an impression? The mere fact that Jesus was unable to bring about any transformation worth the name, and to make any impression either on his friends or foes, is a sufficient testimony that the stories of miracles were invented afterwards.

The poorness of the result attained by Jesus Christ notwithstanding all the stories of miracles becomes the more prominent when compared with the wonderful results attained by the great World-Prophet that appeared in Arabia. The Holy Prophet had before him a nation which had never before been guided to truth, among whom no prophet had appeared before him, the attempts at whose reformation by both the Jews and the Christians had proved an utter failure. This nation had, both as regards material civilization and moral calibre, been sunk in the depth of degradation, and for centuries the voice of the reformers had fallen on deaf ears. Yet within less than a quarter of a century a wonderful transformation was brought about. The old evils had all disappeared, and ignorance and superstition had given place to love of knowledge and learning. From the disunited elements of a people who did not deserve the name of a nation had sprung up a living and united nation before whose onward march in the world the greatest nations of the world were powerless and whose civilization and knowledge fed the world for long centuries. But this material advancement was only the result of an inner change, of a moral and spiritual transformation, the equal of which has not been witnessed in the world. Thus both morally and materially, Muhammad, may peace and the blessings of God be upon him, raised a nation from the depths of degradation to the highest plane of advancement. As against this what did Jesus do? He had before him the Jewish nation read in scriptures and practising many virtues at least externally. He also found them living under a civilized Government with advantages of a material civilization to help their progress. In spite of these advantages he was unable to produce the least change in the life of that nation as a whole. If the effect was so poor, it is impossible that any thing great was done. In this light, the stories of the miracles are clearly pure inventions or exaggerations made to compensate for the apparent failure.

A critical examination of the Gospels leads to the same conclusion. Mark 8:12 contains a plain denial of signs: "And he sighed deeply in his spirit, and saith, Why doth this generation seek after a sign? Verily I say unto you, There shall no sign be given unto this generation." Similar statements are contained in the other Gospels; see Matthew 7:39, Matthew 16:4, Luke 11:29. "Then certain of the Scribes and the Pharisees answered, saying, Master, we would see a sign from thee. But he answered and said unto them, An evil and adulterous generation seeketh after a sign; and there shall no sign be given to it, but the sign of the prophet Jonas." (Matthew 12:38-39) Here we have a plain denial to show any sign except the one sign of Jonas, which is understood by some commentators as meaning the sign of preaching, by others as remaining in the grave (alive of course, as Jonas was) for three days and three nights. If Jesus worked such great wonders, how was it that the Pharisees asked for a sign and how was it that Jesus refused to show any sign? In answer to their demand, he ought to have referred to the testimony of the thousands that had been healed; in fact, the masses around him should have silenced the questioners by their evidence. But no such thing happened. The commentators say that the Pharisees asked for a greater sign than the healing of the sick "to which they were *accustomed.*" If it was indeed so, then too it is clear that Jesus' healing of the sick was nothing extraordinary. And why did not Jesus refer to his raising of the dead?

Again, Mark tells us that Jesus was unable to do any mighty work in Nazareth, save healing a few sick persons: "And he could there do no mighty work, save that he laid his hands upon a few sick folk, and healed them." This too shows Jesus' inability to work any miracle, the healing of the sick being looked upon as a very ordinary occurrence. These statements are a clear evidence that the stories of wonderful works were invented afterwards, or at least there is much exaggeration in them.

The mightiest work of Jesus is said to be the raising of the dead to life, and it is in this, we are told, that the proof of Christ's divinity is met with. Here is the argument:

"Christ's raising the dead to life is admitted by the Moslems on the basis of the Holy Koran, and raising the dead to life is beyond the power of man and only an attribute of the Divine Being. . . . And in this attribute of Divinity no other mortal partakes with Jesus."

As to what the Holy Koran says, we shall see later on. Let us first closely consider the claim made on the basis of the Christian sacred scriptures. The argument is that Jesus is a Divine person because he raised the dead to life. This argument could only be advanced by a man who believed that no other mortal had ever raised the dead to life. But the Bible belies this argument. It contains instances of other mortals who raised the dead to life, and therefore even if Jesus actually wrought this miracle, the inference of his divinity from it is quite illogical; or if he was Divine because he raised the dead to life, Elisha had as much of divinity in him. In II Kings 4, we are told that a child had died and his death had been well made sure when Elisha came in:

> "And when Elisha was come into the house, behold, the child was dead, and laid upon his bed. He went in therefore, and shut the door upon them twain, and prayed unto the Lord. . . . and the child sneezed seven times, and the child opened his eyes." (II Kings 4:32-35)

Elijah also raised the dead to life.

> "And he cried unto the Lord, and said, O Lord, my God, hast thou also brought evil upon the widow with whom I sojourn, by slaying her son? . . . I pray thee, let this child's soul come into him again. And the Lord heard the voice of Elijah; and the soul of the child came into him again and he revived." (I Kings 17:19-22)

Thus the Bible does not give to Jesus any exclusive claim to divinity on the score of raising the dead to life. Indeed, in one respect Elisha's power of raising the dead to life was greater than that of Jesus, for even his dry bones after his death had the efficacy of giving life to a dead man: "And it came to pass as they were burying a man . . . and they cast the man into the sepulchre of Elisha: and when the man was let down and touched the bones of Elisha, he revived and stood up on his feet." (II Kings 13:21) It is sometimes asserted that Jesus wrought the miracles by his own power while in the other prophets, it was God who worked the miracles through the prophets. This fantastic distinction does not prove of much value, for in the case of Jesus too it was God who did the miracles: "Ye men of Israel, hear these words; Jesus of Nazareth, a man approved of God among you by miracles and wonders and signs, which God did by him in the midst of you." (Acts 2:22)

It is very probable that the stories of Elijah and Elisha raising the dead to life produced the pious desire in the minds of the early followers of Jesus Christ to ascribe similar deeds to their Master. There are clear traces of this in the narratives themselves. Matthew, Mark and Luke narrate the raising of the ruler's daughter about whom Matthew quotes Jesus as saying: "The maid is not dead but sleepeth." (Matthew 9:24) The others omit these words, but their presence in Matthew is sufficient to disclose the nature of this miracle. It is remarkable that John does not speak of this miracle at all but mentions instead a miracle which is not known to the Synoptists, viz., the raising of Lazarus after he had been in the grave for four days. (John 11:38-44) How did it happen that the Synoptists, one and all, had no knowledge of such a great miracle, and how was it that John had no knowledge of the raising of the ruler's daughter? The inference is clear that John, writing later, had his doubts about the raising of the ruler's daughter, and he instead made some symbolical story read as if it were an actual occurrence. In addition to these two miracles, Luke alone mentions a third case, the raising of the widow's son at Nain (Luke 7:11-17), which is known neither to the other Synoptists nor to John.

We may, however, refer here to the height of absurdity to which the love of wonderful stories carried the early Christian writers. Matthew was not satisfied with the single miracle of raising the sleeping girl, and he therefore makes the dead rise out of the graveyard and walk into Jerusalem as soon as Jesus gave up the ghost: "And behold the veil of the temple was rent in twain from the top to the bottom; and the earth did quake, and the rocks rent; and the graves were opened; and many bodies of the saints which slept arose, and came out of the graves after his resurrection and went into the holy city and appeared unto man." (Matthew 27:51-53) This wonderful miracle passes all imagination: only the evangelist does not give the details as to what clothes these skeletons had on as they walked into the city; as in the case of Lazarus, the writer is careful enough to add that the dead man came forth bound hand and foot with grave clothes: and his face was bound about with a napkin and an order to loose him had to be given by Jesus Christ. Probably the grave clothes of these saints who had perhaps been dead for centuries, or at any rate for long years, had been preserved intact to assist in the performance of the miracle. Not all the commentators have the courage to read this wonderful story literally, and accordingly we have the following comment by the Rev. J. R. Dummelow: "This incident seems to be a pictorial setting forth of the truth that in the Resurrection of Christ is involved the Resurrection of all his saints, so that on Easter Day all Christians may be said in a certain sense to have risen with him."

Herein lies the truth about all the miracles of raising the dead to life. Jesus talked in parables, and symbolical language was used by him freely. "Let the dead bury their dead," said he. (Matthew 8:22) And again: "Verily, verily, I say unto you, He that heareth my word and believeth on him that sent me, hath everlasting life, and shall not come into condemnation, but is passed from death unto life. Verily, verily, I say unto you, The hour is coming, and now is, when the dead shall hear the voice of the son of God: and they that hear shall live. . . . Marvel not at this; for the hour is coming in which all that are in the graves shall hear his voice and shall come forth." Now in all these cases, by the *dead*, even by *those in the graves*, are meant the spiritually dead, those dead in sin, and by life is meant the life spiritual. Similar figurative language was used by the Jews. Acording to a Jewish tradition, "the wicked, though living, are termed dead." Jesus Christ sent word to John the Baptist: "Go and show John again those things which ye do hear and see: The blind receive their sight, and the lame walk, the lepers are cleansed, and the deaf hear, the dead are raised up, and the poor have the gospel preached to them." (Matthew 11:4-5) The concluding words of this message throw light on what Jesus meant, for he was not actually preaching the Gospel to only *the poor*. He was talking symbolically, but his words being misunderstood, it was thought necessary to add to the story of his life these stories of the raising of the dead to life. The whole fault lies in Jesus' too free use of symbolic language so that it was not the Jews alone who had to be told that they did not understand his symbolic language (John 8:43), but even the disciples often misunderstood him, taking his symbolic language in a literal sense. The following incident is worth noting:

"Now the disciples had forgotten to take bread. . . . And he charged them, saying, Take heed, beware of the leaven of the Pharisees, and of the leaven of Herod. And they reasoned among themselves, saying, It is because we have no bread. And when Jesus knew it, he saith unto them, Why reason ye, because ye have no bread? Perceive ye not yet, neither understand? Have ye your heart hardened? Having eyes see ye not?" (Mark 8:14-17)

Indeed we find the disciples themselves complaining of his resorting too much to symbolic language and pleading their inability to follow him. Herein lies the solution of the stories of raising the dead to life.

Next we come to what the Holy Koran says about the raising of the dead to life. To say that the Holy Koran speaks of Jesus exclusively as raising the dead to life betrays sheer ignorance of its contents. It speaks as clearly of the Holy Prophet raising the dead to life. Thus it says: "O you who believe! answer the call of Alláh and His Apostle when he calls you to that which gives you life." (Koran 8:24) The mistake arises from the invidious distinction made between the prophets of God, so that when the Holy Koran speaks of the Holy Prophet's raising the dead to life, the meaning is said to be the giving of spiritual life to those who were dead in ignorance, but when it speaks of Jesus' raising the dead to life, the words are looked upon as meaning the bringing back to life of those who were dead physically. Why should not the same meaning be attached to the same words in both places? As to what that meaning is, the Holy Koran explains itself. It speaks of the dead again and again and means the spiritually dead. It speaks of raising them to life and means the life spiritual. I will give a few examples to show this, as this point has been much misunderstood. It says in one place: "Is he who was dead, then We raised him to life, and made for him a light by which he walks among the people, like him whose likeness is that of one in utter darkness whence he cannot come forth?" (Koran 6:123) Here we have the *dead man raised to life* in clear words, yet by this description is meant not one whose soul has departed from, and been brought back to, this body of clay, but one whose death and life are both spiritual. In another place we have: "Surely you do not make the dead to hear, nor make the deaf to hear, when they go back retreating." (Koran 27:77) Mark the combination here of the *dead* with the *deaf*. They are both placed in the same category. The Prophet cannot make them *hear* when they do not stay to listen and go back *retreating*. In the same sense it is stated elsewhere: "Neither are the living and the dead alike. Surely Alláh makes whom He pleases hear, and you cannot make those hear who are in the graves" (Koran 35:22) Here it is not only the *dead*, but those who are *in the graves.* Yet the dead bodies that rest in their coffins beneath the earth are not meant. Nor are the words to be taken as meaning that the Prophet cannot give life to those who are spiritually in the graves. What is implied is only this that the Prophet as a mere mortal could not do what was almost impossible, the giving of life to those who were in their graves: it was the hand of Alláh working in the Prophet that would bring about such a mighty change.

It is clear from this that when the Holy Koran speaks of the prophets of God as raising the dead to life, it is spiritual death and spiritual life to which it refers, and it is in this sense that it speaks of the Holy Prophet Muhammad and Jesus Christ as raising the dead to life. This becomes the more clear when it is considered that according to the Holy Koran the dead shall actually be raised to life only on the day of Judgment and their *return to this life* before the Great day is prohibited in the clearest words. Thus: "Alláh takes the souls at the time of their death, and those that die not, during their sleep; then He withholds those on whom He has passed the decree of death and sends the others back till an appointed time." (Koran 39:42) This verse affords a conclusive proof that the Holy Koran does not admit the return to life in this world of those who are actually dead. Once the decree of death is passed, the soul is withheld and under no circumstances is it sent back. The same principle is affirmed in the following verses: "Until when death overtakes one of them, he says: Send me back, my Lord, send me back, haply I may do good in that which I have left. By no means! it is a mere word that he speaks, and against them is a barrier until the day they are raised." (Koran 23:99-100) Thus we are told in the clearest possible words that no one who has passed through the door of death into the state of *barzakh* is allowed to go back into the previous state. A third verse may also be quoted: "And it is binding on a town which We destroy that they shall not return." (Koran 21:95) A few words of comment may be added to this last verse from a saying of the Holy Prophet. The following incident is recorded in *Nisai* and *Ibn-i-Maja*, two out of the six authentic collections of reports. Jabir's father Abdulla was slain in a battle with the enemies of Islám. The Holy Prophet one day saw Jabir dejected. "What makes you dejected?" asked the affectionate Teacher of his sorrowful companion. "My father died and he has left behind a large family and a heavy debt" was the reply. "May I not give you the good news of the great favour that your father met with from Alláh" said the Holy Prophet. . . . "God said, O My servant! express a wish and I will grant you. He said, My Lord! give me life so that I may fight in Thy cause again and be slain once more. The word has gone forth from Me, said the Mighty Lord, that they shall not return." The pious wish of Abdullah to come back to life and fight the enemies of Islám had only one barrier in its way—"*that they shall not return,*" these words being exactly the concluding words of the verse I have quoted last. Similar evidence as to the Holy Prophet's comment on this verse is met with in the *Sahih Muslim*, where the martyrs are generally spoken of in almost the same words. "What more do you desire?" they are asked by the Almighty. "What more may we wish for, our Lord" is the reply. The question is repeated and they say: "Our Lord, we desire that Thou shouldst send us back to the world that we may fight again in Thy cause." And what is the reply to this holy wish at a time when the addition of a single person to the ranks of Islám was looked upon as the greatest Divine favour? "*I have written that they shall not return.*" Nothing in the world can subvert the clear dictum of the Holy Koran that those once dead shall not return to life in this world; and the return to life shall only take place on the great day of Resurrection.

Although Jesus' miracles of healing do not occupy a very high place in the record of miracles, not even among the great and wonderful deeds which man may do, yet it is probable that most of these stories had their origin in figurative speech or in exaggeration. Here too Elijah and Elisha stand on the same footing with him. Elisha healed Naaman of leprosy (II Kings 5:1-14), and restored eyes to a whole people who were first made blind miraculously: "And when they came down to him, Elisha prayed unto the Lord, and said, Smite this people, I pray thee, with blindness. And he smote them with blindness according to the word of Elisha. . . . And it came to pass, when they were come into Samaria, that Elisha said, Lord, open the eyes of these men, that they may see. And the Lord opened their eyes, and they saw." (II Kings 6:17-20)

If these great miracles of healing the sick had been limited to the prophets, as they are in the Old Testament, they would have retained at least the halo of dignity about them. But when we come to the New Testament period, the miracles of healing become a very common thing. When accused by the Pharisees that he cast out devils with the help of Beelzebub, Jesus answered: "And if I by Beelzebub cast out devils, by whom do your children cast them out?" (Matthew 12:27; Luke 11:19) Here therefore is a plain admission put into the mouth of Jesus that even the disciples of the Pharisees who were opposed to Jesus Christ could work miracles of healing, or of casting out the devils, as the writers of the Gospels would have it. Again we are told that a man who did not follow Jesus was working the same miracles as Jesus in those very days: "Master, we saw one casting out devils in thy name, and he followeth not us. . . . But Jesus said, Forbid him not; for there is no man which shall do a miracle in my name, that can lightly speak evil of me." (Mark 9:38-39) And similarly those whom Jesus rejects in the final judgment as workers of iniquity did wonderful works: "Many will say to me in that day, Lord, Lord, have we not prophesied in thy name? and in thy name have cast out devils? and in thy name done many wonderful works?" (Matthew 7:22) Nay, even false prophets could show great signs: "For there shall arise false Christs, and false prophets, and shall show great signs and wonders." (Matthew 24:24)

The strangest of all is the story of the healing pool which St. John records in his Gospel: "Now there is at Jerusalem by the sheep-market a pool, which is called in the Hebrew tongue Bethesda, having five porches. In these lay a great multitude of impotent folk, of blind, halt, withered, waiting for the moving of the water. For an angel went down at a certain season into the pool, and troubled the water: whosoever then first after the troubling of the water stepped in was made whole of whatsoever disease he had." (John 5:2-4) The revised version omits the latter portion as an interpolation but even then the difficulty of the healing-pool having the same power as the "son of God" is not surmounted.

In addition to the influence of exaggeration on the stories of the marvellous, there was the mistaking of the spiritual for the physical, as I have already shown in the discussion on the miracles relating to the raising of the dead to life. This is clearly indicated by the words in which the message to John the Baptist is conveyed: "The blind receive their sight, and the lame walk, the lepers are cleansed, and the deaf hear, the dead are raised up, and the poor have the Gospel preached to them." And when the disciples of Jesus failed to turn out a devil, Jesus remarked: "This kind goeth not but by prayer and fasting." (Matthew 17:21) It is by prayer and fasting that the power is attained to drive devils out of men, and clearly these are the devils which affect the spirit and not the physique of man.

The light cast upon this subject by the Holy Koran clears away all doubts. On three different occasions, the Holy Koran is spoken of as a *Healing:* 10:57, 17:82, and 41:44. In fact, this is one of the names by which the Holy Book is known. The adoption of this name is a significant fact. It shows that the healing effected by the prophets of God is of a different nature from the removal of physical ailments. And again and again are the deaf and the dumb and the blind mentioned in the Holy Koran; but these are not the armies of the sick by whom Jesus is supposed to have been followed: "And great multitudes followed him and he healed all." (Matthew 12:15) Nay, the Holy Koran itself tells us what it means by the blind and the deaf, etc.: "They have hearts with which they do not understand, and they have eyes with which they do not see, and they have ears with which they do not hear." (Koran 7:179) "For surely it is not the eyes that are blind, but blind are the hearts which are in the breasts." (Koran 22:46) Similar statements abound in the Holy Koran, but in view of the clearness and conclusiveness of what has been here quoted I need not multiply instances. What is left obscure by the Gospels is thus made clear by the Holy Koran, and it is in this light that the Holy Book speaks of the healing effected by the prophets of God, of whom Jesus Christ is one.

SHORT BIBLIOGRAPHY

The following books deal primarily with Christianity and its relation to the other world religions. The list is by no means complete. Selections were limited to books of the last twenty-five years.

Ashby, Philip H., *The Conflict of Religions,* New York, 1955.

Bonquet, A. C., *Christian Faith and Non-Christian Religions,* New York, 1958.

Hocking, William E., *Living Religions and a World Faith,* New York, 1940.

Jurji, Edward, ed., *The Great Religions of the Modern World,* Princeton, N. J., 1947.

Kraemer, Hendrik, *The Christian Message in a Non-Christian World,* London, 1938.

———, *World Cultures and World Religions: The Coming Dialogue,* London, 1960.

Neill, Stephen, *Christian Faith and Other Faiths,* London, 1961.

Ohm, Thomas, *Asia Looks at Western Christianity,* New York, 1959.

Radhakrishnan, S., *Eastern Religions and Western Thought,* London, 1940.

Schweitzer, Albert, *Christianity and the Religions of the World,* New York, 1951.

Slater, R. L., *Can Christians Learn from Other Religions?,* New York, 1963.

———, *World Religions and World Community,* New York, 1963.

Tillich, Paul, *Christianity and the Encounter of the World Religions,* New York, 1963.

Toynbee, A. J., *Christianity among the Religions of the World,* New York, 1957.

Wach, Joachim, *The Comparative Study of Religions,* New York, 1958.

———, *Types of Religious Experience: Christian and Non-Christian,* Chicago, 1951.

Zaehner, R. C., *The Comparison of Religions,* London, 1958.

CHRISTIANITY: Some Non-Christian Appraisals

David W. McKain has made the study of comparative religions a field of special interest since his graduation from the University of Connecticut.

Robert Lawson Slater is Professor of World Religions and Director of the Center for the Study of World Religions at the Harvard Divinity School.